ALIENATED ™

Published by

BOOM!
S T U D I O S

BOOM! STUDIOS

ALIENATED, November 2020. Published by BOOM! Studios, a division
of Boom Entertainment, Inc. ALIENATED is ™ & © 2020 Simon Spurrier Ltd. &
Christian Mathew Wildgoose. Originally published in single magazine form
as ALIENATED No. 1-6. ™ & © 2020 Simon Spurrier Ltd. & Christian Mathew
Wildgoose. All rights reserved. BOOM! Studios™ and the BOOM! Studios
logo are trademarks of Boom Entertainment, Inc., registered in various
countries and categories. All characters, events, and institutions depicted
herein are fictional. Any similarity between any of the names, characters,
persons, events, and/or institutions in this publication to actual names,
characters, and persons, whether living or dead, events, and/or institutions
is unintended and purely coincidental. BOOM! Studios does not read or accept
unsolicited submissions of ideas, stories, or artwork.

BOOM! Studios, 5670 Wilshire Boulevard, Suite 400, Los Angeles, CA 90036-
5679. Printed in USA. First Printing.

ISBN: 978-1-68415-527-9, eISBN: 9-781-64144-693-8

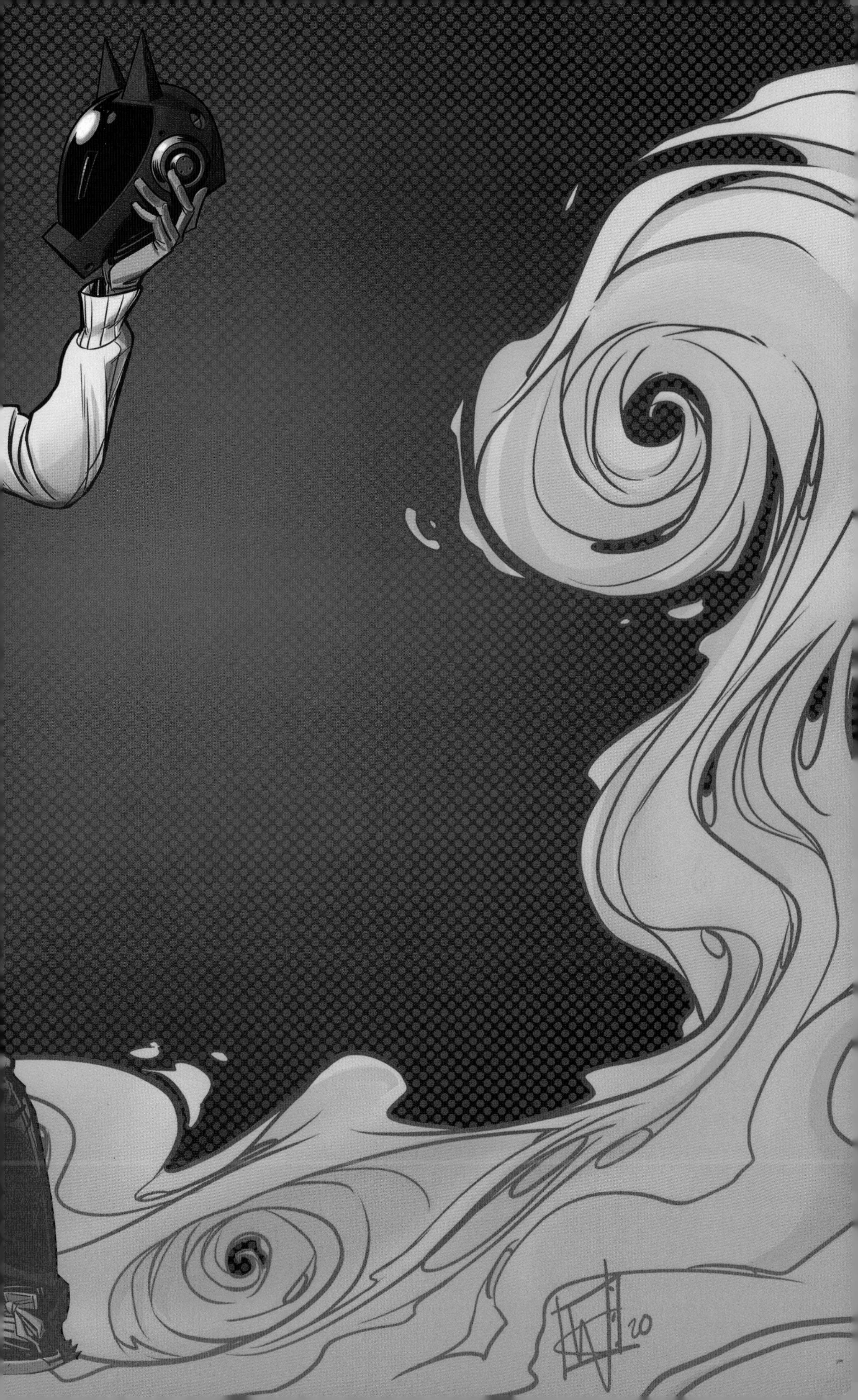

ALIENATED™

CREATED BY SIMON SPURRIER & CHRIS WILDGOOSE

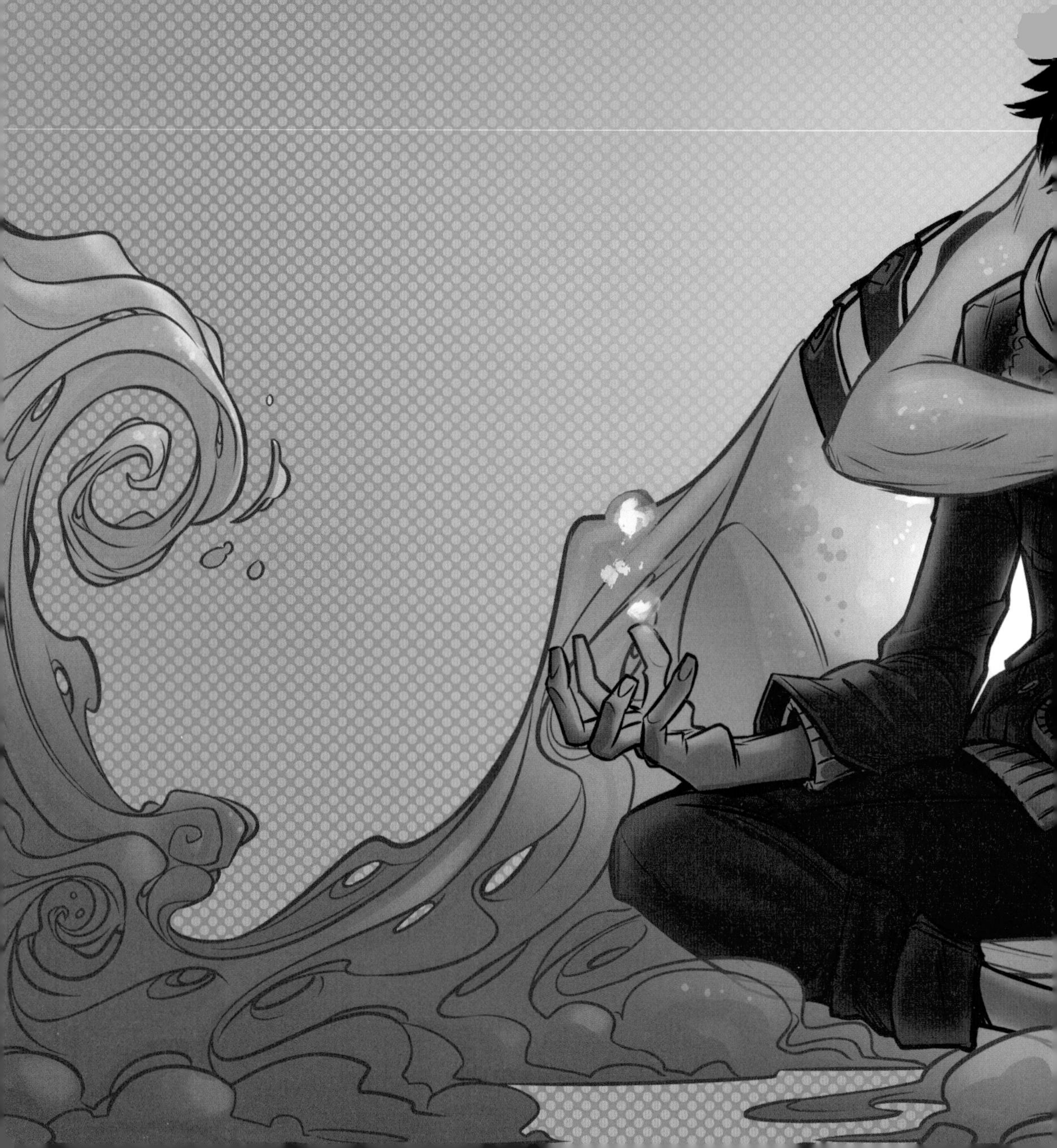

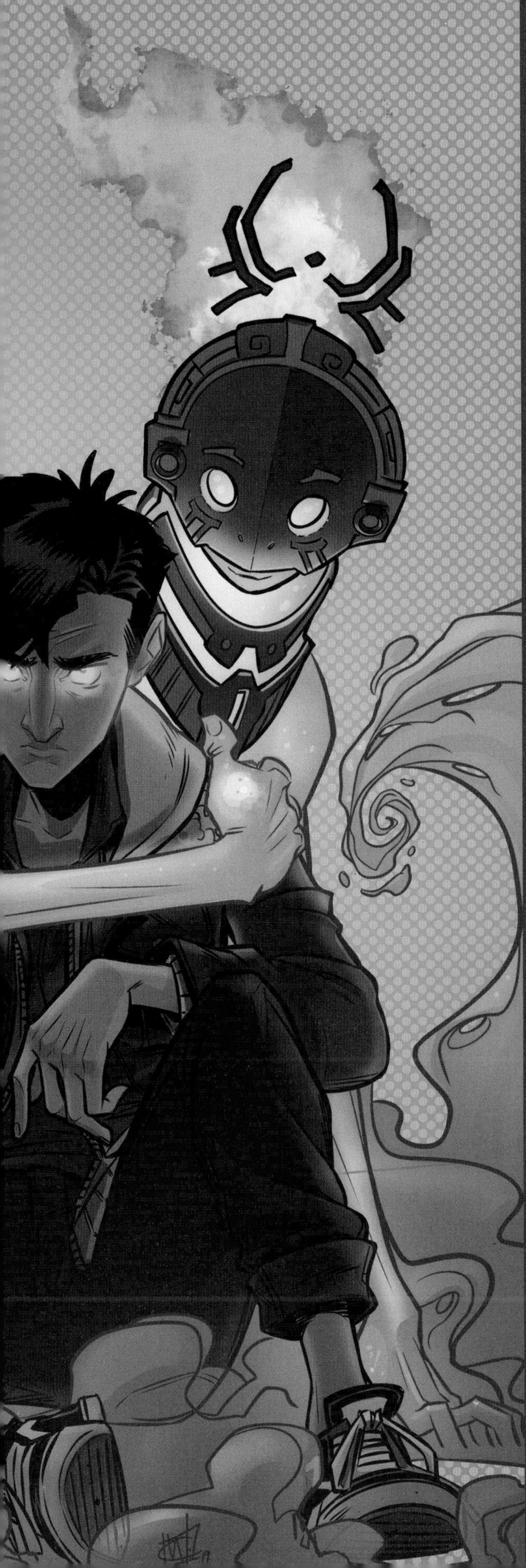

WRITTEN BY
SIMON SPURRIER

ILLUSTRATED BY
CHRIS WILDGOOSE

COLORED BY
ANDRÉ MAY

LETTERED BY
JIM CAMPBELL

COVER AND CHAPTER
BREAK ARTWORK BY
CHRIS WILDGOOSE

SERIES DESIGNER
SCOTT NEWMAN

COLLECTION DESIGNER
CHELSEA ROBERTS

ASSISTANT EDITORS
RAMIRO PORTNOY &
GAVIN GRONENTHAL

EDITOR
ERIC HARBURN

CHAPTER ONE

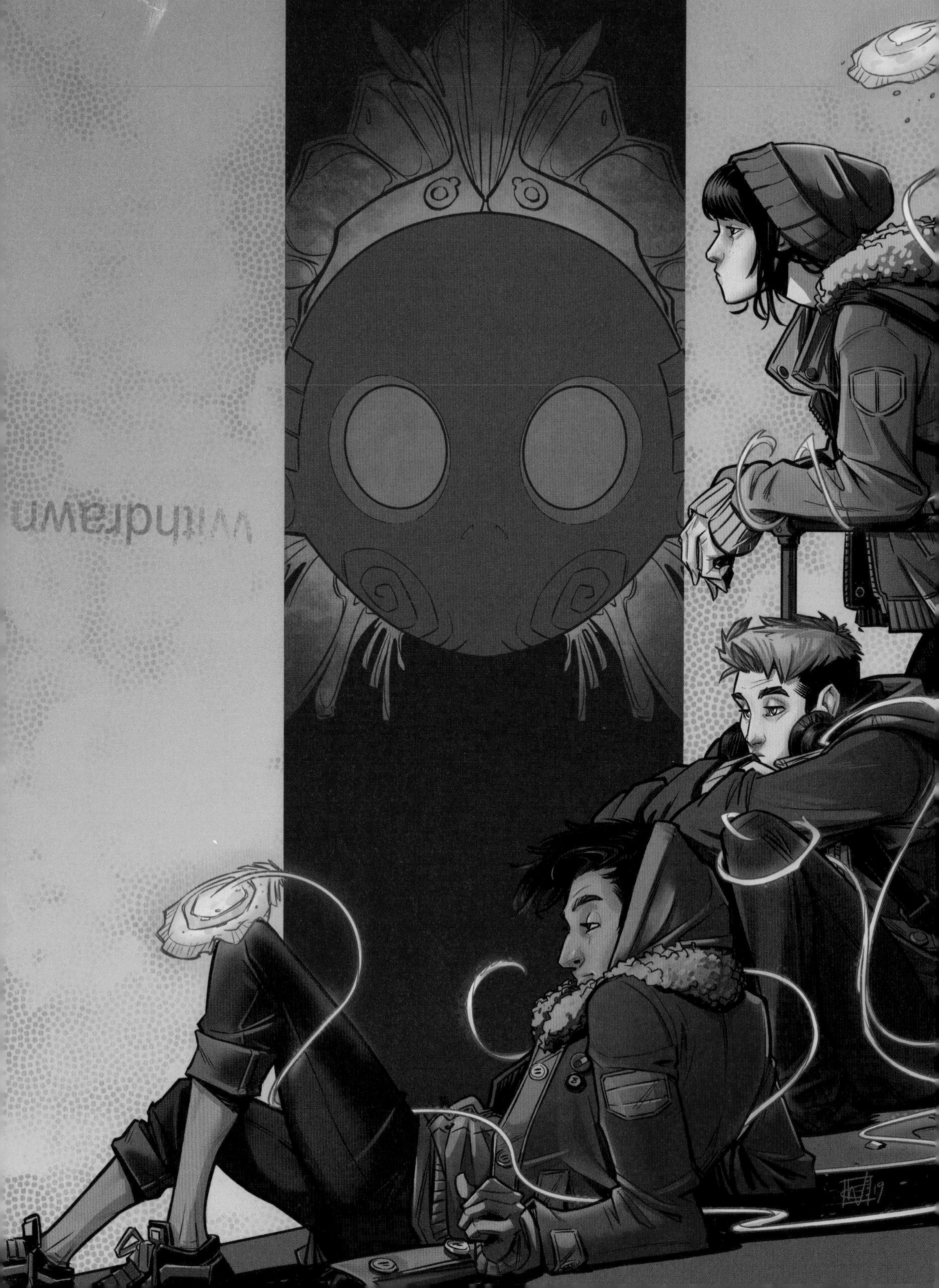

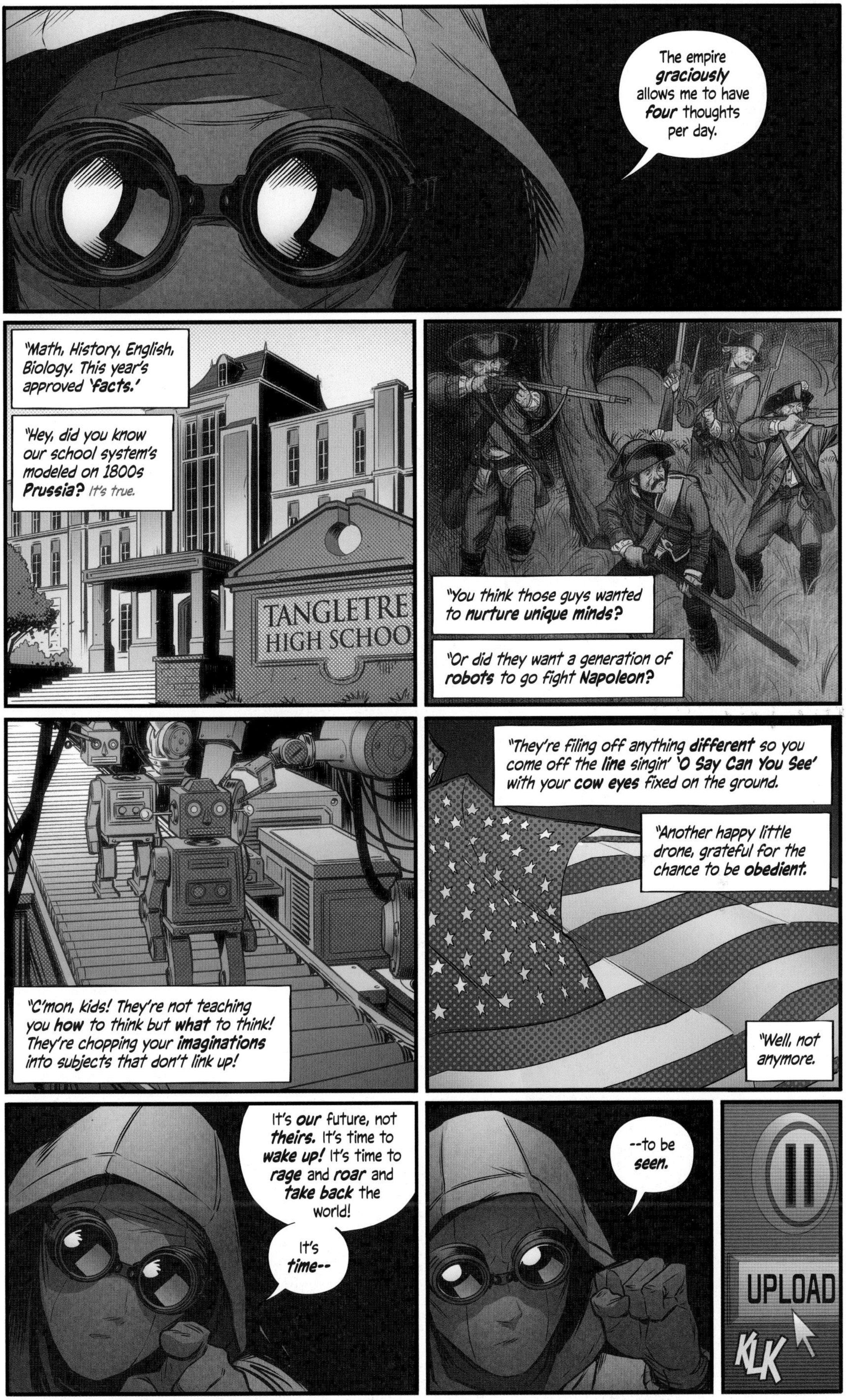
The empire graciously allows me to have four thoughts per day.
"Math, History, English, Biology. This year's approved 'facts.'
"Hey, did you know our school system's modeled on 1800s Prussia? It's true.
TANGLETREE HIGH SCHOOL
"You think those guys wanted to nurture unique minds?
"Or did they want a generation of robots to go fight Napoleon?
"C'mon, kids! They're not teaching you how to think but what to think! They're chopping your imaginations into subjects that don't link up!
"They're filing off anything different so you come off the line singin' 'O Say Can You See' with your cow eyes fixed on the ground.
"Another happy little drone, grateful for the chance to be obedient.
"Well, not anymore.
It's our future, not theirs. It's time to wake up! It's time to rage and roar and take back the world!
It's time--
--to be seen.
UPLOAD
KLK

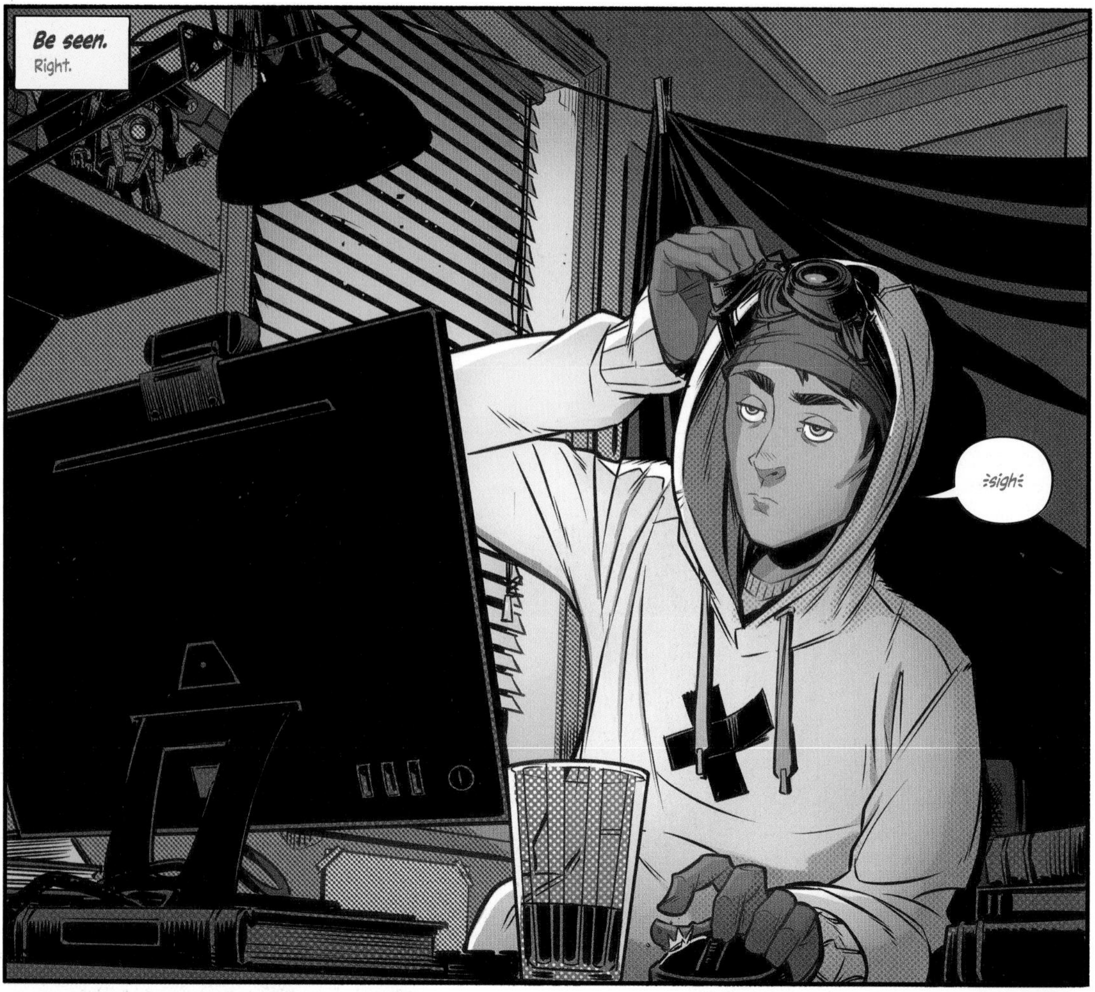
Be seen.
Right.
sigh

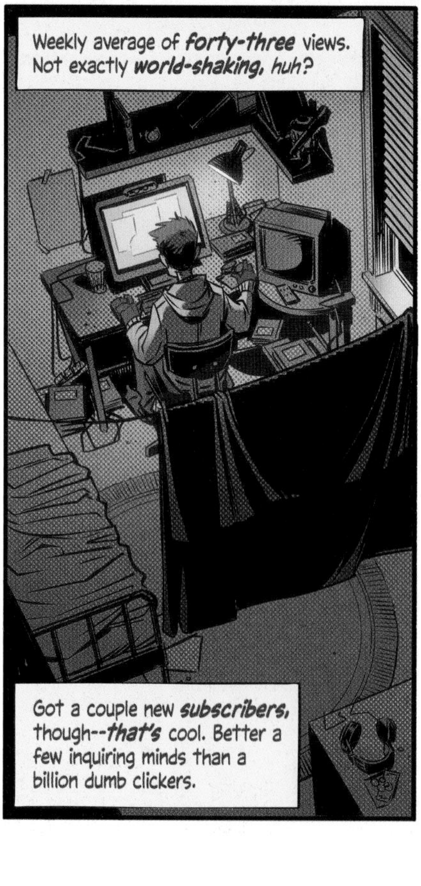
Weekly average of ***forty-three*** views. Not exactly ***world-shaking, huh?***
Got a couple new ***subscribers,*** though--***that's*** cool. Better a few inquiring minds than a billion dumb clickers.

"Factions speak louder than herds"-- that's one of the golden rules.

The others are ***"Don't read the comments"*** and ***"Keep the damn content flowing, dummy."***

Because...c'mon.

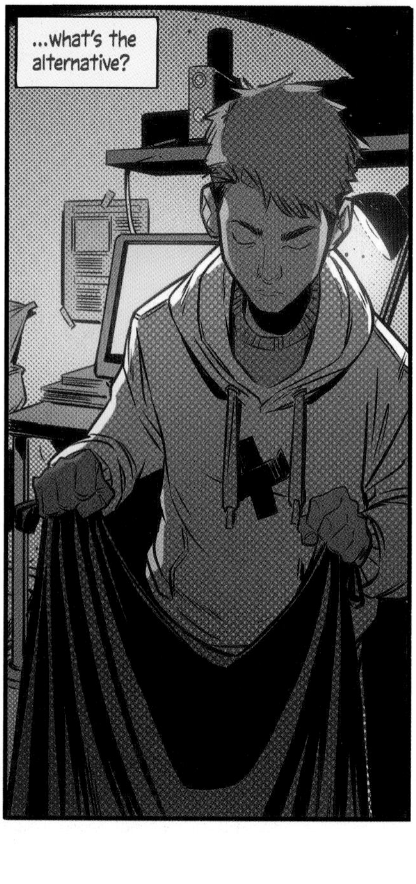
...what's the alternative?

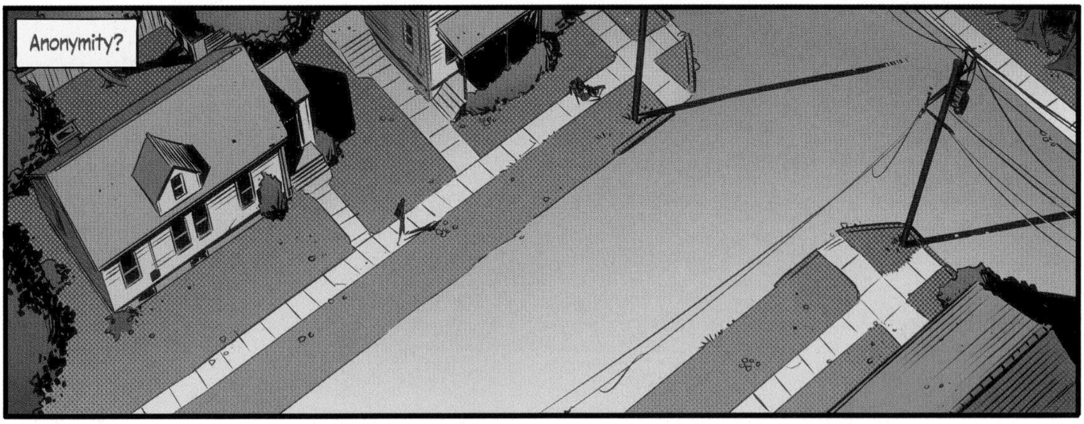
Anonymity?

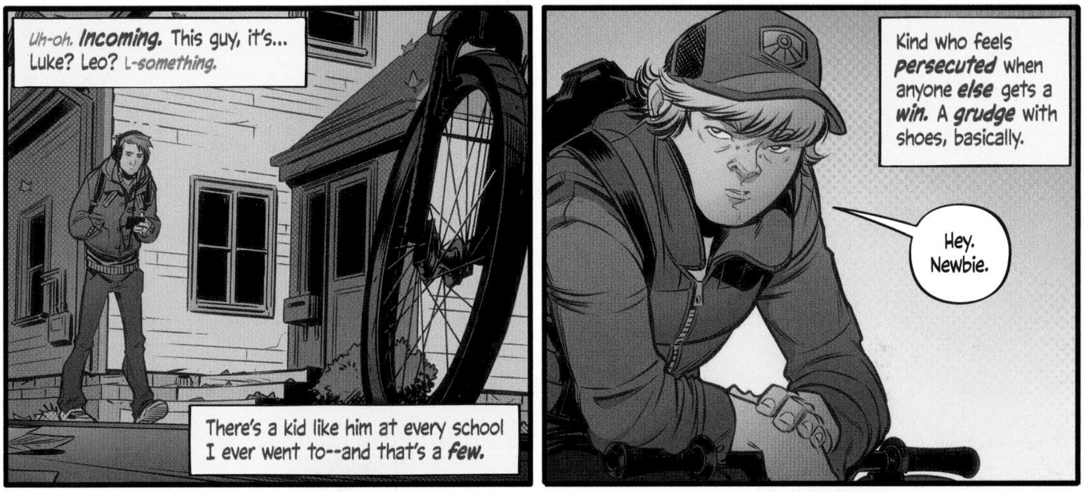
Uh-oh. Incoming. This guy, it's... Luke? Leo? L-something.
There's a kid like him at every school I ever went to--and that's a few.
Kind who feels persecuted when anyone else gets a win. A grudge with shoes, basically.
Hey. Newbie.

Probably got a shopping list of *small arms* in the pocket of his favorite trenchcoat. One of *those* guys.

Just my luck he's the only one so far who even *noticed* me.

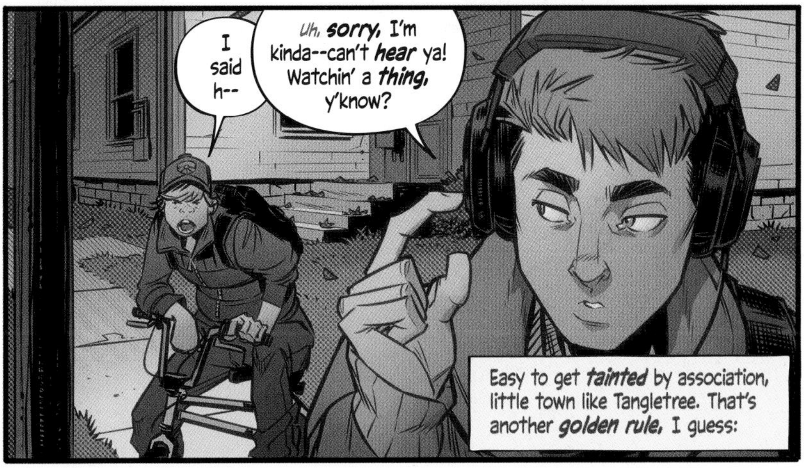
I said h--
Uh, sorry, I'm kinda--can't hear ya! Watchin' a thing, y'know?
Easy to get tainted by association, little town like Tangletree. That's another golden rule, I guess:

S A M U E L

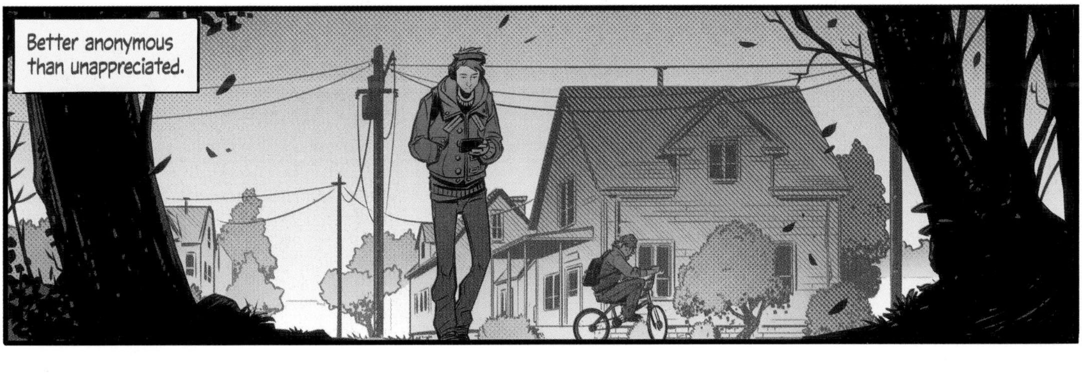
Better anonymous than unappreciated.

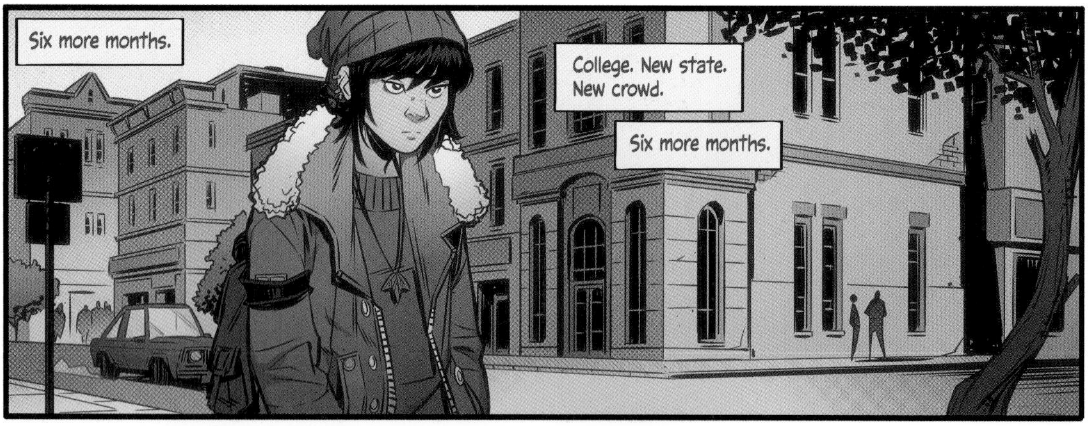
Six more months.
College. New state. New crowd.
Six more months.

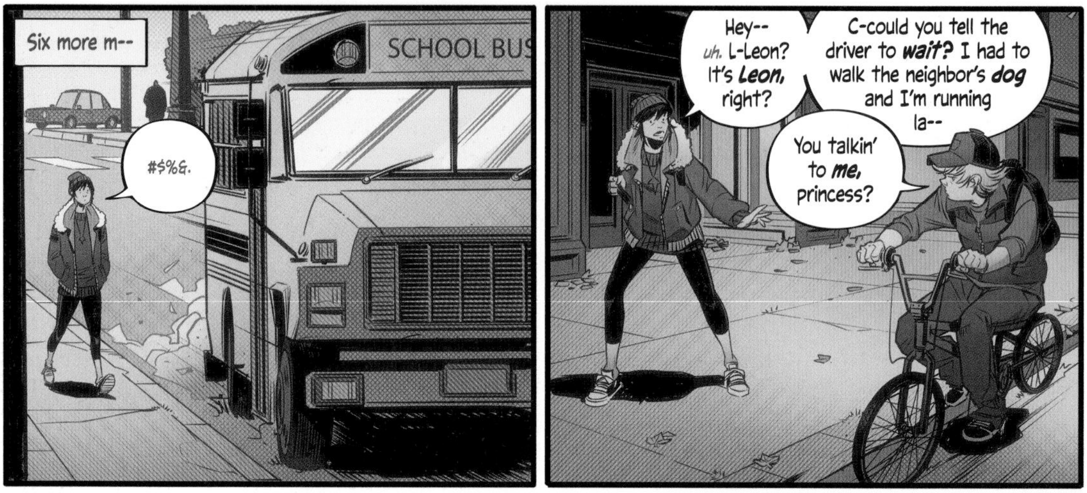
Six more m--
SCHOOL BUS
#$%&.
Hey-- uh. L-Leon? It's Leon, right?
C-could you tell the driver to wait? I had to walk the neighbor's dog and I'm running la--
You talkin' to me, princess?

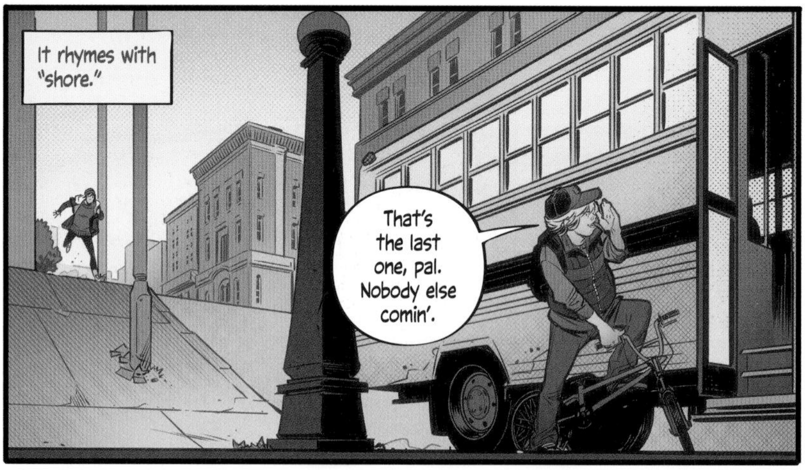
It rhymes with "shore."
That's the last one, pal. Nobody else comin'.

He slows the bike and he says that's the first time I ever said his name.

I'm about to ***apologize*** for that --I'm blushing, even-- when he meets my eye and says a ***word.***

S A M A N T H A

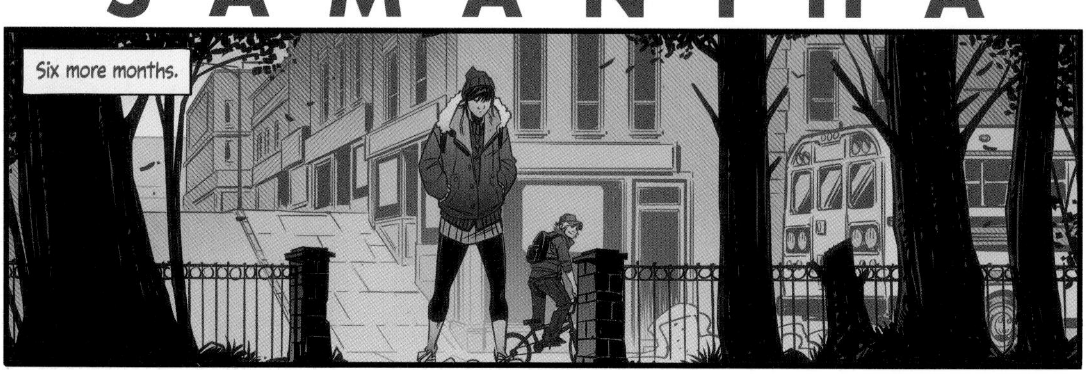
Six more months.

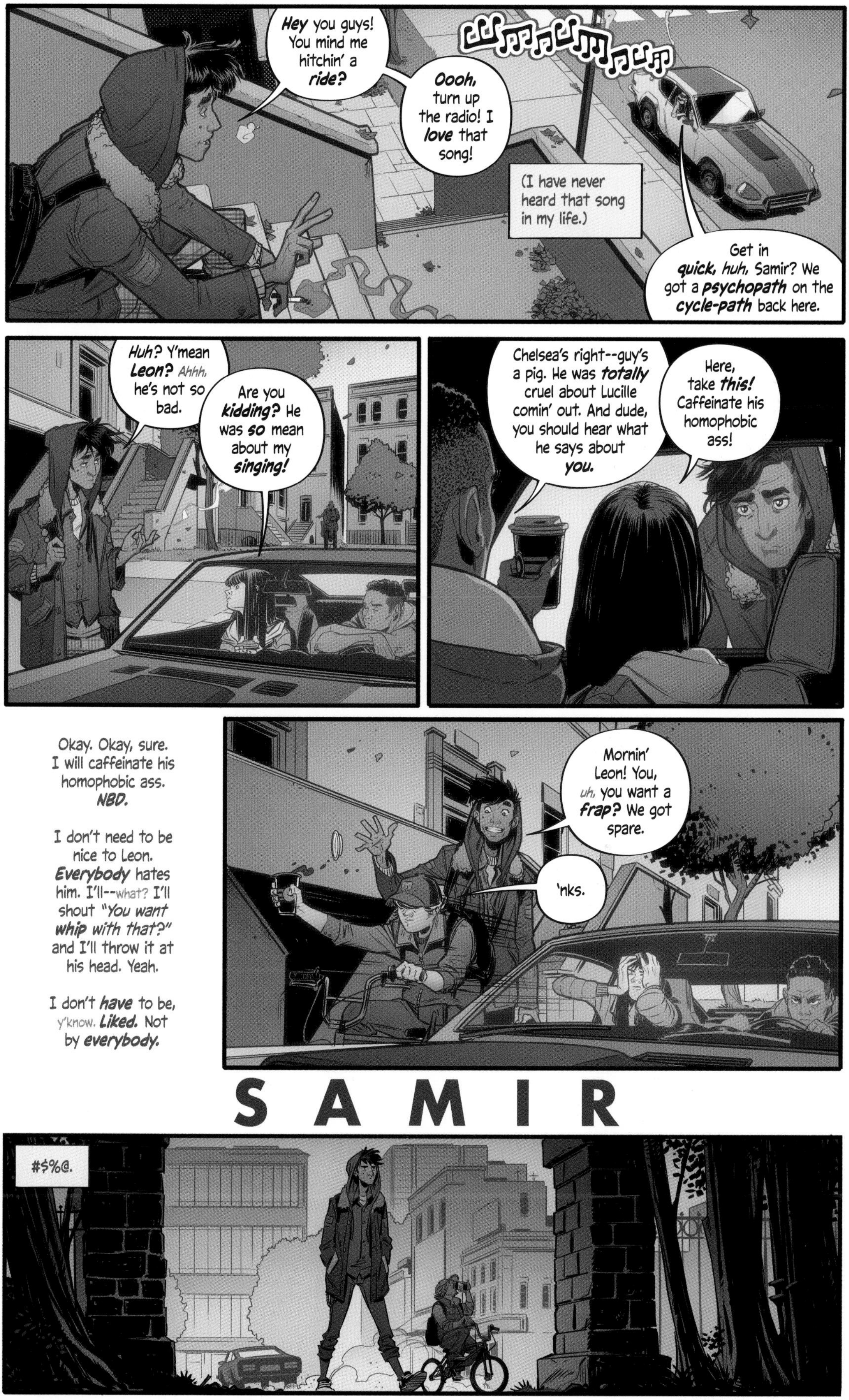

Hey you guys! You mind me hitchin' a ride?
Oooh, turn up the radio! I love that song!
(I have never heard that song in my life.)
Get in quick, huh, Samir? We got a psychopath on the cycle-path back here.
Huh? Y'mean Leon? Ahhh, he's not so bad.
Are you kidding? He was so mean about my singing!
Chelsea's right--guy's a pig. He was totally cruel about Lucille comin' out. And dude, you should hear what he says about you.
Here, take this! Caffeinate his homophobic ass!
Okay. Okay, sure. I will caffeinate his homophobic ass. NBD.
I don't need to be nice to Leon. Everybody hates him. I'll--what? I'll shout "You want whip with that?" and I'll throw it at his head. Yeah.
I don't have to be, y'know. Liked. Not by everybody.
Mornin' Leon! You, uh, you want a frap? We got spare.
'nks.
SAMIR
#$%@.

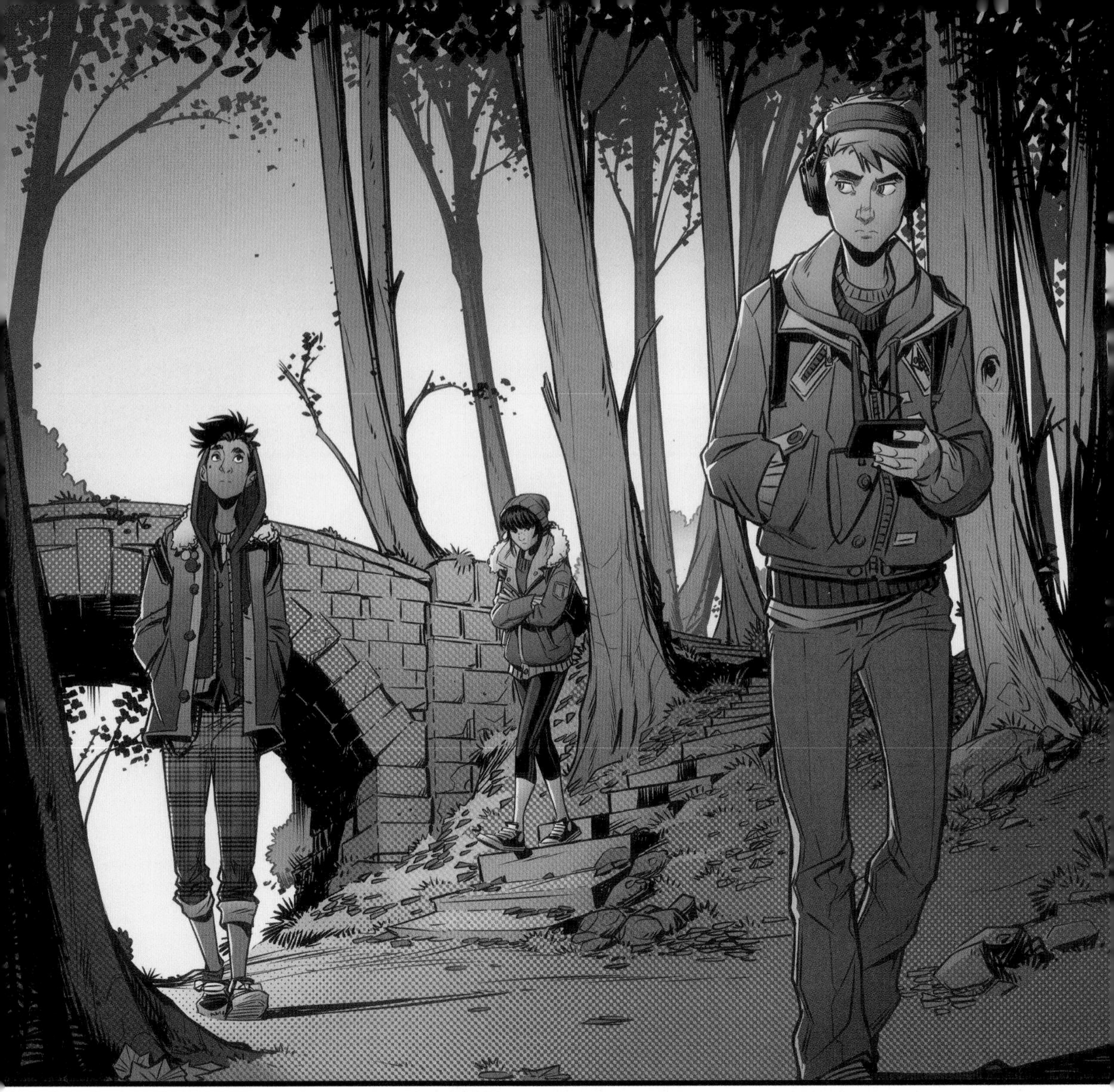

Chapter 1:
THREE KIDS CALLED SAM GO WALKING IN THE WOODS

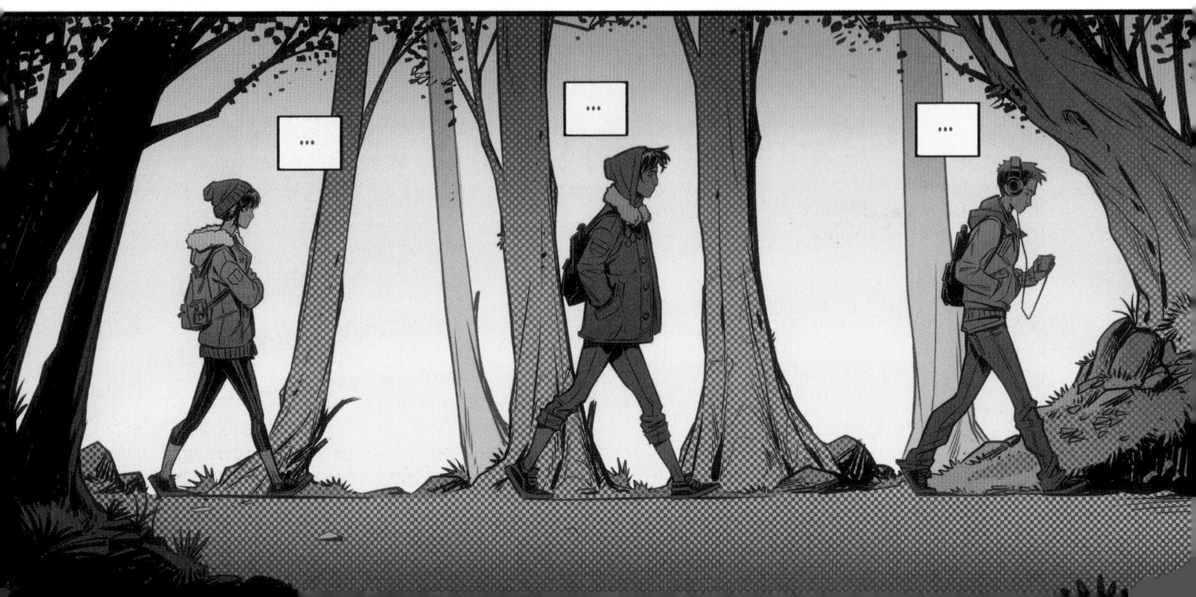
...
...
...

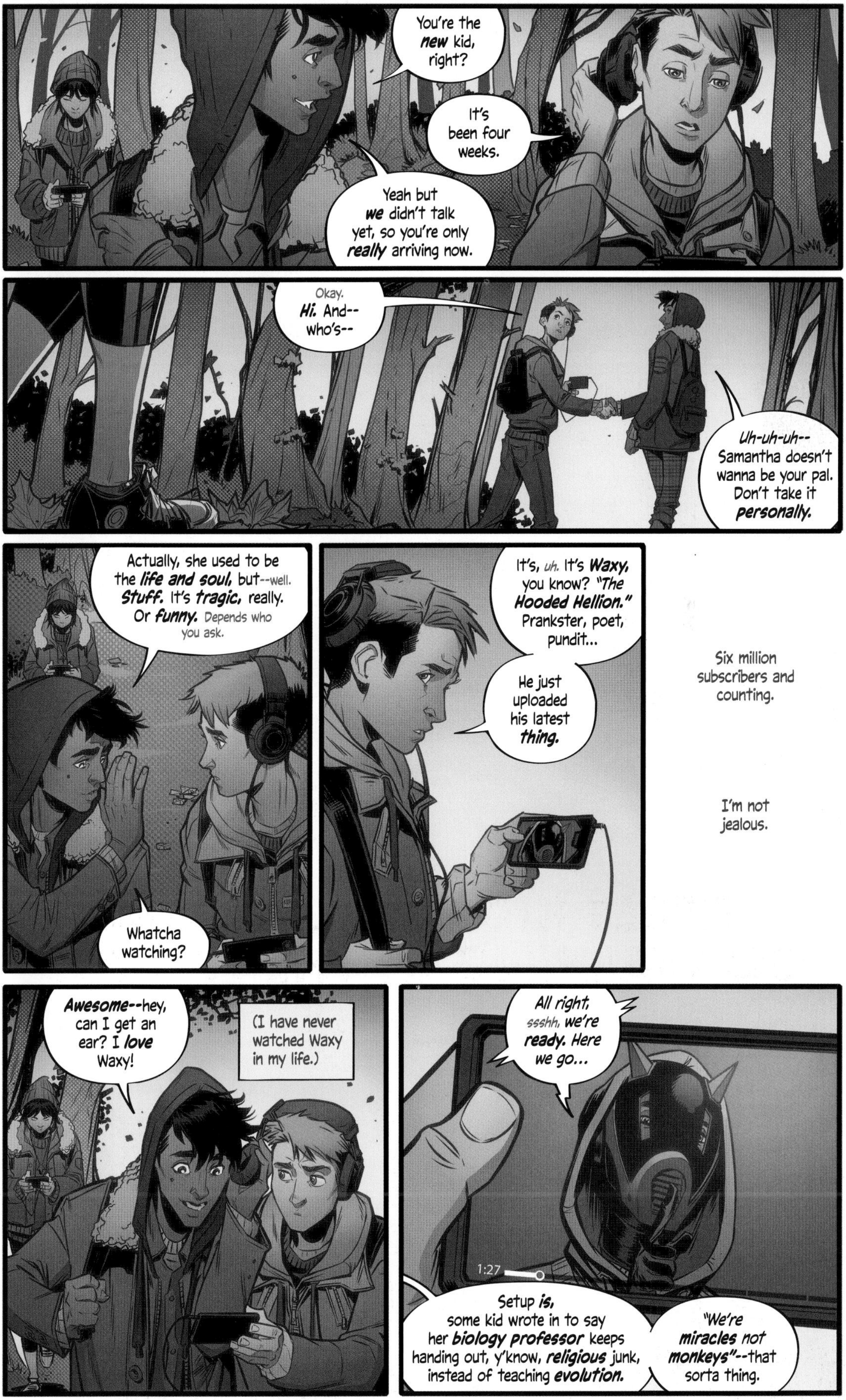
You're the new kid, right?
It's been four weeks.
Yeah but we didn't talk yet, so you're only really arriving now.
Okay. Hi. And-- who's--
Uh-uh-uh-- Samantha doesn't wanna be your pal. Don't take it personally.
Actually, she used to be the life and soul, but--well. Stuff. It's tragic, really. Or funny. Depends who you ask.
Whatcha watching?
It's, uh. It's Waxy, you know? "The Hooded Hellion." Prankster, poet, pundit...
He just uploaded his latest thing.
Six million subscribers and counting.
I'm not jealous.
Awesome--hey, can I get an ear? I love Waxy!
(I have never watched Waxy in my life.)
All right, ssshh, we're ready. Here we go...
1:27
Setup is, some kid wrote in to say her biology professor keeps handing out, y'know, religious junk, instead of teaching evolution.
"We're miracles not monkeys"--that sorta thing.

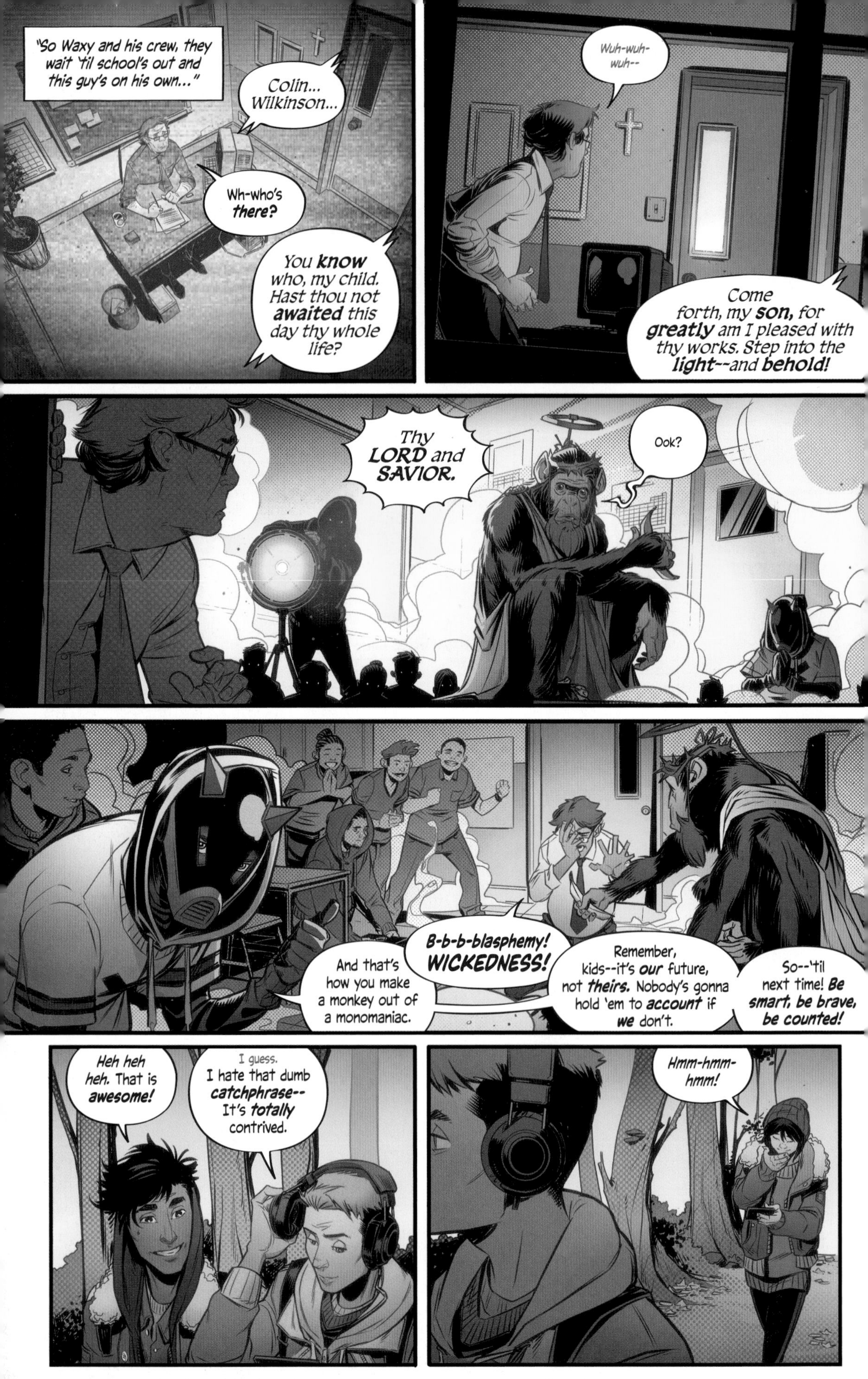
"So Waxy and his crew, they wait 'til school's out and this guy's on his own..."
Colin... Wilkinson...
Wh-who's there?
You know who, my child. Hast thou not awaited this day thy whole life?
Wuh-wuh-wuh--
Come forth, my son, for greatly am I pleased with thy works. Step into the light--and behold!
Thy LORD and SAVIOR.
Ook?
And that's how you make a monkey out of a monomaniac.
B-b-b-blasphemy! WICKEDNESS!
Remember, kids--it's our future, not theirs. Nobody's gonna hold 'em to account if we don't.
So--'til next time! Be smart, be brave, be counted!
Heh heh heh. That is awesome!
I guess. I hate that dumb catchphrase-- It's totally contrived.
Hmm-hmm-hmm!

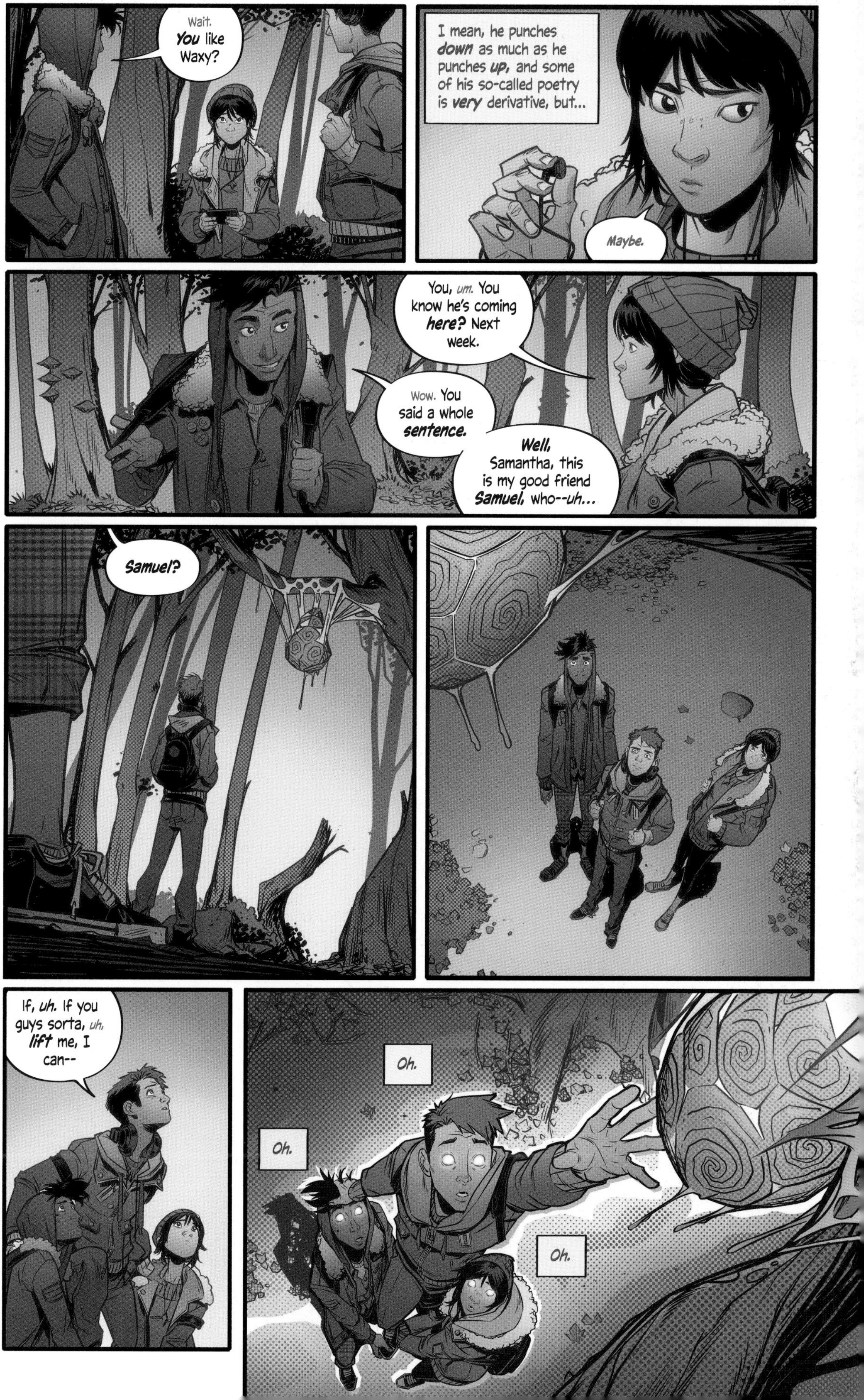
Wait. You like Waxy?
I mean, he punches down as much as he punches up, and some of his so-called poetry is very derivative, but...
Maybe.
You, um. You know he's coming here? Next week.
Wow. You said a whole sentence.
Well, Samantha, this is my good friend Samuel, who--uh...
Samuel?
If, uh. If you guys sorta, uh, lift me, I can--
Oh.
Oh.
Oh.

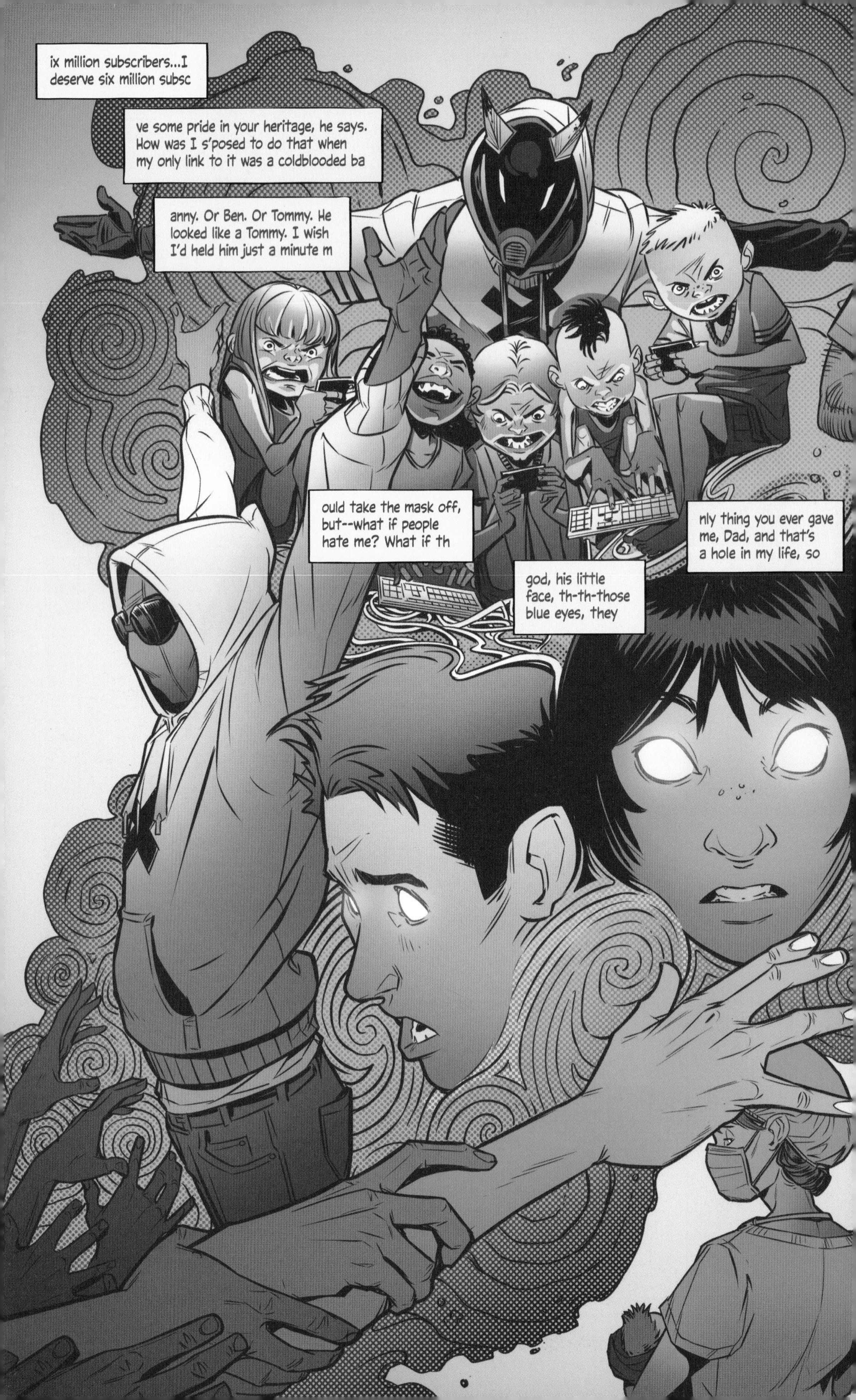
ix million subscribers...I deserve six million subsc
ve some pride in your heritage, he says. How was I s'posed to do that when my only link to it was a coldblooded ba
anny. Or Ben. Or Tommy. He looked like a Tommy. I wish I'd held him just a minute m
ould take the mask off, but--what if people hate me? What if th
nly thing you ever gave me, Dad, and that's a hole in my life, so
god, his little face, th-th-those blue eyes, they

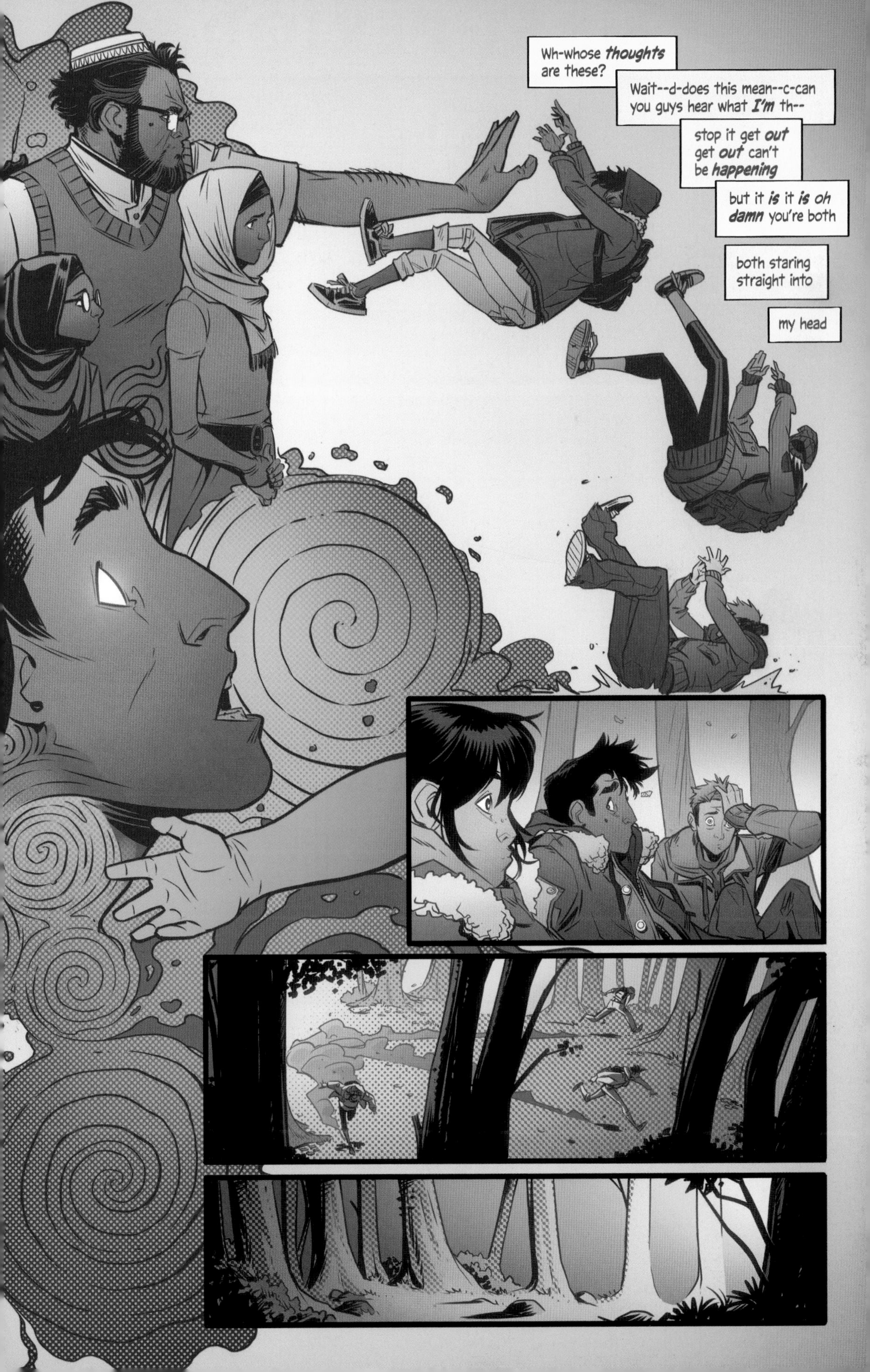
Wh-whose *thoughts* are these?
Wait--d-does this mean--c-can you guys hear what *I'm* th--
stop it get *out* get *out* can't be *happening*
but it *is* it *is oh damn* you're both
both staring straight into
my head

FIRST PERIOD

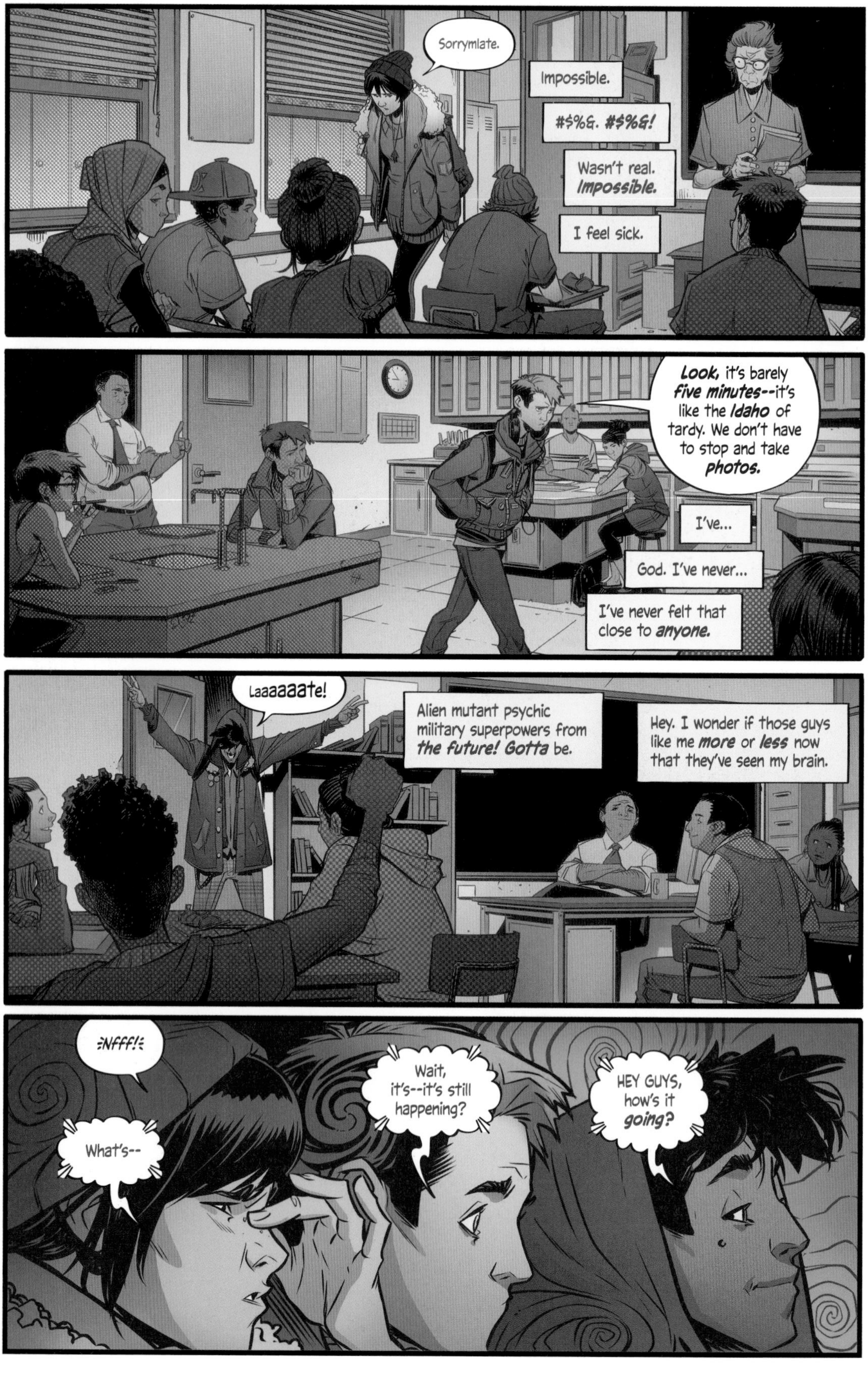

Sorrymlate.
Impossible.
#$%&. #$%&!
Wasn't real. *Impossible.*
I feel sick.
Look, it's barely *five minutes*--it's like the *Idaho* of tardy. We don't have to stop and take *photos.*
I've...
God. I've never...
I've never felt that close to *anyone.*
Laaaaaate!
Alien mutant psychic military superpowers from *the future! Gotta* be.
Hey. I wonder if those guys like me *more* or *less* now that they've seen my brain.
Nfff!
What's--
Wait, it's--it's still happening?
HEY GUYS, how's it *going?*

SECOND PERIOD

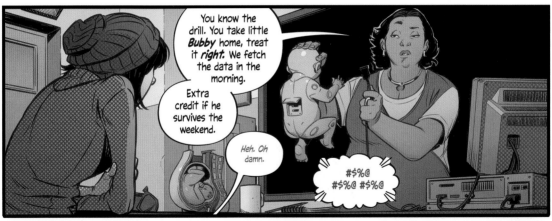

You know the drill. You take little *Bubby* home, treat it *right*. We fetch the data in the morning.

Extra credit if he survives the weekend.

Heh. Oh damn.

#$%@ #$%@ #$%@

I never felt *sorry* for no *toy* before.

bastard bastard bastard bastard

W-What's Leon *mean*? What's the big deal about *babie--*

Get out of my *head* get out of my *head!*

Listen, Leon's not that bad--I'll *talk* to him, okay? Us three gotta *stick together*, now that we're *brainbuds*.

We are *not* brainbu--

F-F-S Samantha, would you calm *down*? Givin' me a migraine over here.

Anyway, he's *totally* into me.

LUNCH BREAK

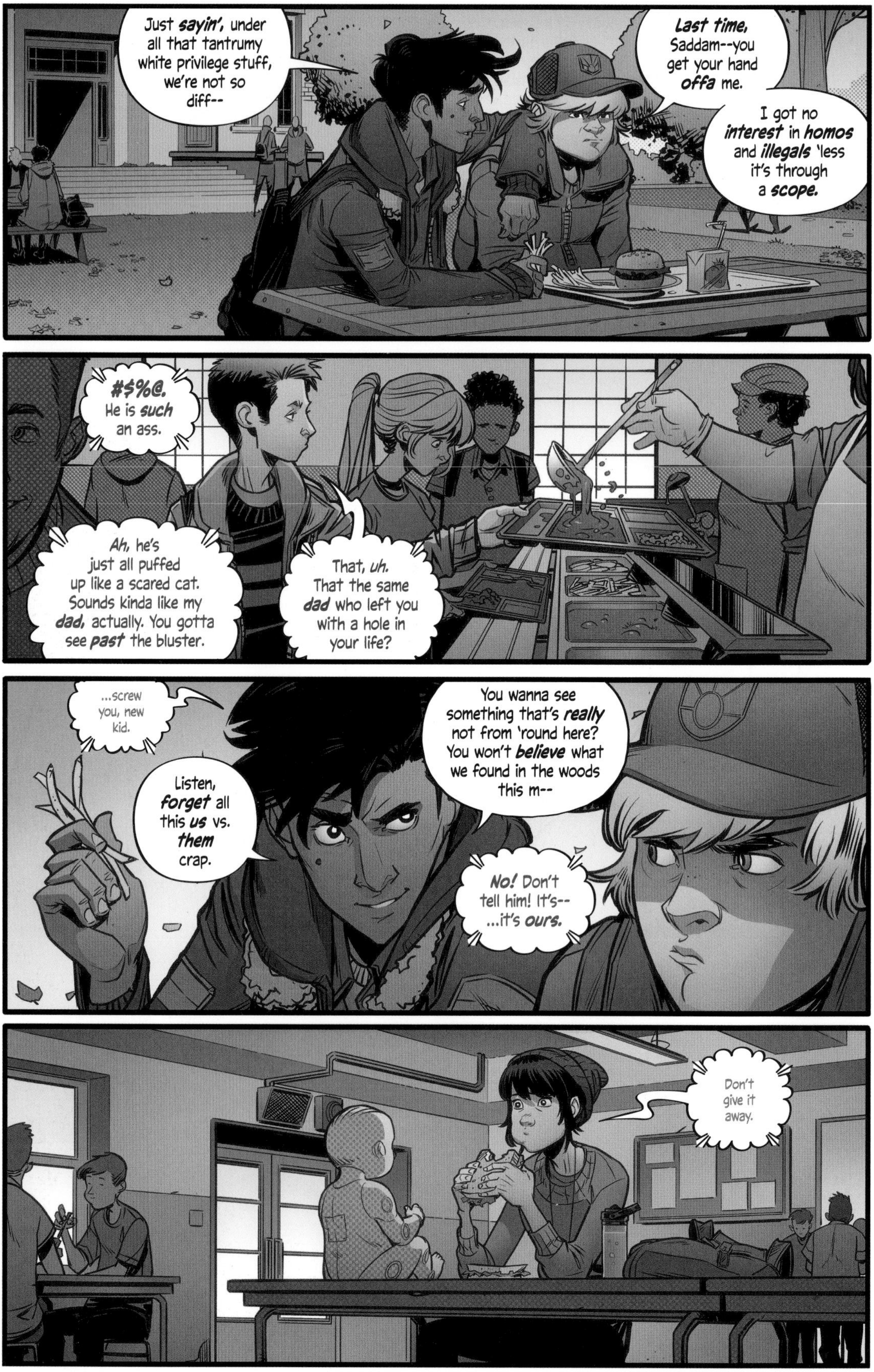
Just sayin', under all that tantrumy white privilege stuff, we're not so diff--
Last time, Saddam--you get your hand offa me.
I got no interest in homos and illegals 'less it's through a scope.
#$%@. He is such an ass.
Ah, he's just all puffed up like a scared cat. Sounds kinda like my dad, actually. You gotta see past the bluster.
That, uh. That the same dad who left you with a hole in your life?
...screw you, new kid.
Listen, forget all this us vs. them crap.
You wanna see something that's really not from 'round here? You won't believe what we found in the woods this m--
No! Don't tell him! It's-- ...it's ours.
Don't give it away.

THIRD PERIOD

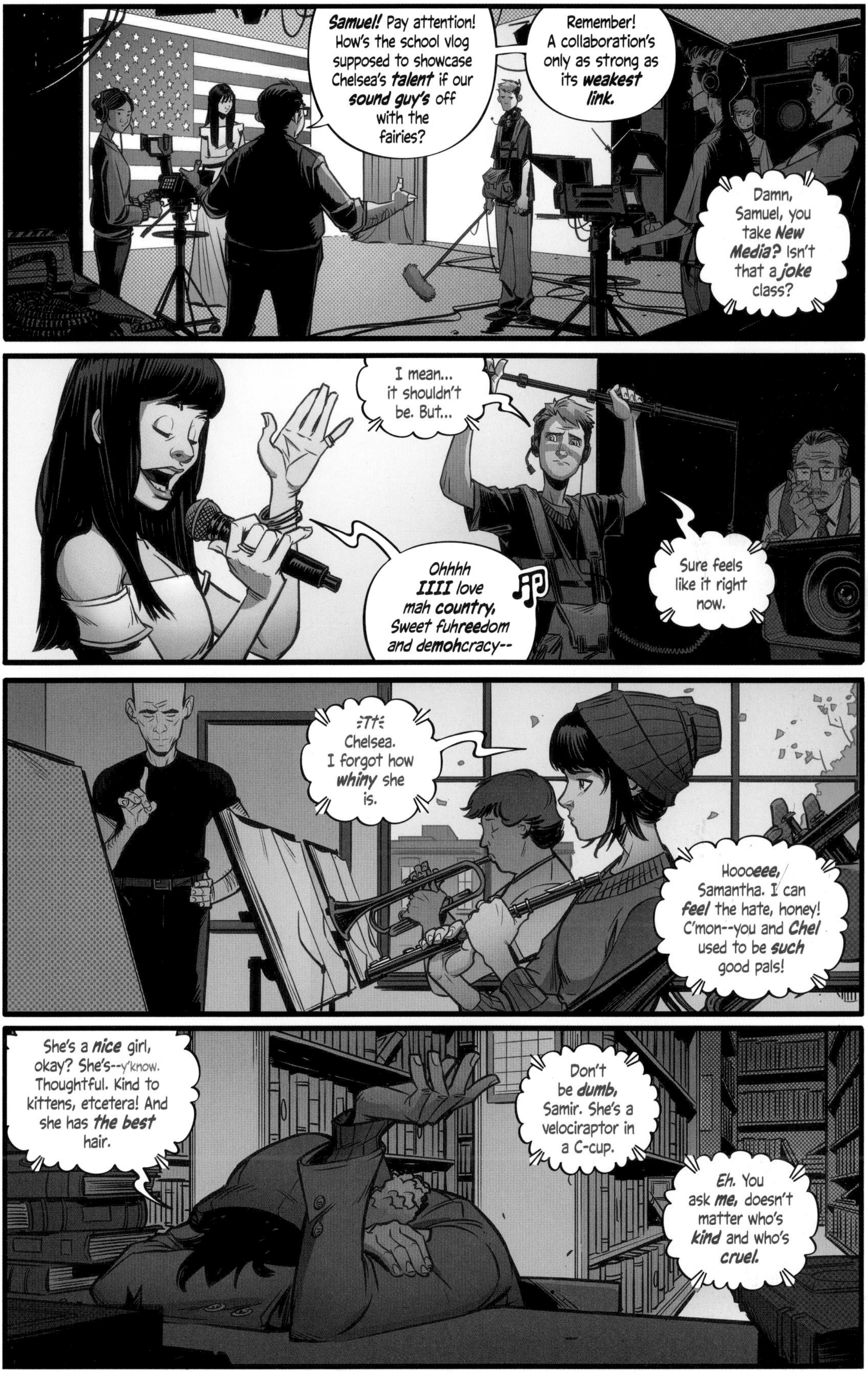
Samuel! Pay attention! How's the school vlog supposed to showcase Chelsea's talent if our sound guy's off with the fairies?
Remember! A collaboration's only as strong as its weakest link.
Damn, Samuel, you take New Media? Isn't that a joke class?
I mean... it shouldn't be. But...
Ohhhh IIII love mah country, Sweet fuhreedom and demohcracy--
Sure feels like it right now.
Tt
Chelsea. I forgot how whiny she is.
Hoooeee, Samantha. I can feel the hate, honey! C'mon--you and Chel used to be such good pals!
She's a nice girl, okay? She's--y'know. Thoughtful. Kind to kittens, etcetera! And she has the best hair.
Don't be dumb, Samir. She's a velociraptor in a C-cup.
Eh. You ask me, doesn't matter who's kind and who's cruel.

FOURTH PERIOD

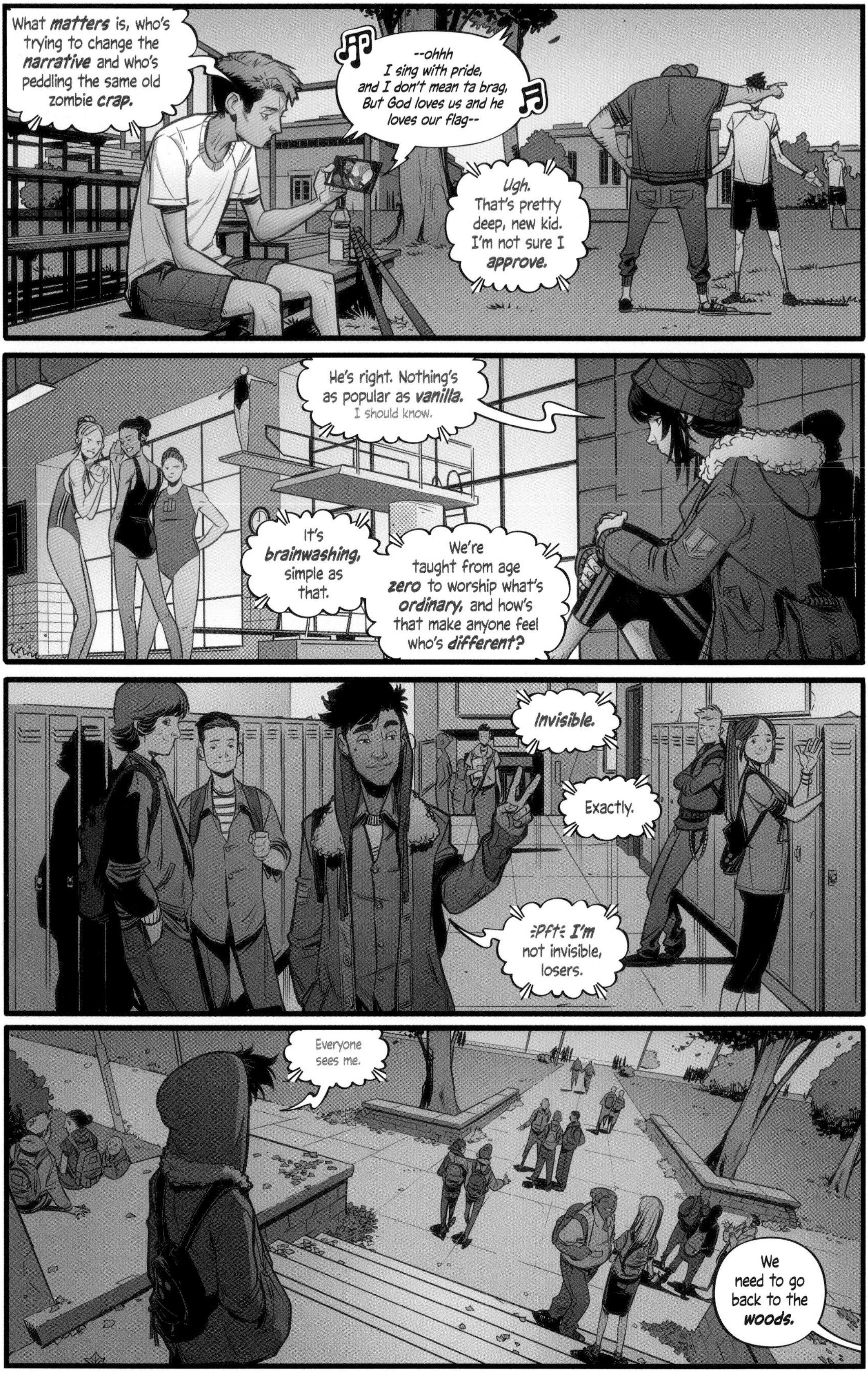
What matters is, who's trying to change the narrative and who's peddling the same old zombie crap.
--ohhh I sing with pride, and I don't mean ta brag, But God loves us and he loves our flag--
Ugh. That's pretty deep, new kid. I'm not sure I approve.
He's right. Nothing's as popular as vanilla. I should know.
It's brainwashing, simple as that.
We're taught from age zero to worship what's ordinary, and how's that make anyone feel who's different?
Invisible.
Exactly.
Pft I'm not invisible, losers.
Everyone sees me.
We need to go back to the woods.

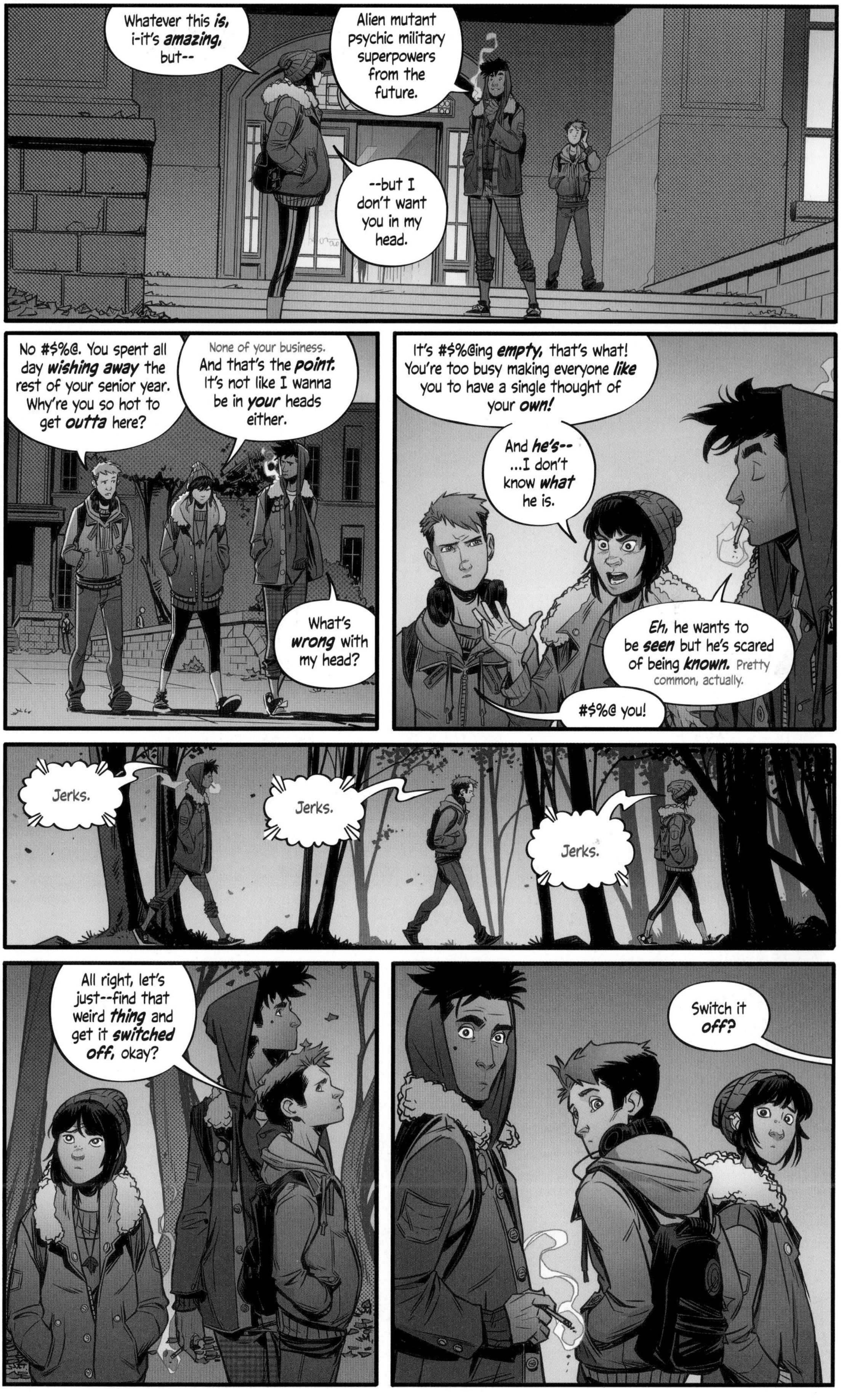
Whatever this is, i-it's amazing, but--
Alien mutant psychic military superpowers from the future.
--but I don't want you in my head.
No #$%@. You spent all day wishing away the rest of your senior year. Why're you so hot to get outta here?
None of your business. And that's the point. It's not like I wanna be in your heads either.
What's wrong with my head?
It's #$%@ing empty, that's what! You're too busy making everyone like you to have a single thought of your own!
And he's-- ...I don't know what he is.
Eh, he wants to be seen but he's scared of being known. Pretty common, actually.
#$%@ you!
Jerks.
Jerks.
Jerks.
All right, let's just--find that weird thing and get it switched off, okay?
Switch it off?

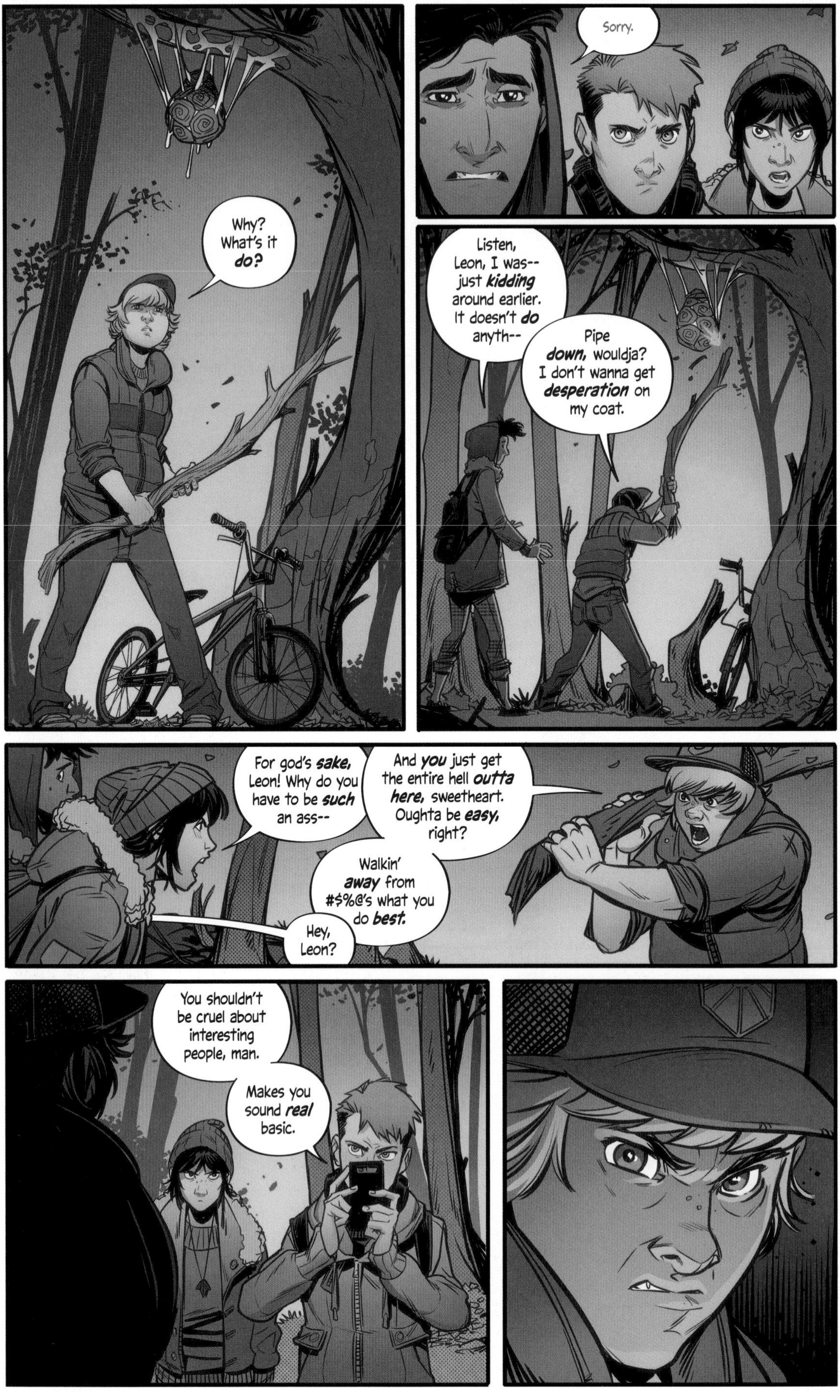
Why? What's it do?
Sorry.
Listen, Leon, I was-- just kidding around earlier. It doesn't do anyth--
Pipe down, wouldja? I don't wanna get desperation on my coat.
For god's sake, Leon! Why do you have to be such an ass--
And you just get the entire hell outta here, sweetheart. Oughta be easy, right?
Walkin' away from #$%@'s what you do best.
Hey, Leon?
You shouldn't be cruel about interesting people, man.
Makes you sound real basic.

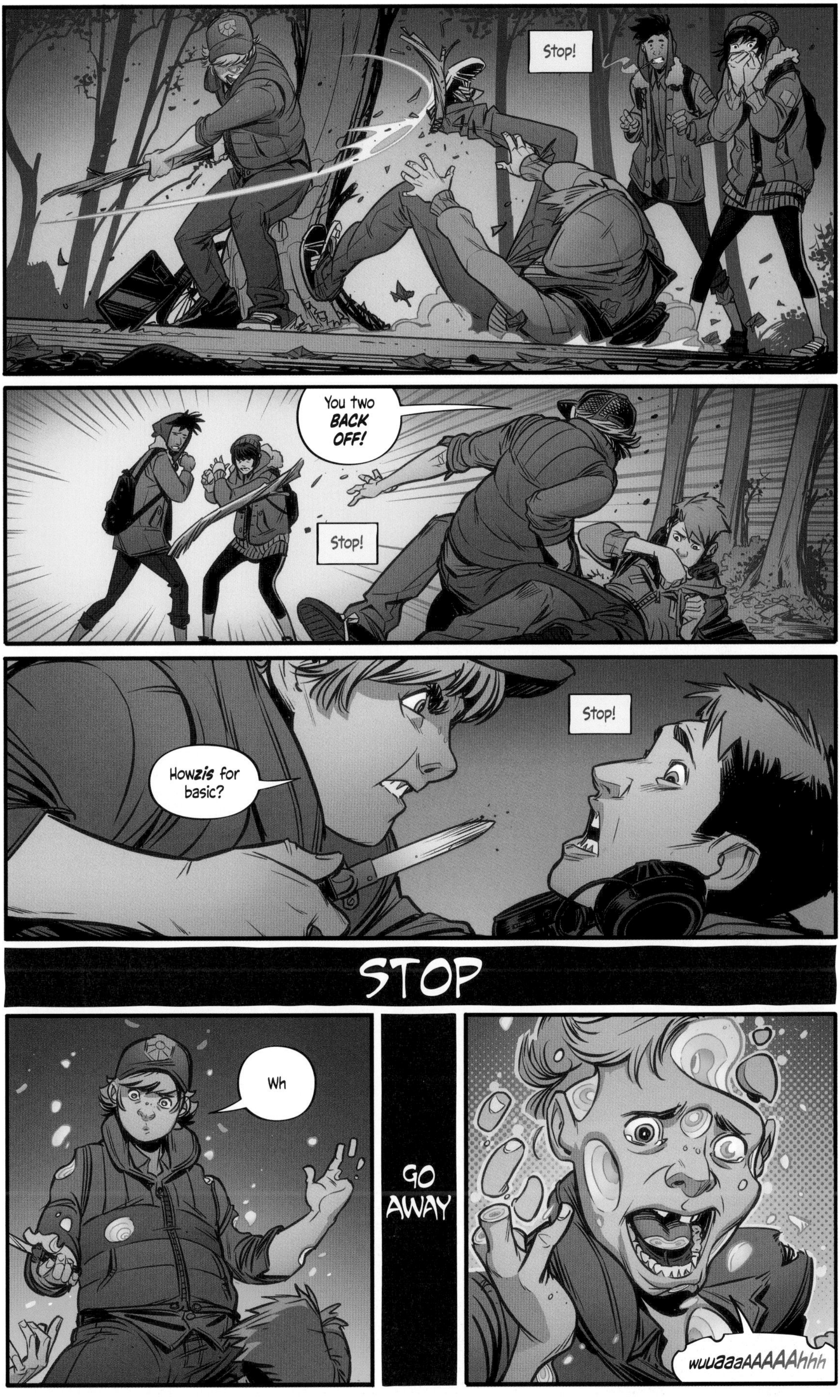
Stop!
You two BACK OFF!
Stop!
Stop!
Howzis for basic?
STOP
Wh
GO AWAY
wuuaaaAAAAAhhh

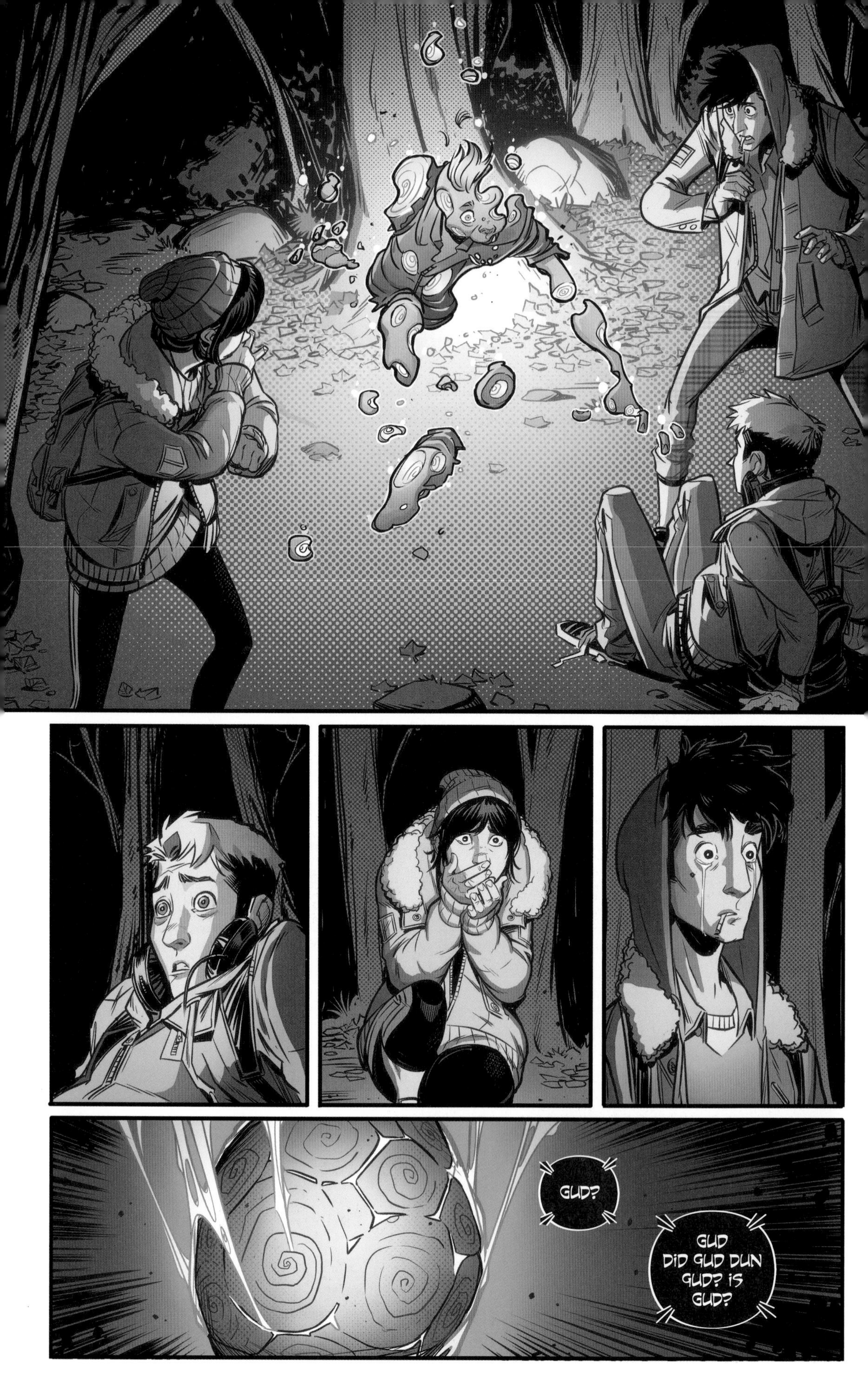
GUD?
GUD
DID GUD DUN
GUD? IS
GUD?

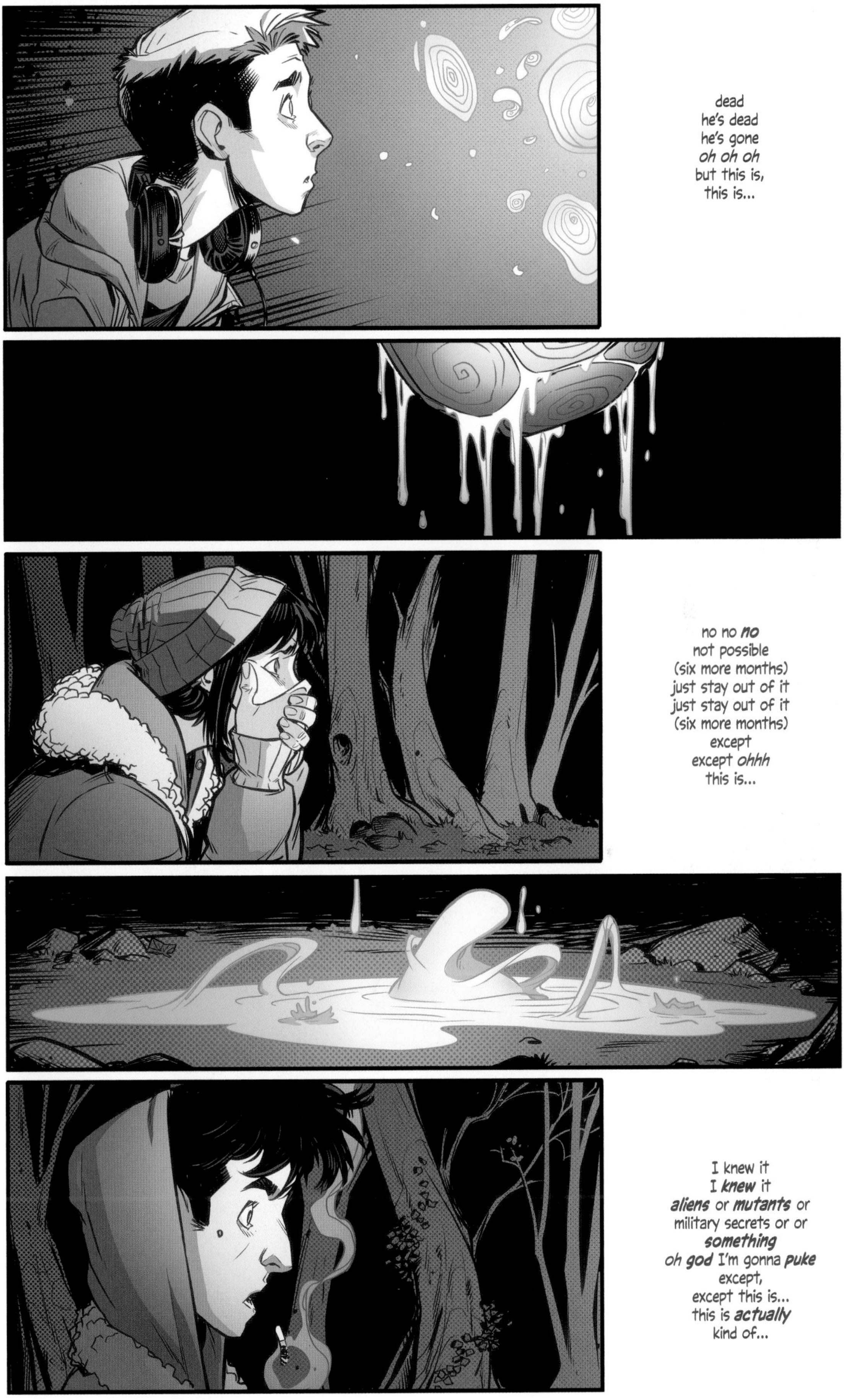
dead
he's dead
he's gone
oh oh oh
but this is,
this is...
no no no
not possible
(six more months)
just stay out of it
just stay out of it
(six more months)
except
except ohhh
this is...
I knew it
I knew it
aliens or mutants or
military secrets or or
something
oh god I'm gonna puke
except,
except this is...
this is actually
kind of...

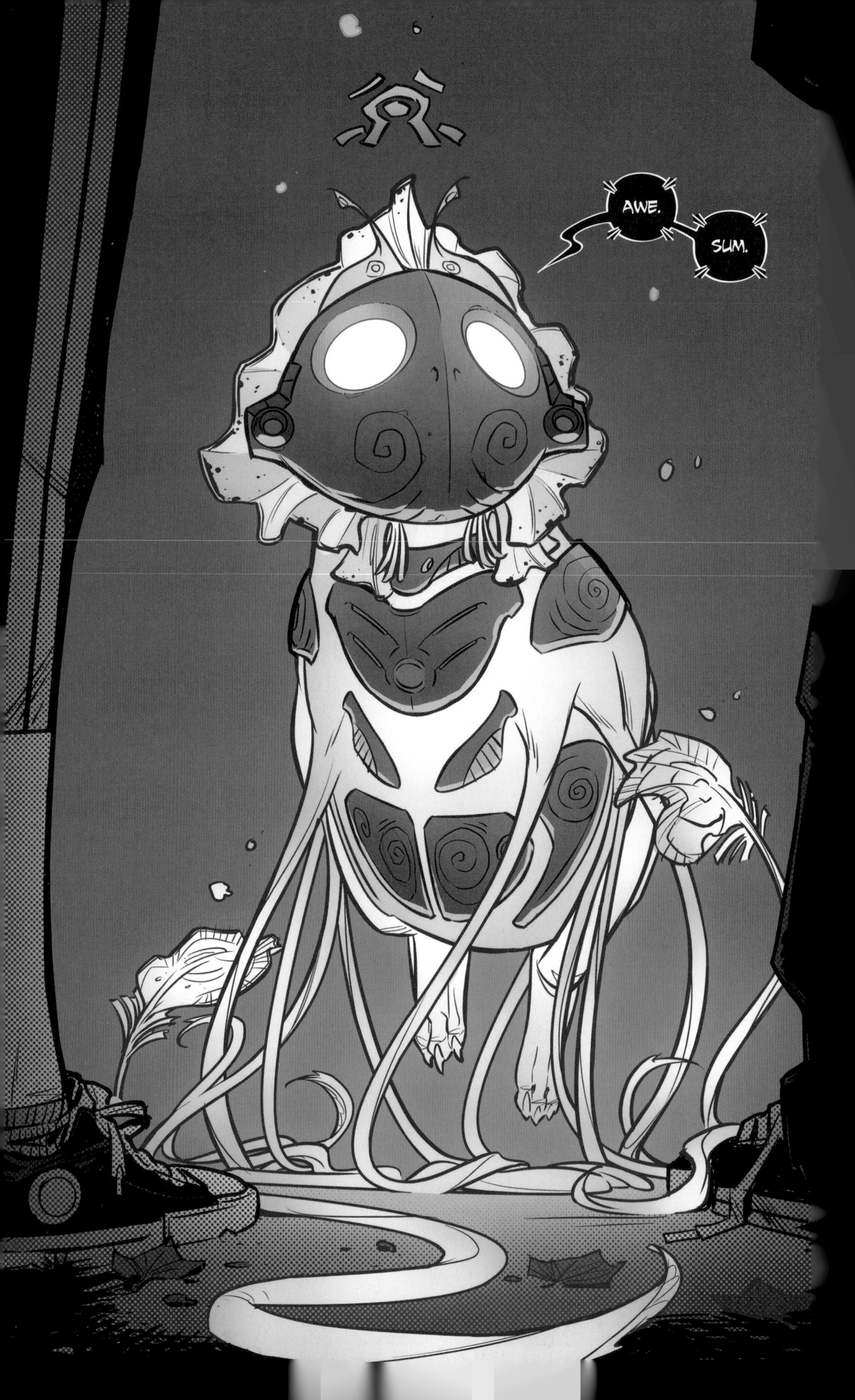
AWE.
SUM.

CHAPTER TWO

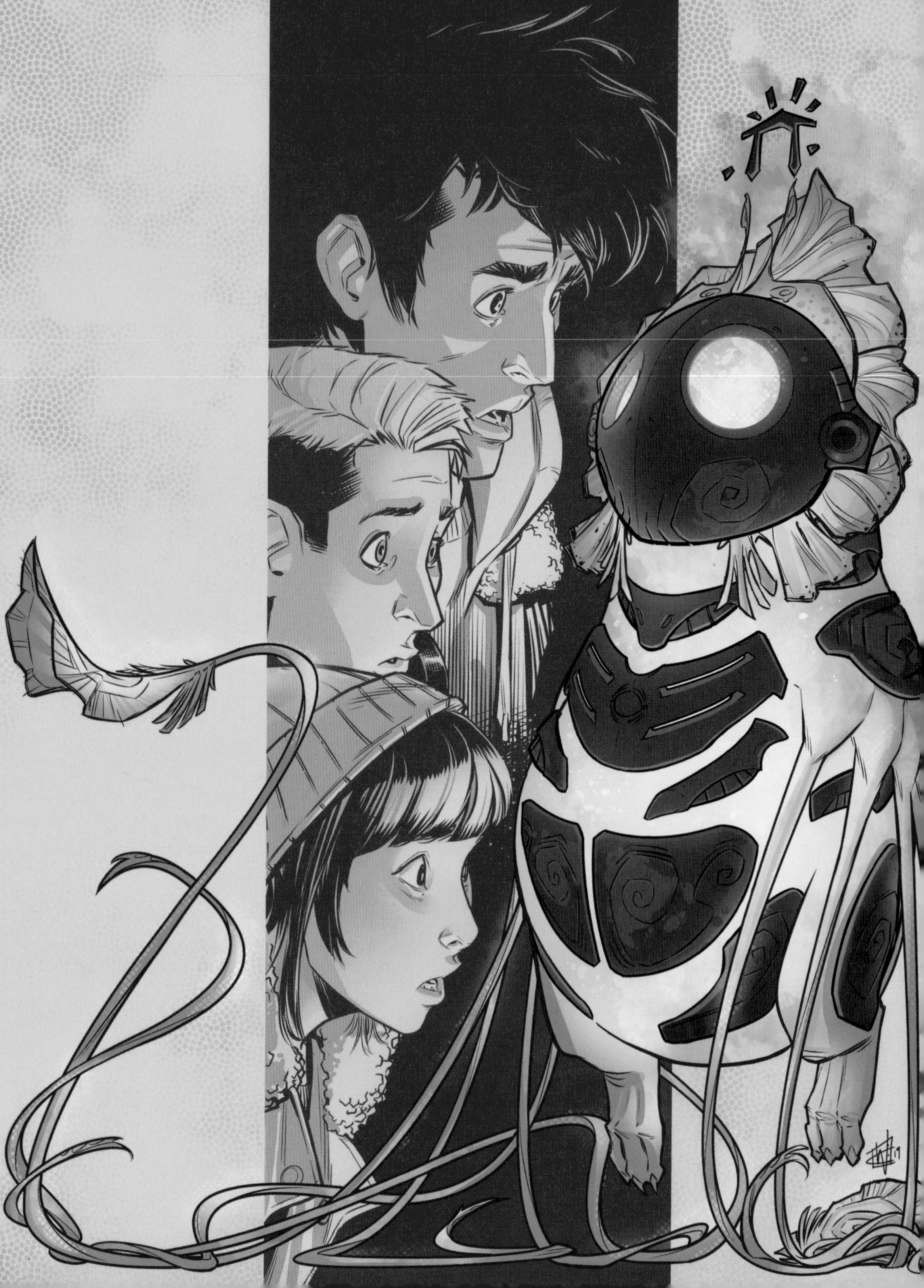

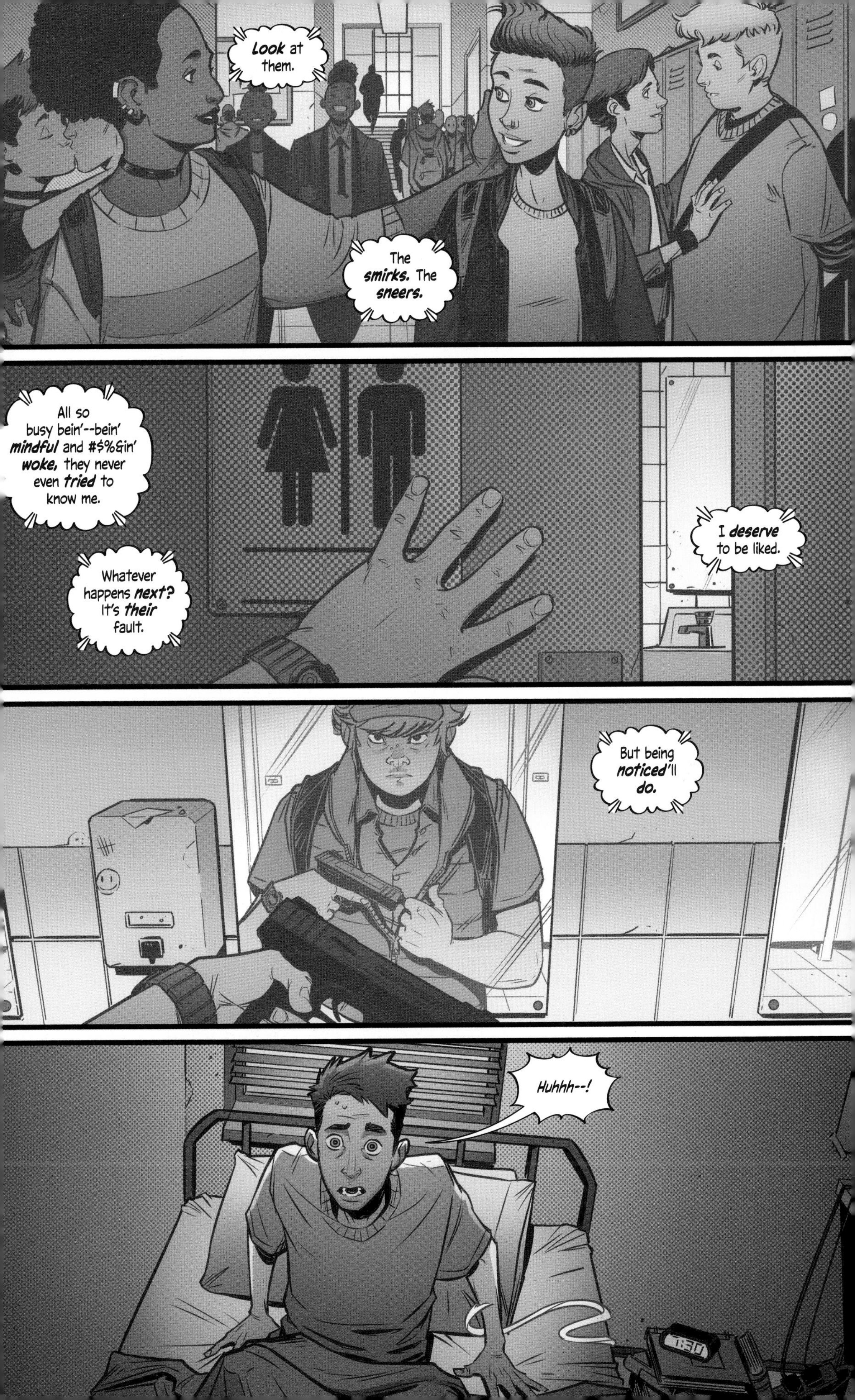
Look at them.
The smirks. The sneers.
All so busy bein'--bein' mindful and #$%&in' woke, they never even tried to know me.
Whatever happens next? It's their fault.
I deserve to be liked.
But being noticed'll do.
Huhhh--!
7:30

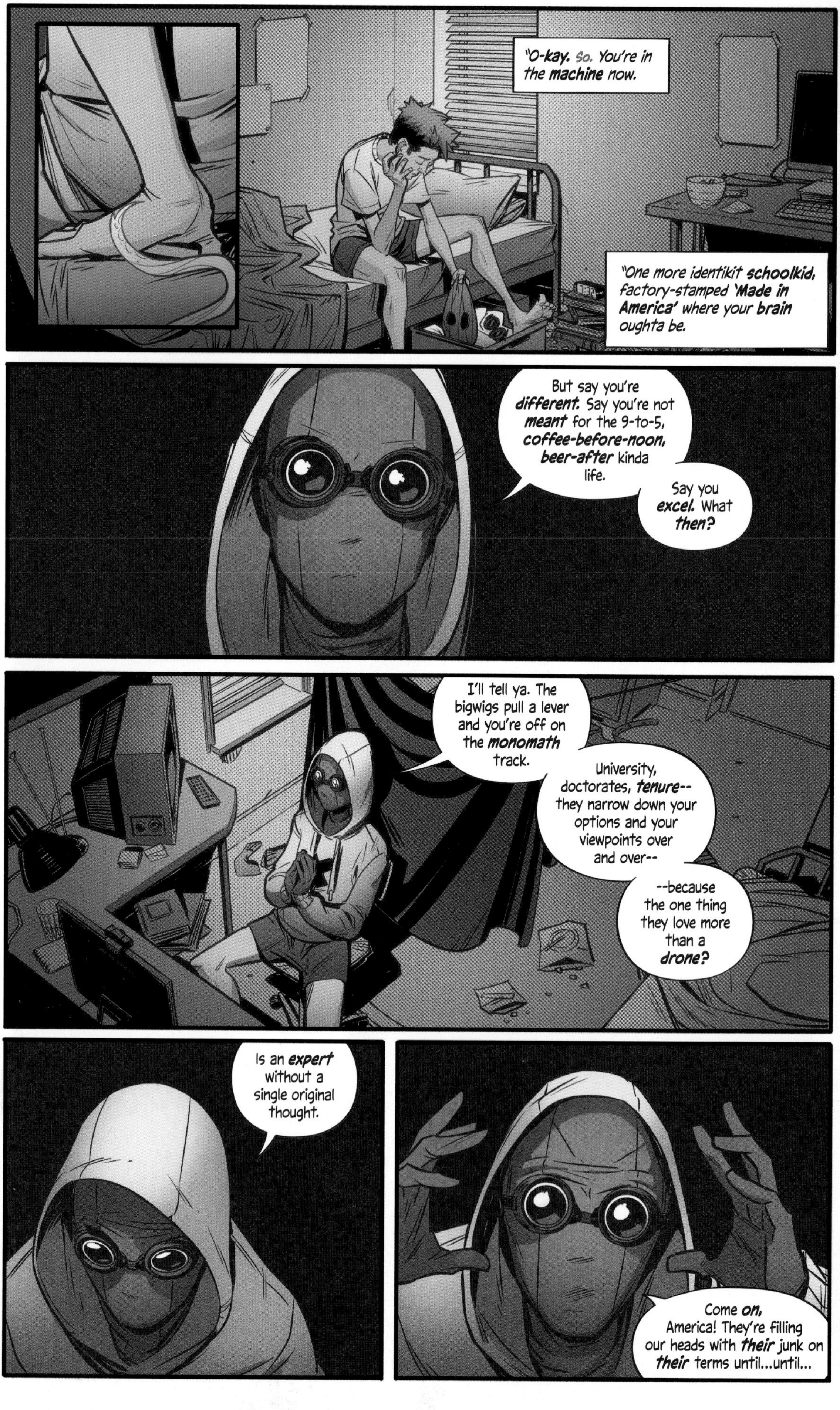
"O-kay. So. You're in the machine now.
"One more identikit schoolkid, factory-stamped 'Made in America' where your brain oughta be.
But say you're different. Say you're not meant for the 9-to-5, coffee-before-noon, beer-after kinda life.
Say you excel. What then?
I'll tell ya. The bigwigs pull a lever and you're off on the monomath track.
University, doctorates, tenure-- they narrow down your options and your viewpoints over and over--
--because the one thing they love more than a drone?
Is an expert without a single original thought.
Come on, America! They're filling our heads with their junk on their terms until...until...

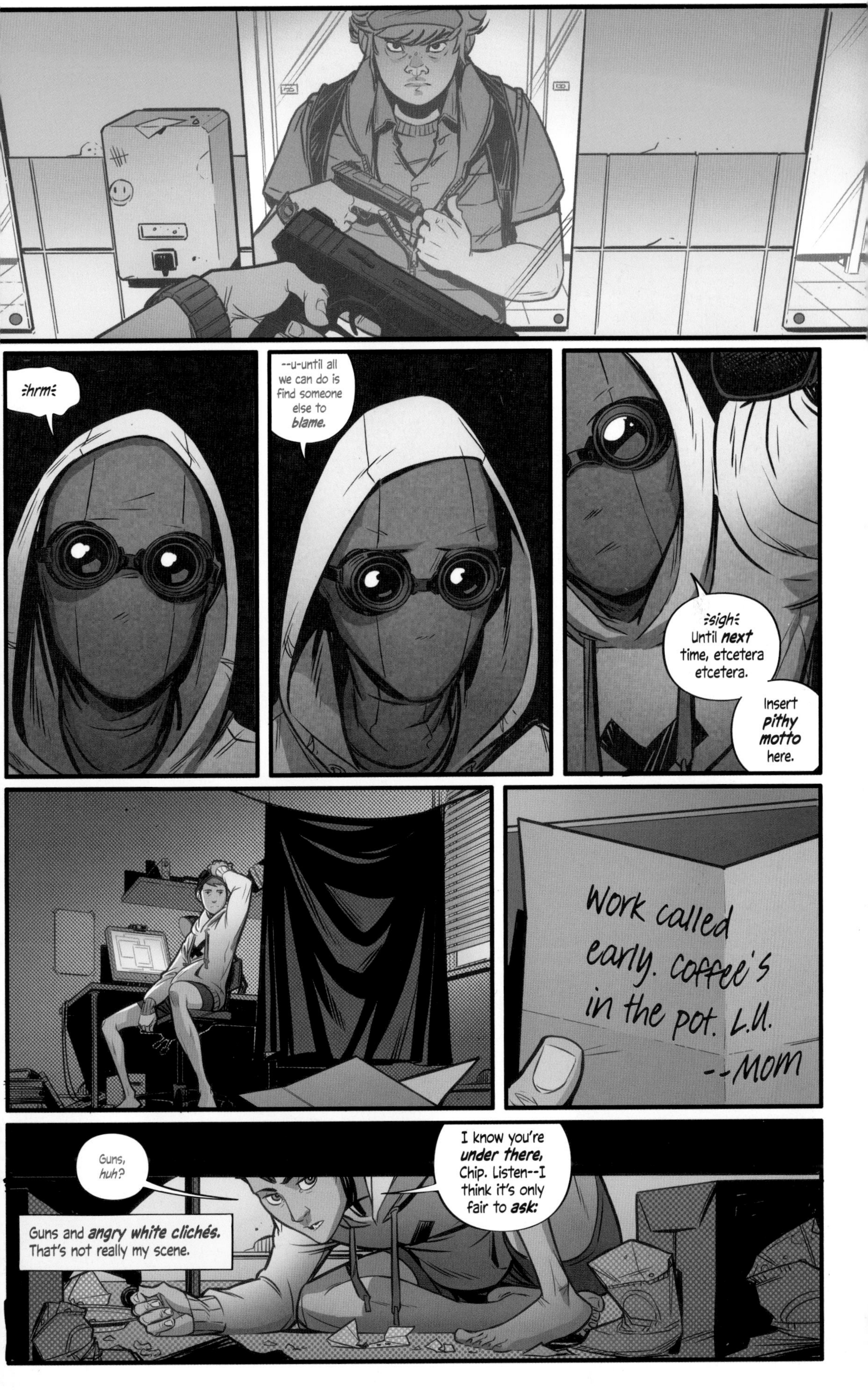
≈hrm≈
--u-until all we can do is find someone else to blame.
≈sigh≈ Until next time, etcetera etcetera.
Insert pithy motto here.
Work called early. coffee's in the pot. L.U. --Mom
Guns, huh?
Guns and angry white clichés. That's not really my scene.
I know you're under there, Chip. Listen--I think it's only fair to ask:

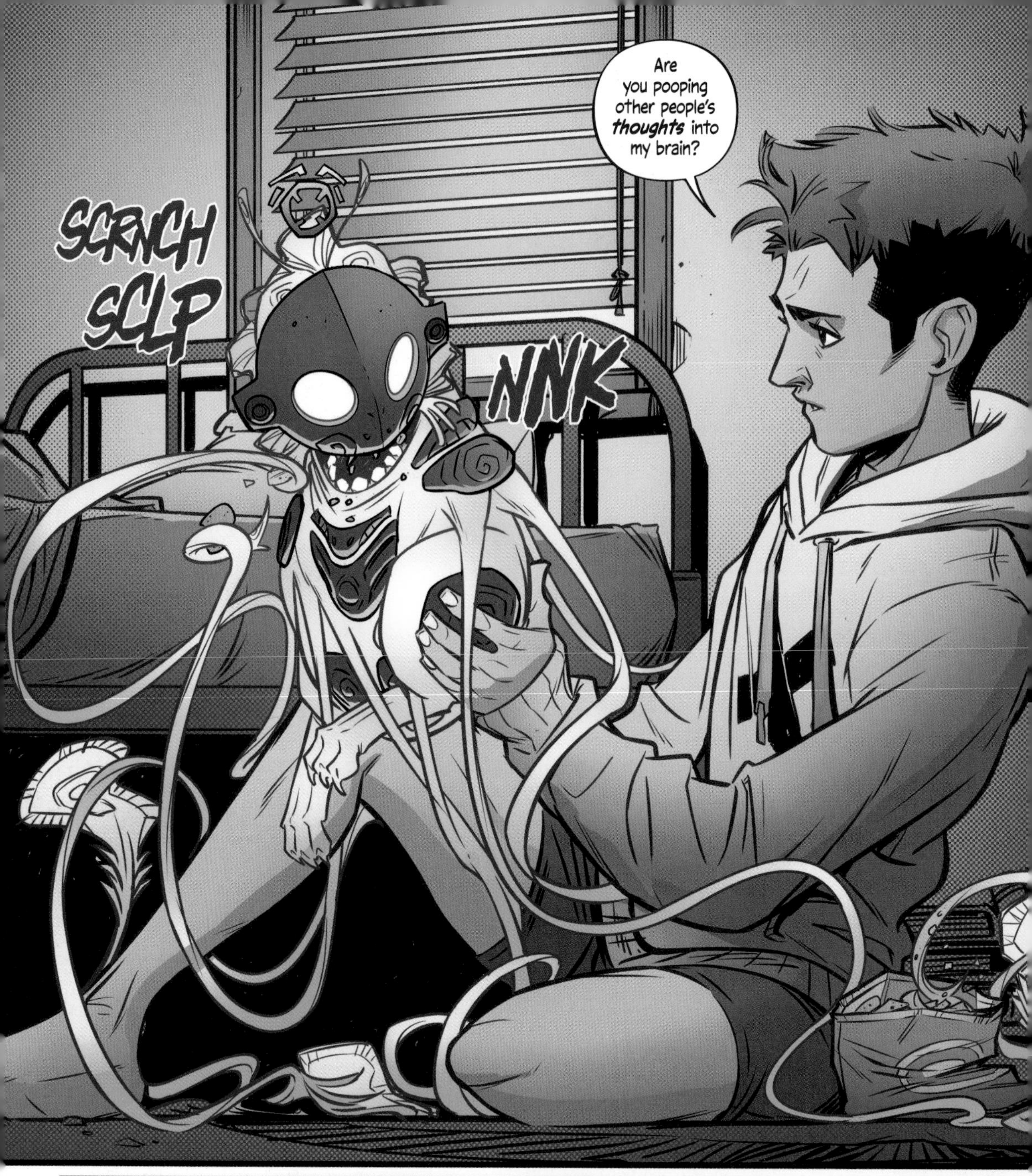
SCRNCH
SCLP
NNK
Are you pooping other people's ***thoughts*** into my brain?

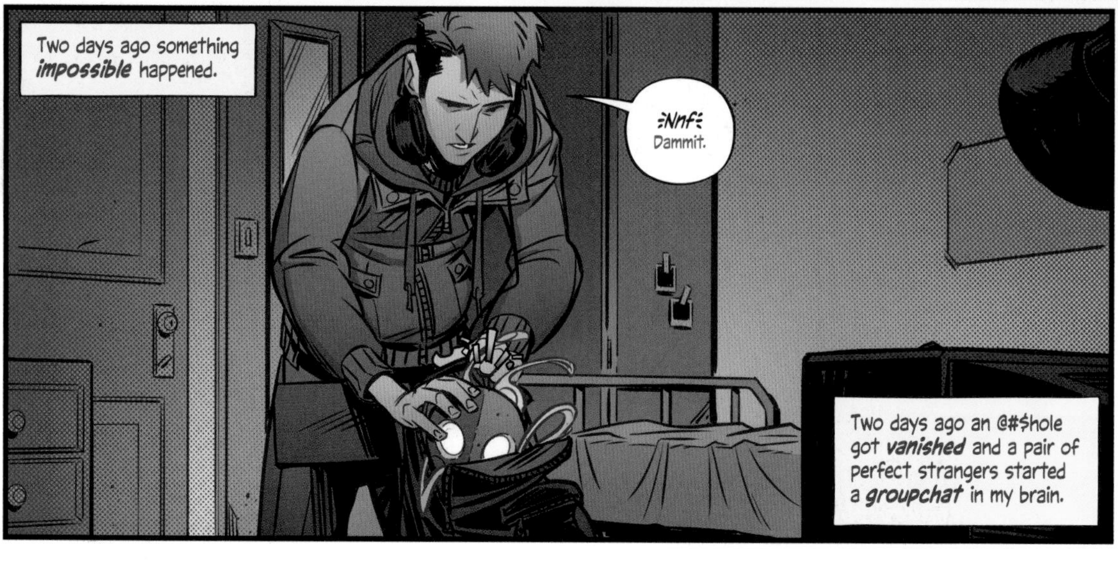
Two days ago something ***impossible*** happened.
≈Nnf≈
Dammit.
Two days ago an @#$hole got ***vanished*** and a pair of perfect strangers started a ***groupchat*** in my brain.

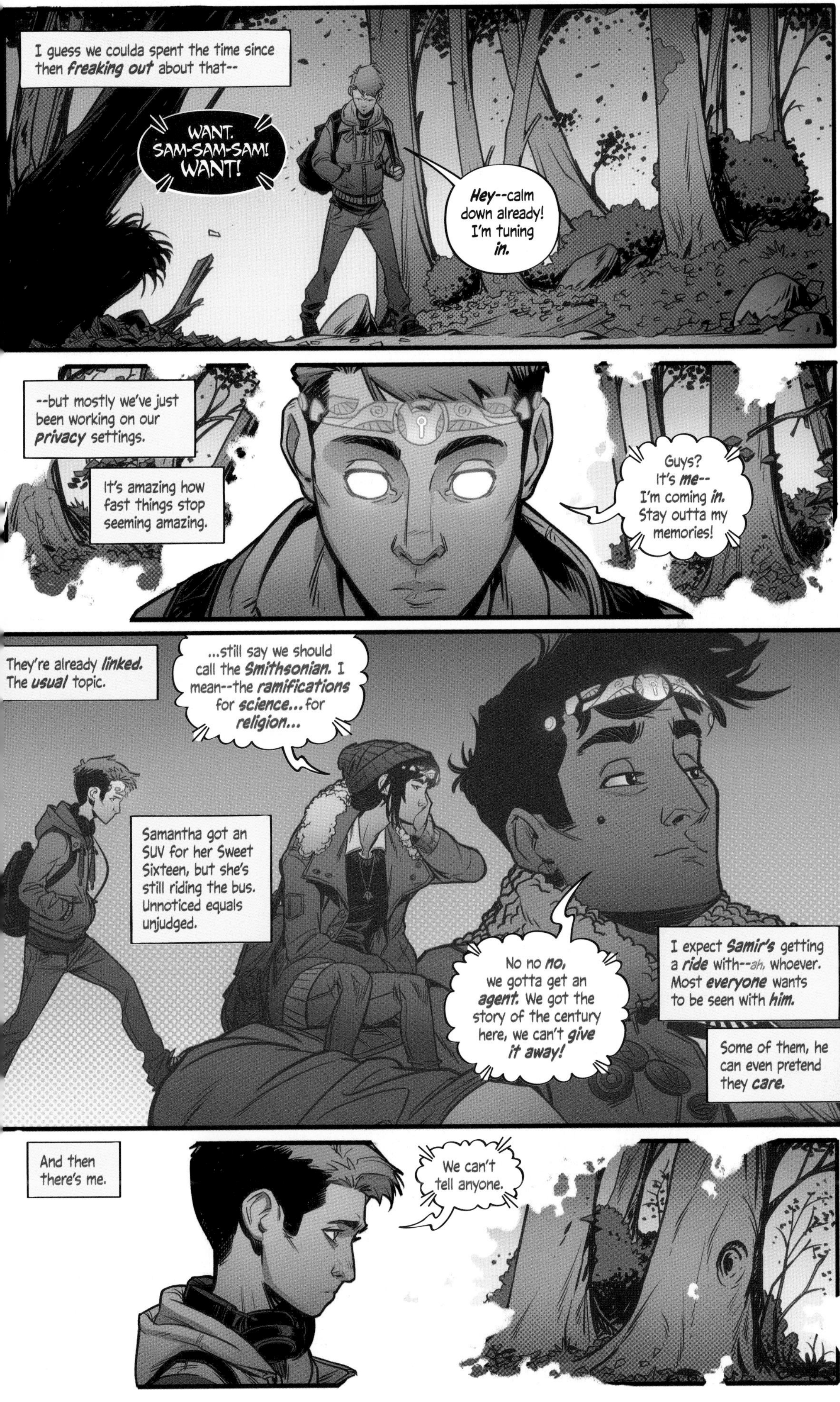
I guess we coulda spent the time since then *freaking out* about that--
WANT. SAM-SAM-SAM! WANT!
Hey--calm down already! I'm tuning *in.*
--but mostly we've just been working on our *privacy* settings.
It's amazing how fast things stop seeming amazing.
Guys? It's *me*-- I'm coming *in.* Stay outta my memories!
They're already *linked.* The *usual* topic.
...still say we should call the *Smithsonian.* I mean--the *ramifications* for *science...* for *religion...*
Samantha got an SUV for her Sweet Sixteen, but she's still riding the bus. Unnoticed equals unjudged.
No no *no,* we gotta get an *agent.* We got the story of the century here, we can't *give it away!*
I expect *Samir's* getting a *ride* with--*ah,* whoever. Most *everyone* wants to be seen with *him.*
Some of them, he can even pretend they *care.*
And then there's me.
We can't tell anyone.

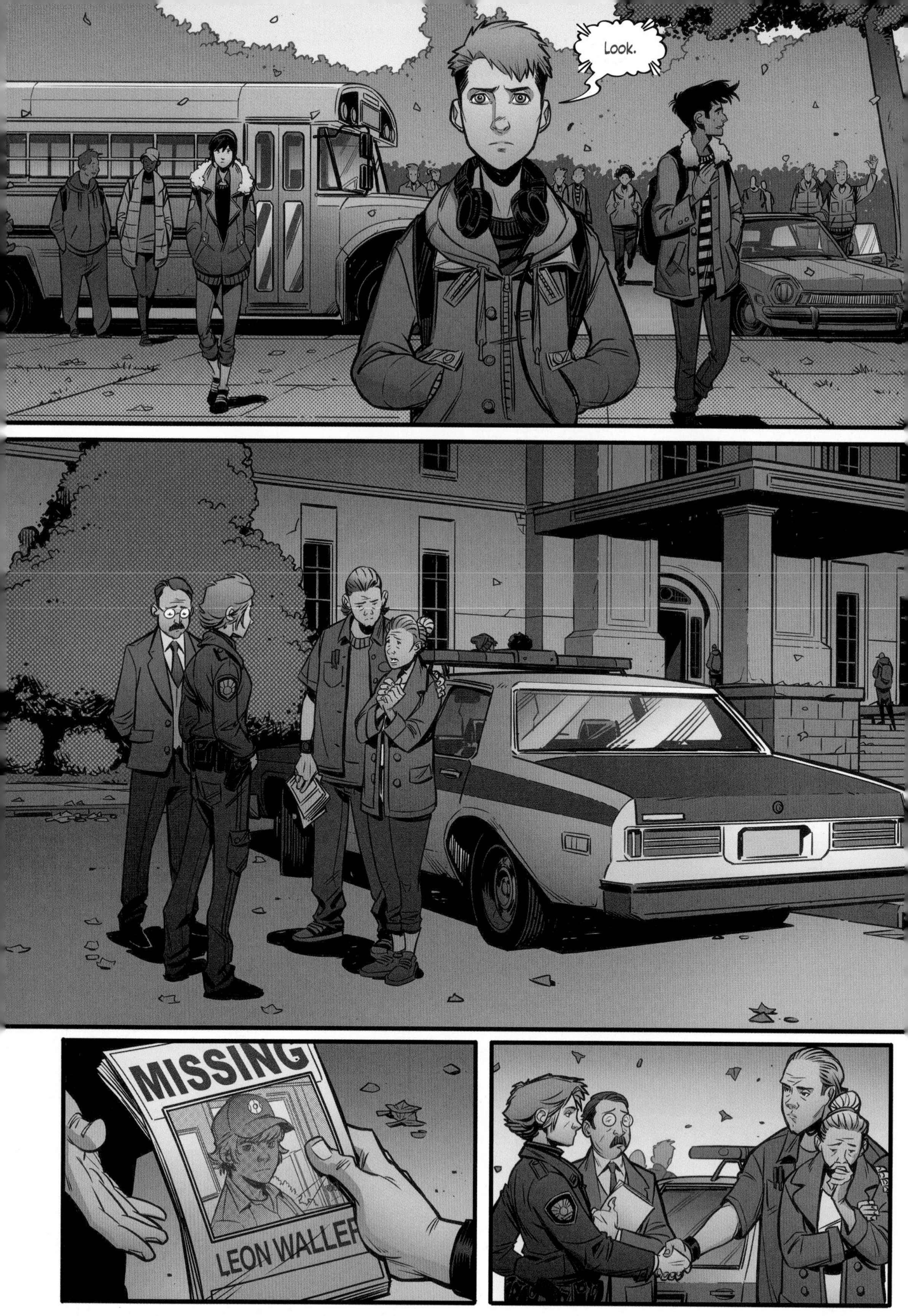
Look.
MISSING
LEON WALLER

Chapter 2:
WE NEED TO TALK

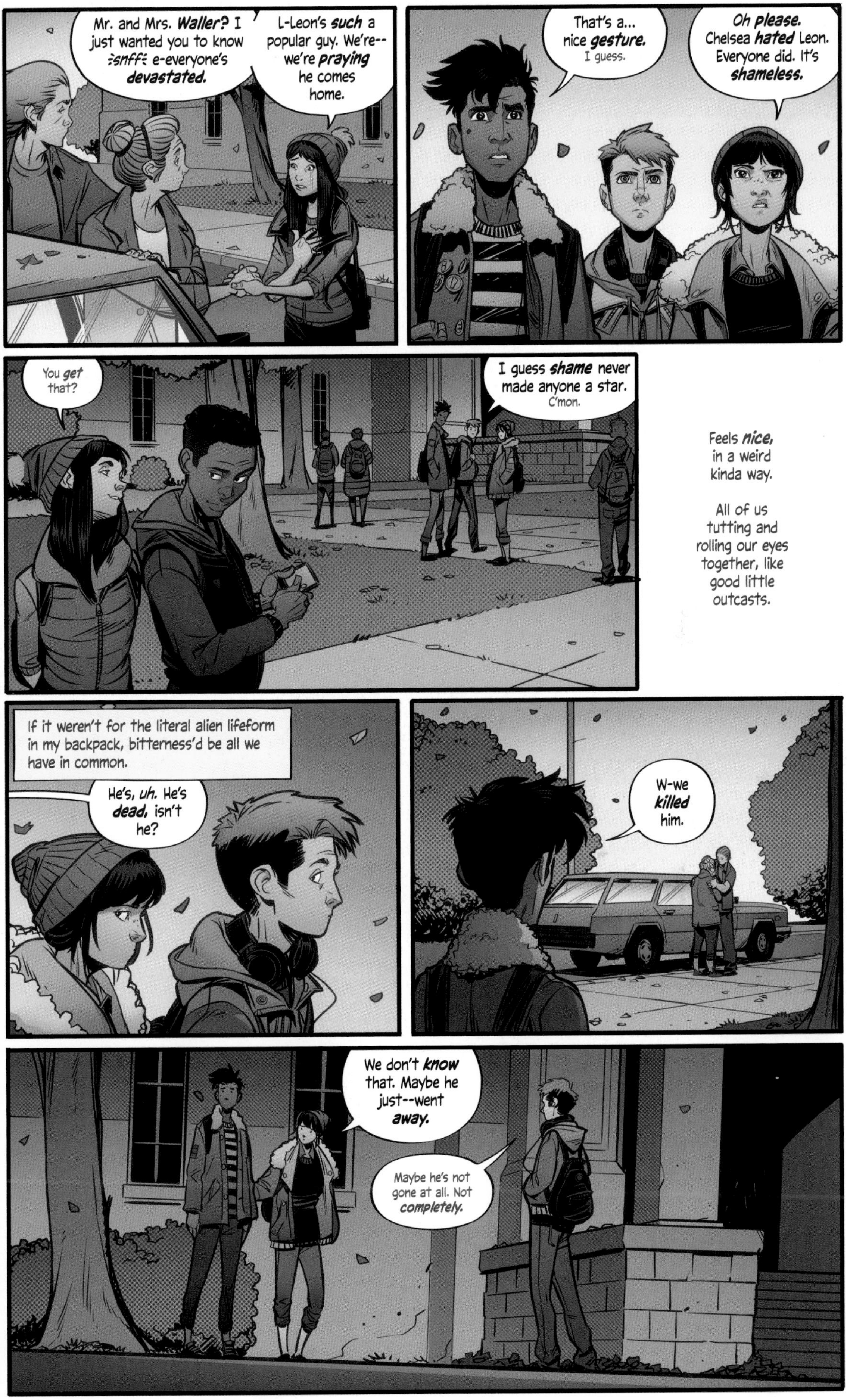

Mr. and Mrs. Waller? I just wanted you to know ≈snff≈ e-everyone's devastated.
L-Leon's such a popular guy. We're-- we're praying he comes home.
That's a... nice gesture. I guess.
Oh please. Chelsea hated Leon. Everyone did. It's shameless.
You get that?
I guess shame never made anyone a star. C'mon.
Feels nice, in a weird kinda way.
All of us tutting and rolling our eyes together, like good little outcasts.
If it weren't for the literal alien lifeform in my backpack, bitterness'd be all we have in common.
He's, uh. He's dead, isn't he?
W-we killed him.
We don't know that. Maybe he just--went away.
Maybe he's not gone at all. Not completely.

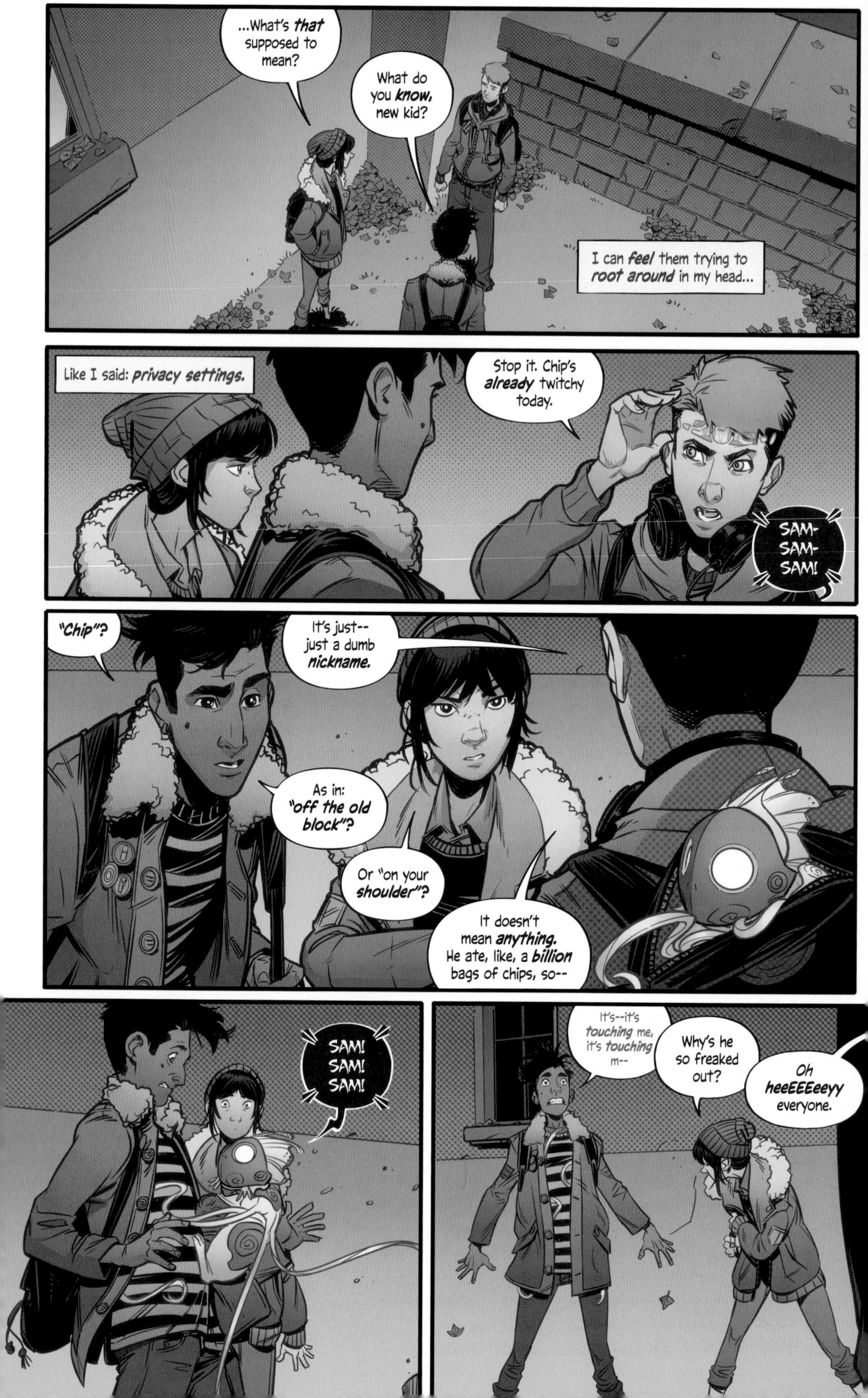
...What's **that** supposed to mean?
What do you **know,** new kid?
I can **feel** them trying to **root around** in my head...
Like I said: **privacy settings.**
Stop it. Chip's **already** twitchy today.
SAM-SAM-SAM!
"Chip"?
It's just-- just a dumb **nickname.**
As in: "off the old block"?
Or "on your **shoulder**"?
It doesn't mean **anything.** He ate, like, a **billion** bags of chips, so--
SAM! SAM! SAM!
It's--it's **touching** me, it's **touching** m--
Why's he so freaked out?
Oh heeEEEeeyy everyone.

Listen you guys, this is tough for **all** of us. Leon's left a hole in our lives. A **hole** that's ⋮snf⋮ that's right...

Oh-- I **promised** myself I wouldn't **lose it**...

Right **here**.

S--so I spoke with the **school counselor** and--she **agreed** it'd be a real **comfort** to just--**share** our pain.

So this morning we're gonna **hug it out**. Okay? Who's **first**?

Samir! **C'mere.**

Uh...**sure**, Chel--but-- listen...

I thought you totally **despised** that g--

Leon will **always** be in our prayers.

Huh. Say. Did you put on some **weight**?

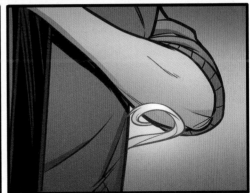

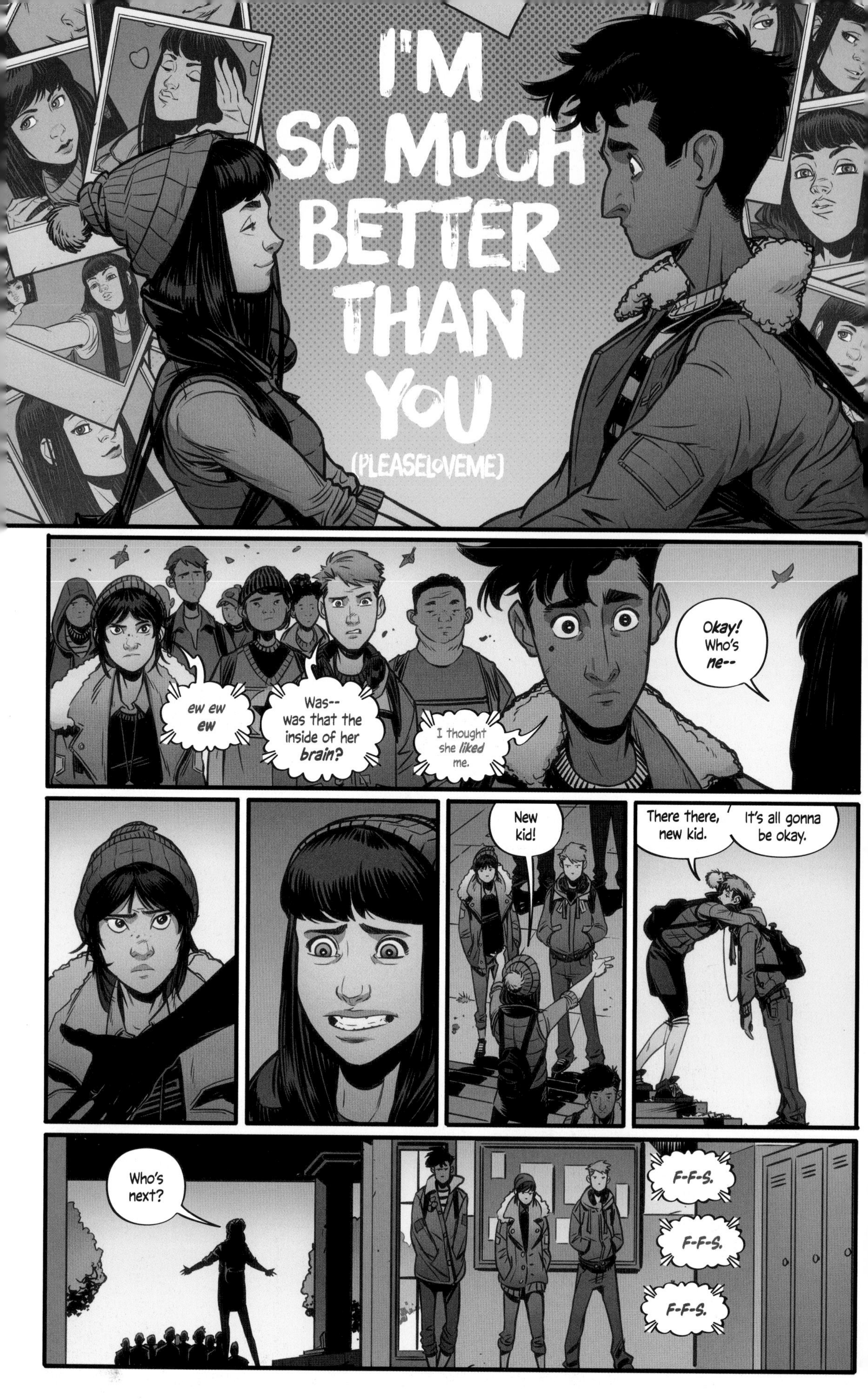
I'M SO MUCH BETTER THAN YOU
(PLEASELOVEME)
ew ew ew
Was-- was that the inside of her brain?
I thought she liked me.
Okay! Who's ne--
New kid!
There there, new kid.
It's all gonna be okay.
Who's next?
F-F-S.
F-F-S.
F-F-S.

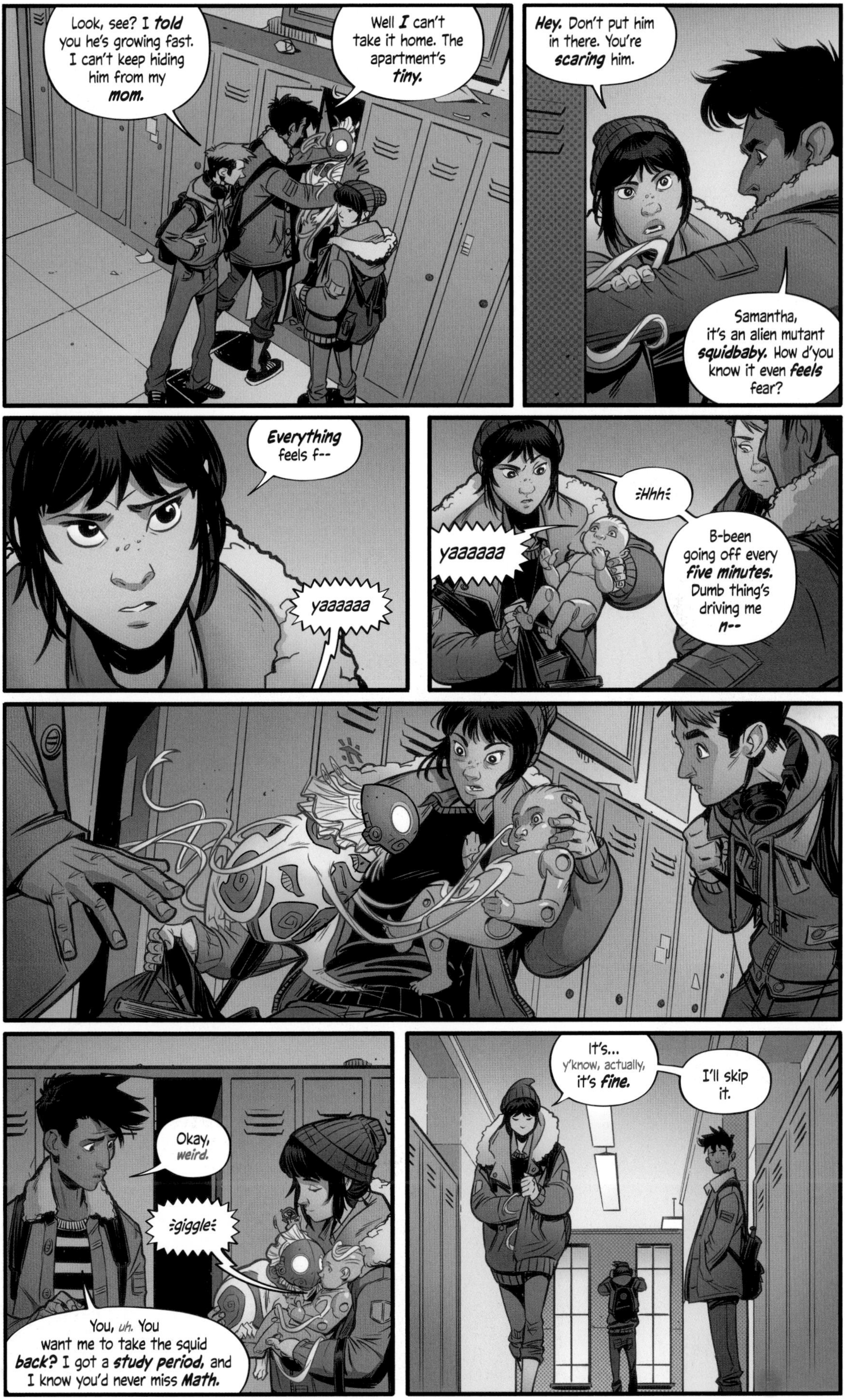

Look, see? I told you he's growing fast. I can't keep hiding him from my mom.
Well I can't take it home. The apartment's tiny.
Hey. Don't put him in there. You're scaring him.
Samantha, it's an alien mutant squidbaby. How d'you know it even feels fear?
Everything feels f--
yaaaaaa
:Hhh:
yaaaaaa
B-been going off every five minutes. Dumb thing's driving me n--
Okay, weird.
:giggle:
You, uh. You want me to take the squid back? I got a study period, and I know you'd never miss Math.
It's... y'know, actually, it's fine.
I'll skip it.

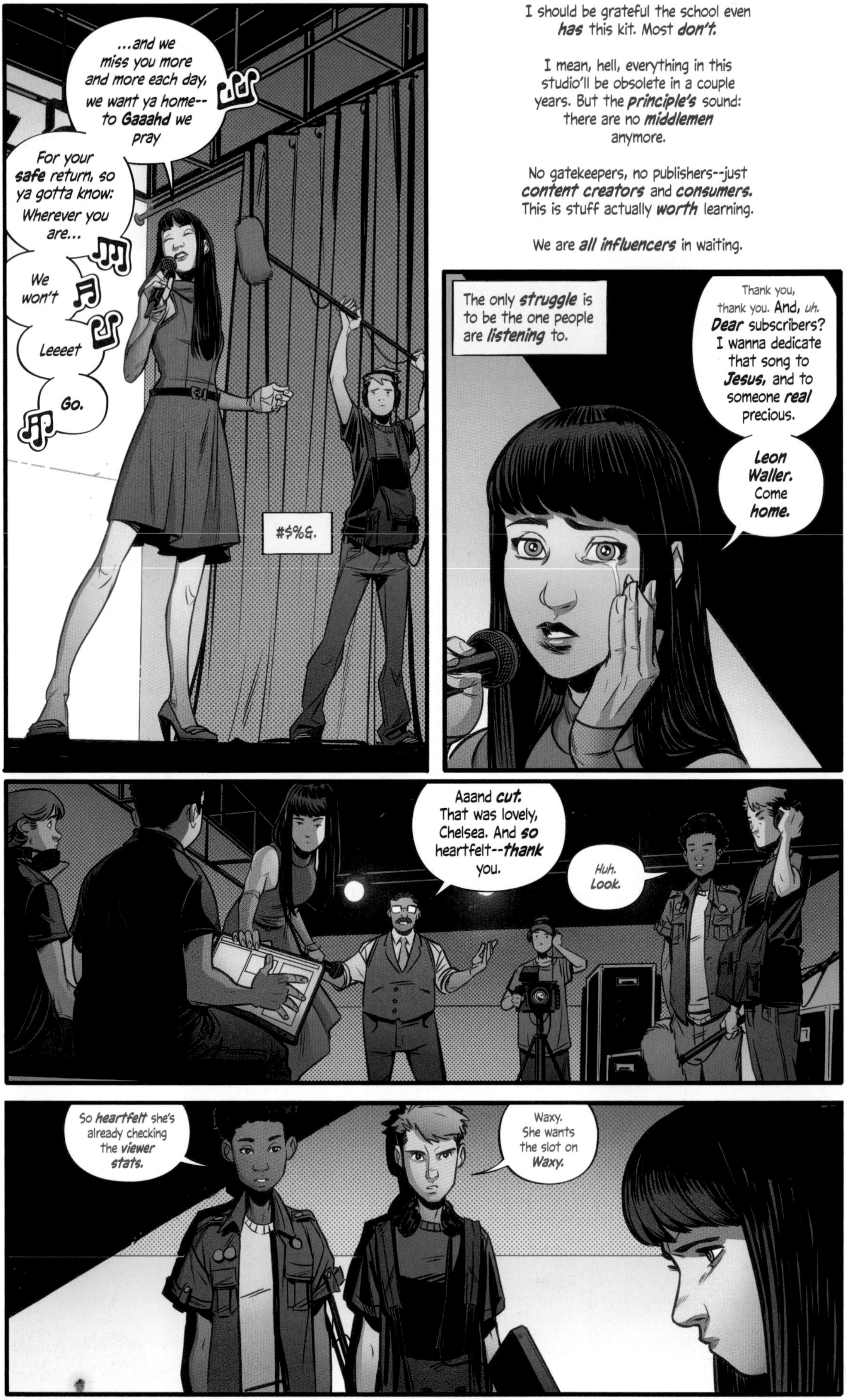
...and we miss you more and more each day, we want ya home-- to Gaaahd we pray
For your safe return, so ya gotta know: Wherever you are...
We won't
Leeeet
Go.
#$%&.
I should be grateful the school even has this kit. Most don't.
I mean, hell, everything in this studio'll be obsolete in a couple years. But the principle's sound: there are no middlemen anymore.
No gatekeepers, no publishers--just content creators and consumers. This is stuff actually worth learning.
We are all influencers in waiting.
The only struggle is to be the one people are listening to.
Thank you, thank you. And, uh. Dear subscribers? I wanna dedicate that song to Jesus, and to someone real precious.
Leon Waller. Come home.
Aaand cut. That was lovely, Chelsea. And so heartfelt--thank you.
Huh. Look.
So heartfelt she's already checking the viewer stats.
Waxy. She wants the slot on Waxy.

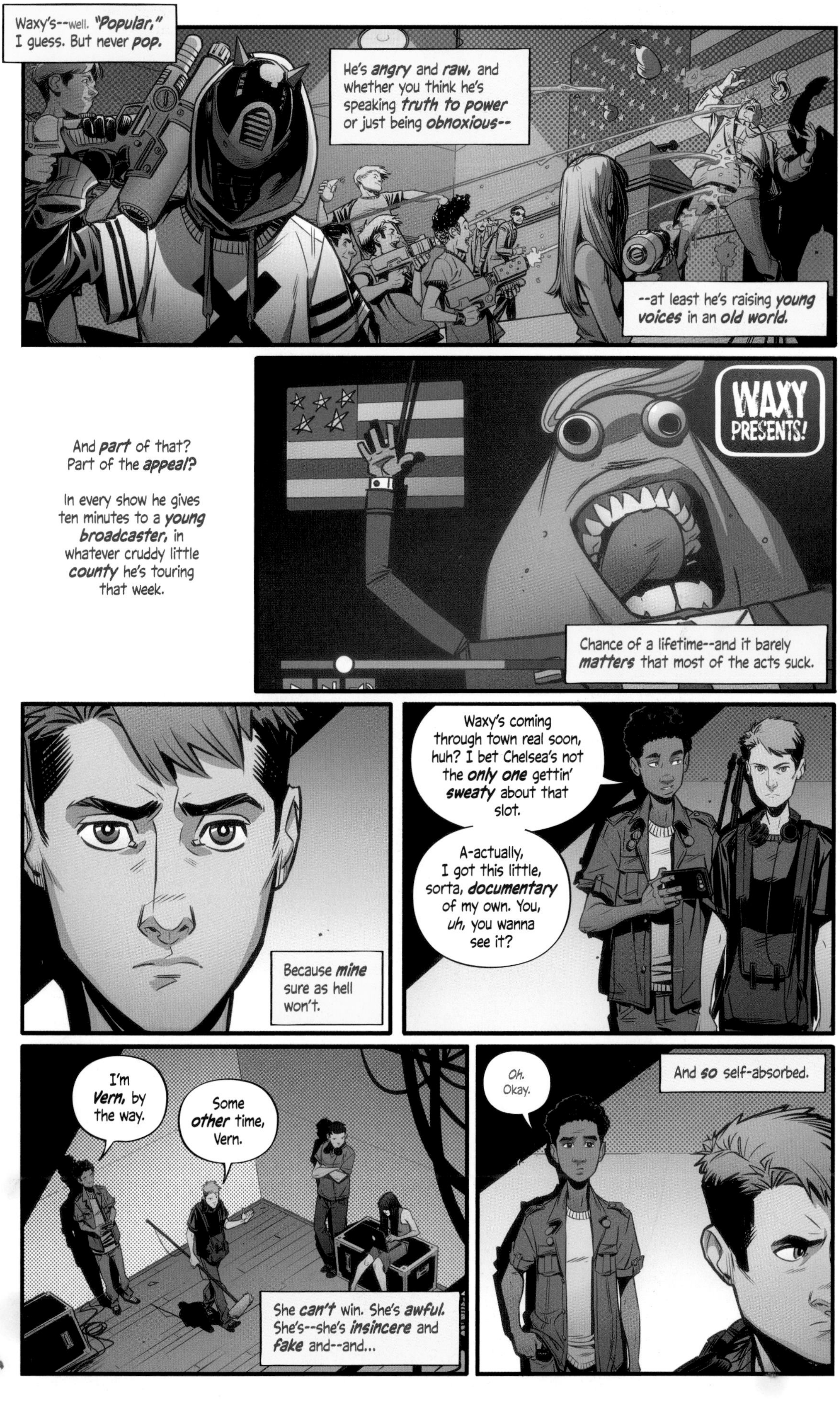
Waxy's--well. "Popular," I guess. But never pop.
He's angry and raw, and whether you think he's speaking truth to power or just being obnoxious--
--at least he's raising young voices in an old world.
WAXY PRESENTS!
And part of that? Part of the appeal?
In every show he gives ten minutes to a young broadcaster, in whatever cruddy little county he's touring that week.
Chance of a lifetime--and it barely matters that most of the acts suck.
Because mine sure as hell won't.
Waxy's coming through town real soon, huh? I bet Chelsea's not the only one gettin' sweaty about that slot.
A-actually, I got this little, sorta, documentary of my own. You, uh, you wanna see it?
I'm Vern, by the way.
Some other time, Vern.
She can't win. She's awful. She's--she's insincere and fake and--and...
Oh. Okay.
And so self-absorbed.

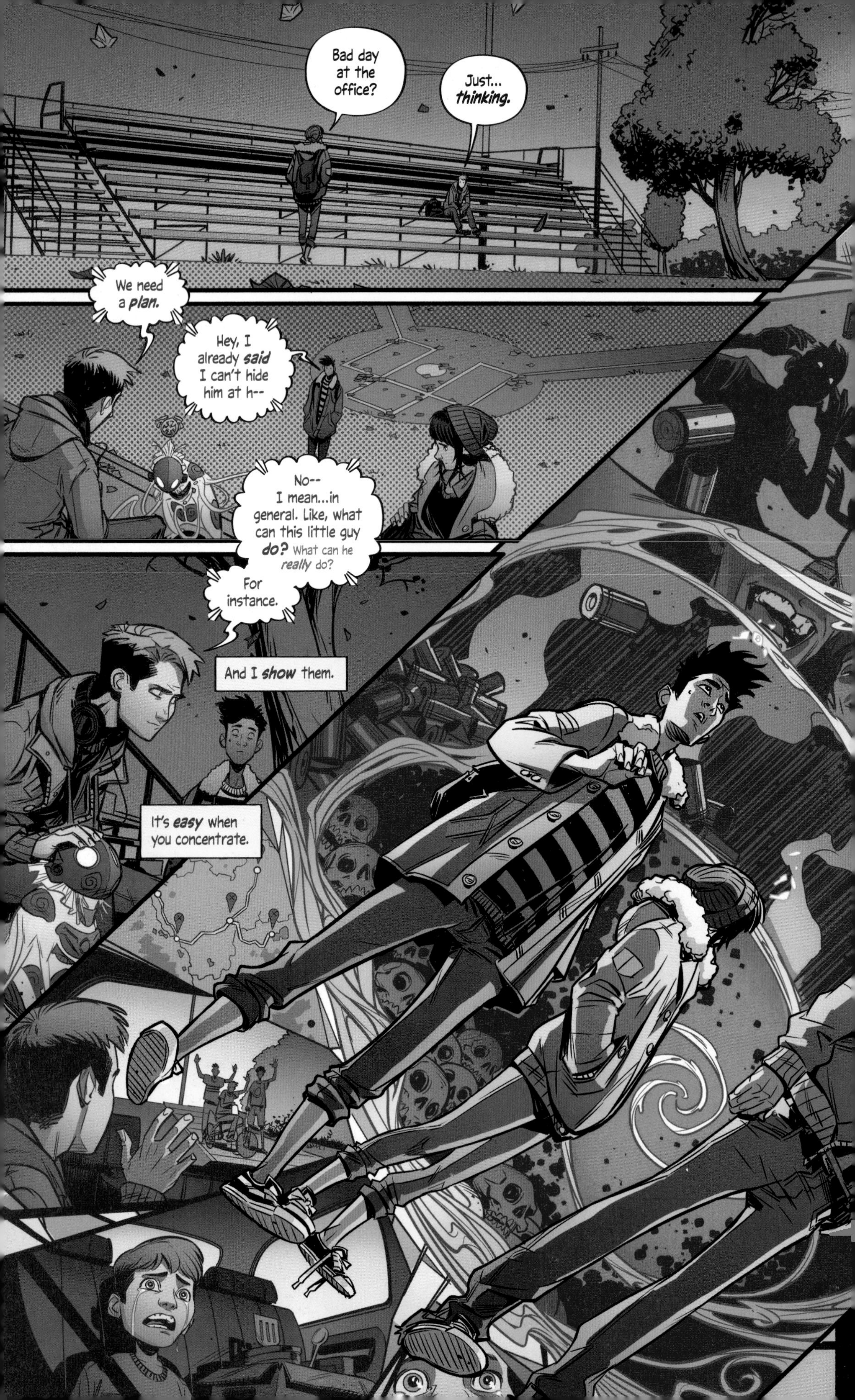
Bad day at the office?
Just... *thinking.*
We need a *plan.*
Hey, I already *said* I can't hide him at h--
No-- I mean...in general. Like, what can this little guy *do?* What can he *really* do?
For instance.
And I *show* them.
It's *easy* when you concentrate.

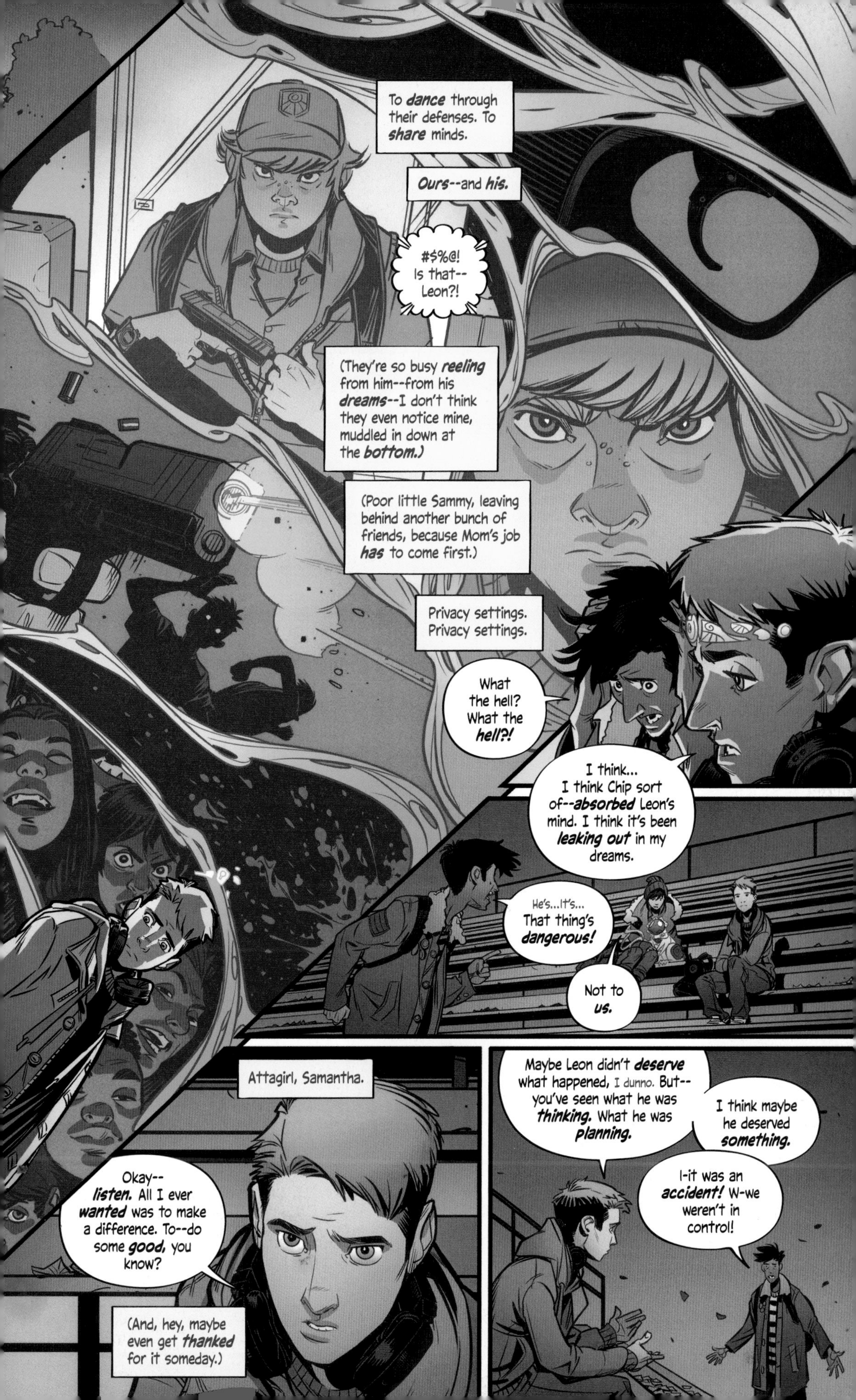
To dance through their defenses. To share minds.
Ours--and his.
#$%@! Is that-- Leon?!
(They're so busy reeling from him--from his dreams--I don't think they even notice mine, muddled in down at the bottom.)
(Poor little Sammy, leaving behind another bunch of friends, because Mom's job has to come first.)
Privacy settings. Privacy settings.
What the hell? What the hell?!
I think... I think Chip sort of--absorbed Leon's mind. I think it's been leaking out in my dreams.
He's...It's... That thing's dangerous!
Not to us.
Attagirl, Samantha.
Okay-- listen. All I ever wanted was to make a difference. To--do some good, you know?
(And, hey, maybe even get thanked for it someday.)
Maybe Leon didn't deserve what happened, I dunno. But--you've seen what he was thinking. What he was planning.
I think maybe he deserved something.
I-it was an accident! W-we weren't in control!

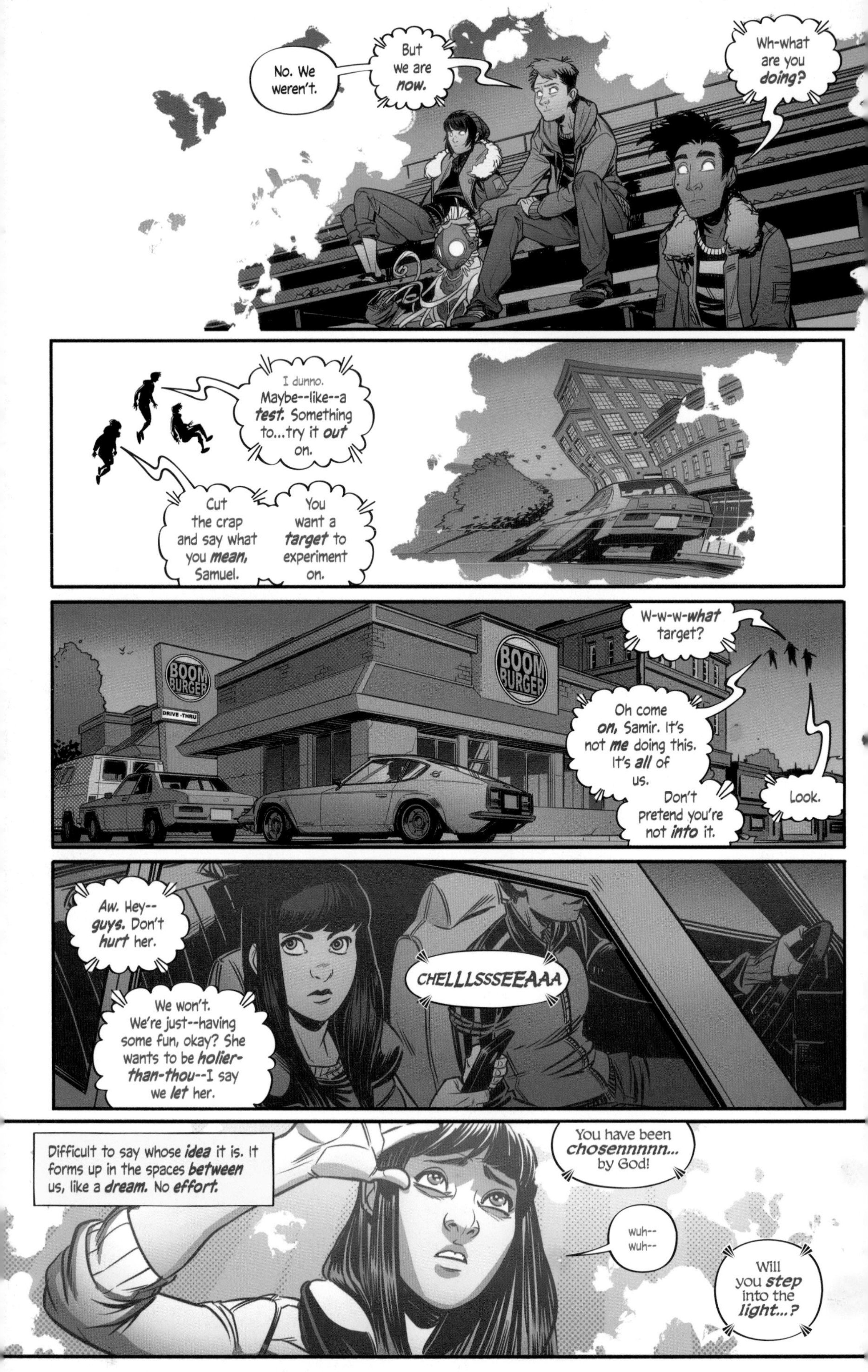
No. We weren't.
But we are *now.*
Wh-what are you *doing?*
I dunno. Maybe--like--a *test.* Something to...try it *out* on.
Cut the crap and say what you *mean,* Samuel.
You want a *target* to experiment on.
BOOM BURGER
DRIVE-THRU
BOOM BURGER
W-w-w-*what* target?
Oh come *on,* Samir. It's not *me* doing this. It's *all* of us.
Don't pretend you're not *into* it.
Look.
Aw. Hey-- *guys.* Don't *hurt* her.
CHELLLSSSEEAAA
We won't. We're just--having some fun, okay? She wants to be *holier-than-thou*--I say we *let* her.
Difficult to say whose *idea* it is. It forms up in the spaces *between* us, like a *dream.* No *effort.*
You have been *chosennnnn...* by God!
wuh-- wuh--
Will you *step* into the *light...?*

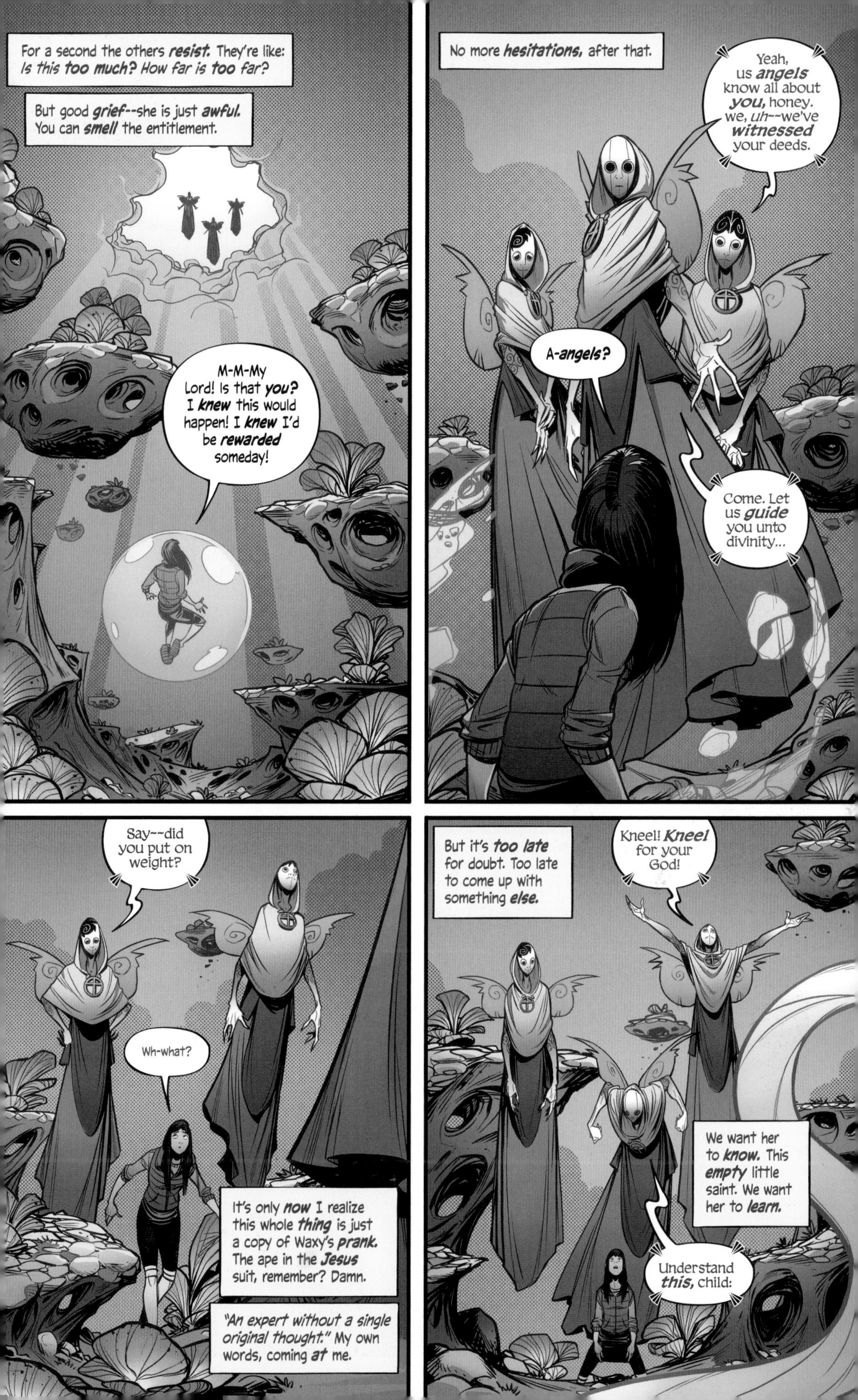
For a second the others *resist.* They're like: *Is this **too much?** How far is **too** far?*
But good ***grief***--she is just ***awful.*** You can ***smell*** the entitlement.
M-M-My Lord! Is that ***you?*** I ***knew*** this would happen! I ***knew*** I'd be ***rewarded*** someday!
No more ***hesitations,*** after that.
Yeah, us ***angels*** know all about ***you,*** honey. we, *uh*--we've ***witnessed*** your deeds.
A-***angels?***
Come. Let us ***guide*** you unto divinity...
Say--did you put on weight?
Wh-what?
It's only ***now*** I realize this whole ***thing*** is just a copy of Waxy's ***prank.*** The ape in the ***Jesus*** suit, remember? Damn.
"An expert without a single original thought." My own words, coming ***at*** me.
But it's ***too late*** for doubt. Too late to come up with something ***else.***
Kneel! ***Kneel*** for your God!
We want her to ***know.*** This ***empty*** little saint. We want her to ***learn.***
Understand ***this,*** child:

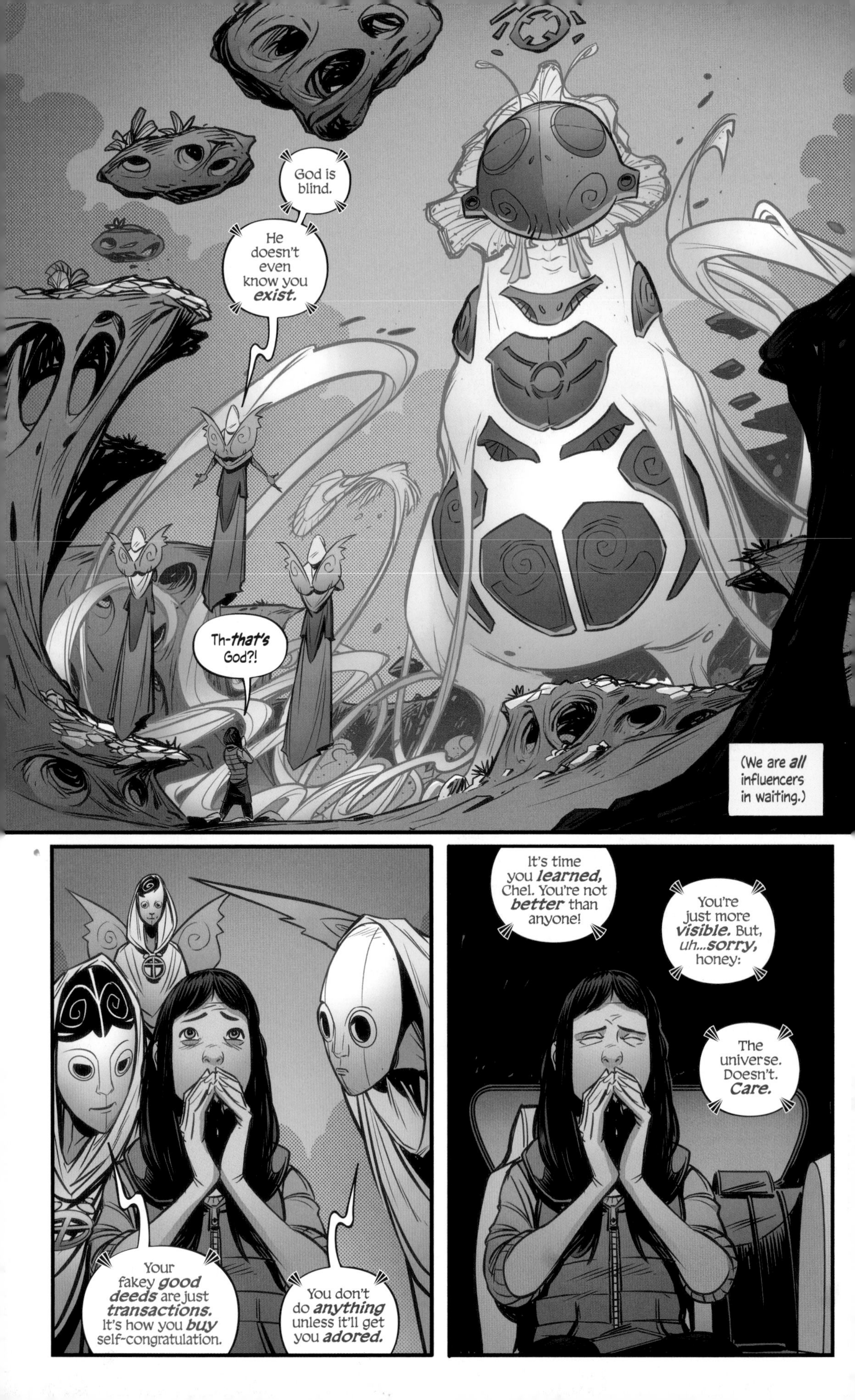
God is blind.
He doesn't even know you exist.
Th-that's God?!
(We are all influencers in waiting.)
Your fakey good deeds are just transactions. It's how you buy self-congratulation.
You don't do anything unless it'll get you adored.
It's time you learned, Chel. You're not better than anyone!
You're just more visible. But, uh...sorry, honey:
The universe. Doesn't. Care.

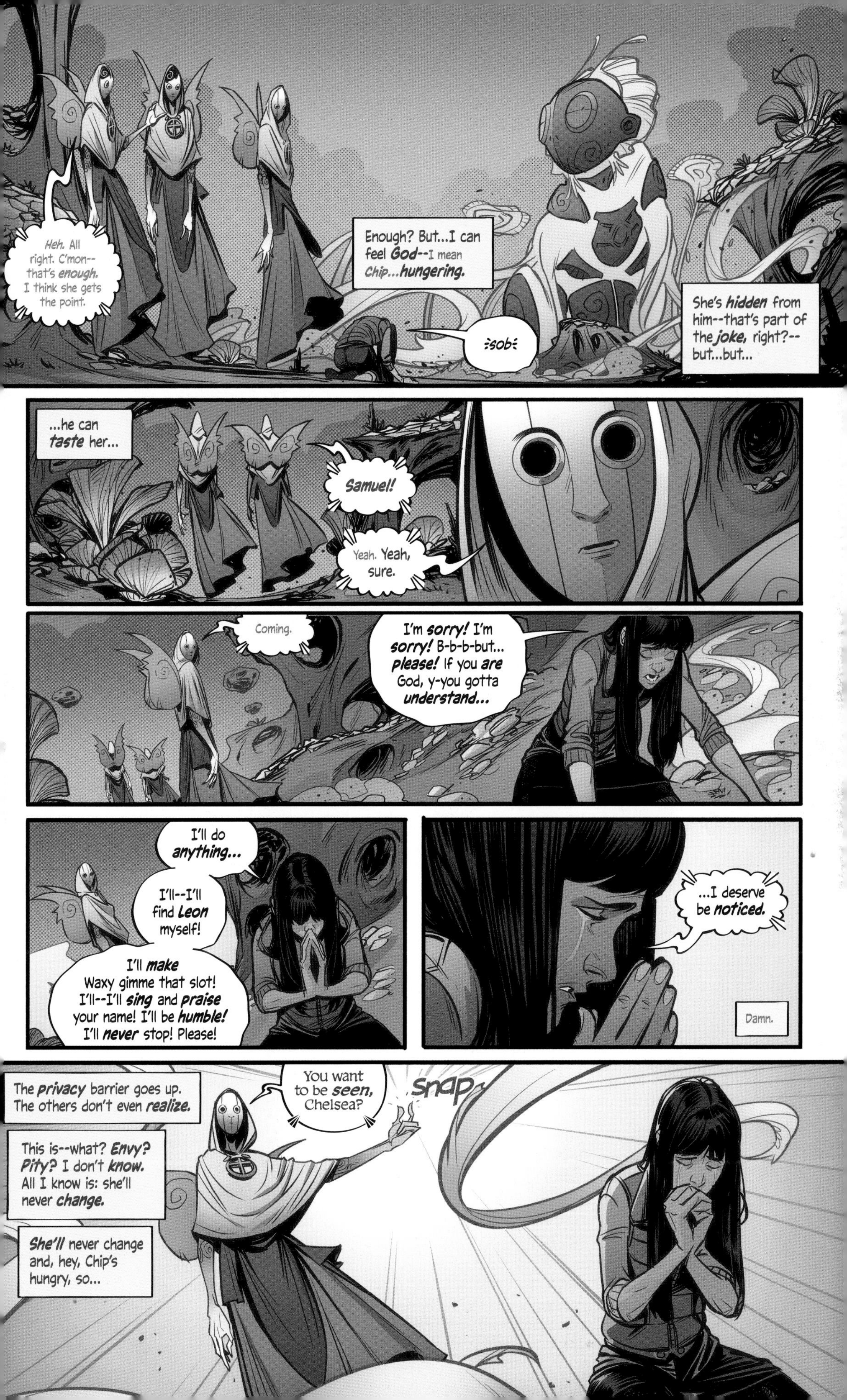
Heh. All right. C'mon--that's enough. I think she gets the point.
Enough? But...I can feel God--I mean Chip...hungering.
sob
She's hidden from him--that's part of the joke, right?--but...but...
...he can taste her...
Samuel!
Yeah. Yeah, sure.
Coming.
I'm sorry! I'm sorry! B-b-b-but... please! If you are God, y-you gotta understand...
I'll do anything...
I'll--I'll find Leon myself!
I'll make Waxy gimme that slot! I'll--I'll sing and praise your name! I'll be humble! I'll never stop! Please!
...I deserve be noticed.
Damn.
The privacy barrier goes up. The others don't even realize.
You want to be seen, Chelsea?
snap
This is--what? Envy? Pity? I don't know. All I know is: she'll never change.
She'll never change and, hey, Chip's hungry, so...

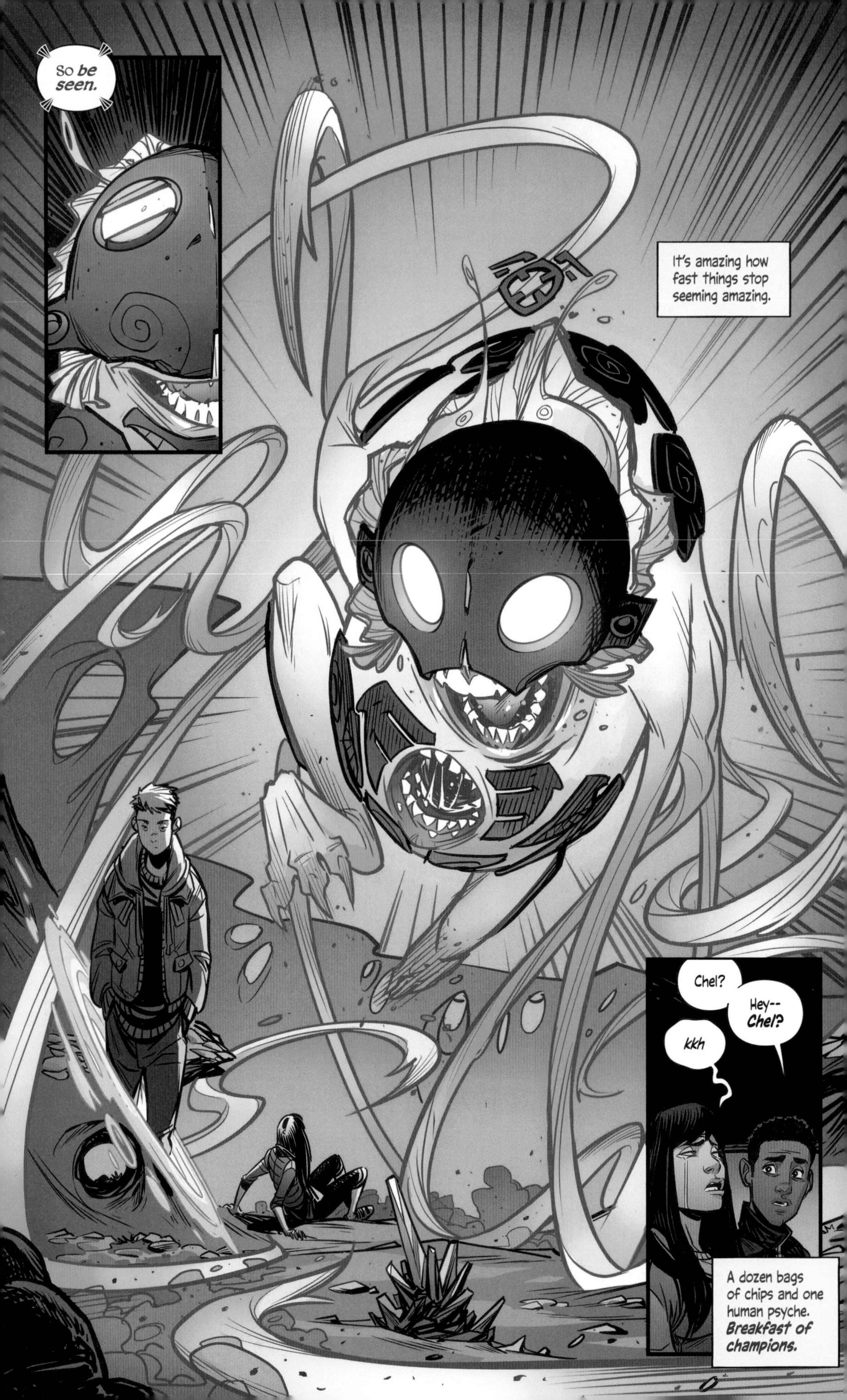
So be seen.
It's amazing how fast things stop seeming amazing.
Chel?
Hey-- Chel?
kkh
A dozen bags of chips and one human psyche. Breakfast of champions.

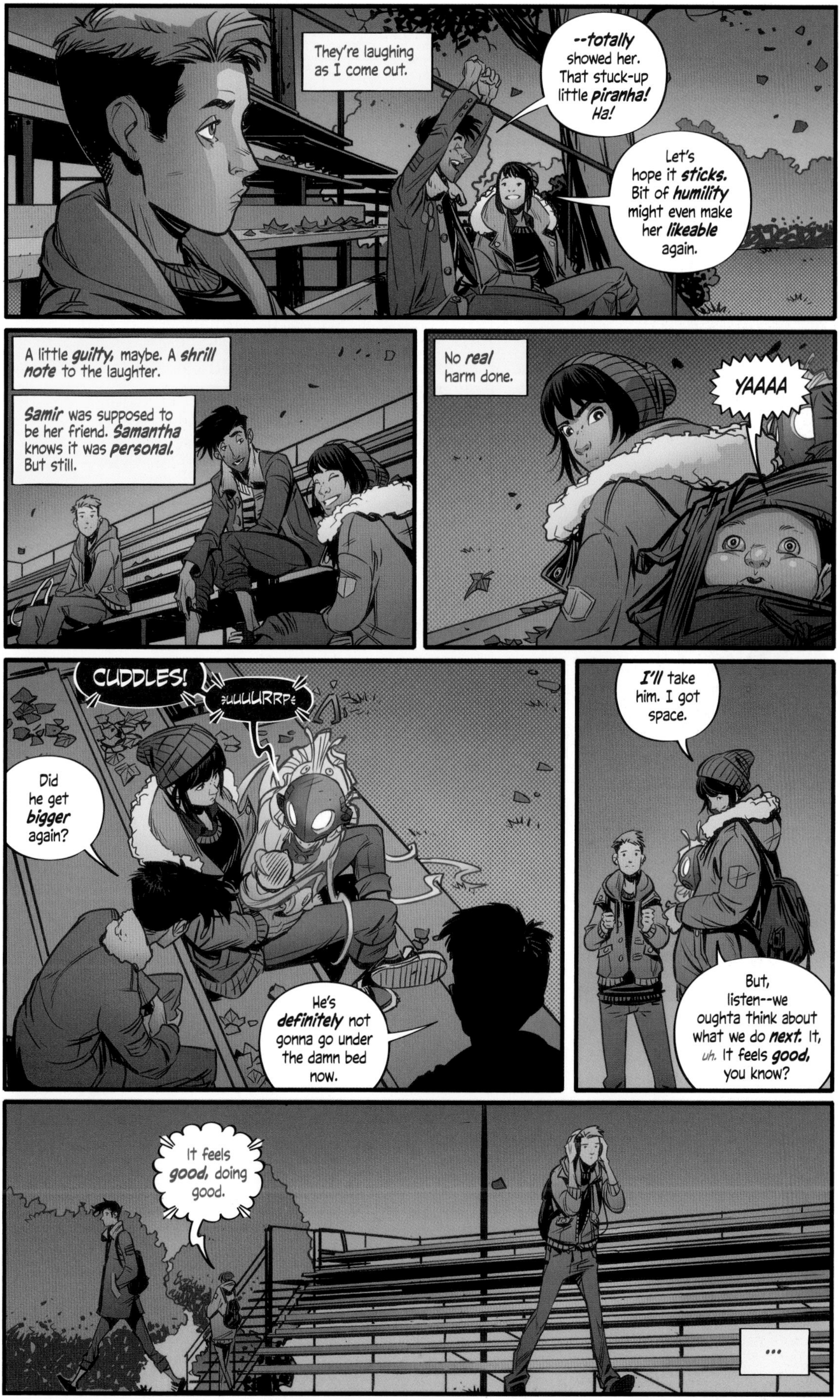
They're laughing as I come out.
--totally showed her. That stuck-up little piranha! Ha!
Let's hope it sticks. Bit of humility might even make her likeable again.
A little guilty, maybe. A shrill note to the laughter.
Samir was supposed to be her friend. Samantha knows it was personal. But still.
No real harm done.
YAAAA
CUDDLES!
uuuURRP
Did he get bigger again?
He's definitely not gonna go under the damn bed now.
I'll take him. I got space.
But, listen--we oughta think about what we do next. It, uh. It feels good, you know?
It feels good, doing good.
...

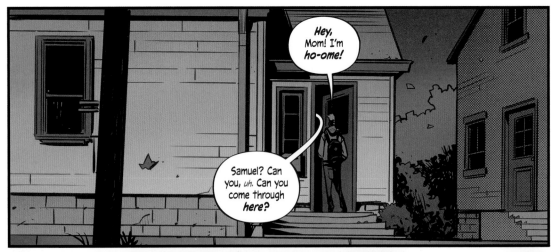

Hey, Mom! I'm *ho-ome!*

Samuel? Can you, *uh.* Can you come through *here?*

Uh-oh. I know *that* tone. Something *bad's* happe--...wait.

Mom, t-tell me you didn't get another *transfer* already? We only just *moved* here!

No, it's-- it's not *that,* hun. We, *uh...*

We need to talk.

CHAPTER THREE

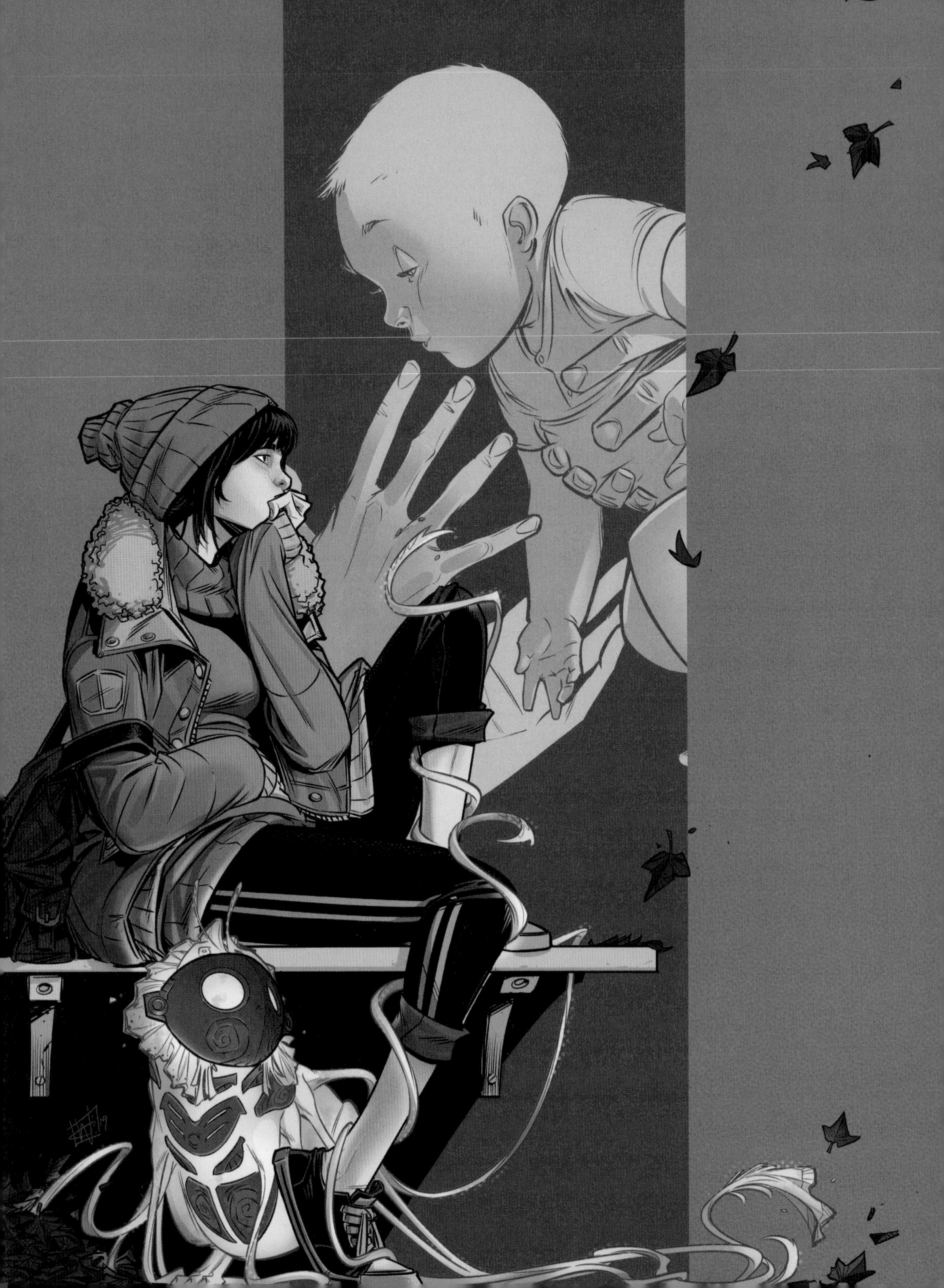

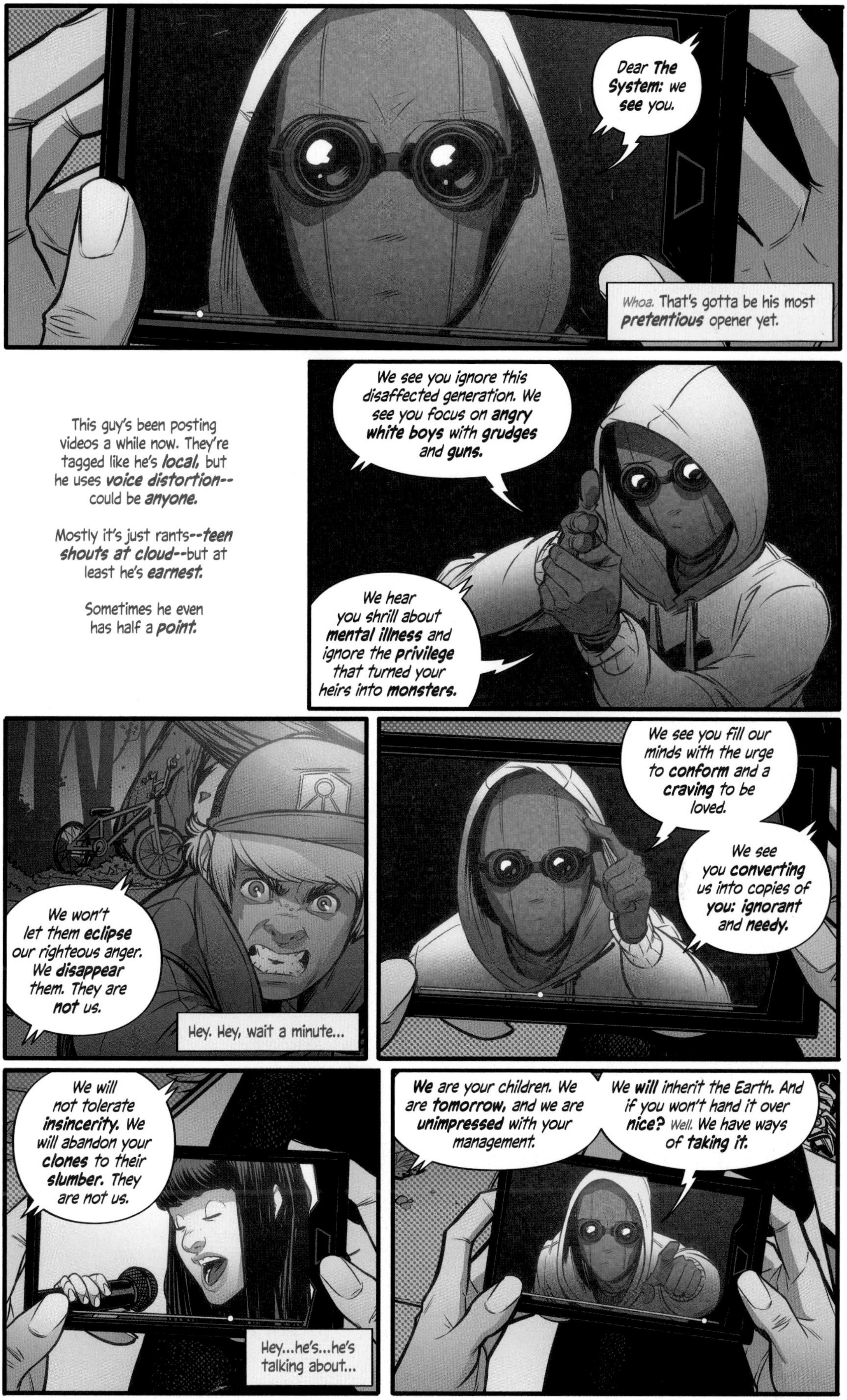

Dear The System: we see you.
Whoa. That's gotta be his most pretentious opener yet.
This guy's been posting videos a while now. They're tagged like he's local, but he uses voice distortion--could be anyone.
Mostly it's just rants--teen shouts at cloud--but at least he's earnest.
Sometimes he even has half a point.
We see you ignore this disaffected generation. We see you focus on angry white boys with grudges and guns.
We hear you shrill about mental illness and ignore the privilege that turned your heirs into monsters.
We won't let them eclipse our righteous anger. We disappear them. They are not us.
Hey. Hey, wait a minute...
We see you fill our minds with the urge to conform and a craving to be loved.
We see you converting us into copies of you: ignorant and needy.
We will not tolerate insincerity. We will abandon your clones to their slumber. They are not us.
Hey...he's...he's talking about...
We are your children. We are tomorrow, and we are unimpressed with your management.
We will inherit the Earth. And if you won't hand it over nice? Well. We have ways of taking it.

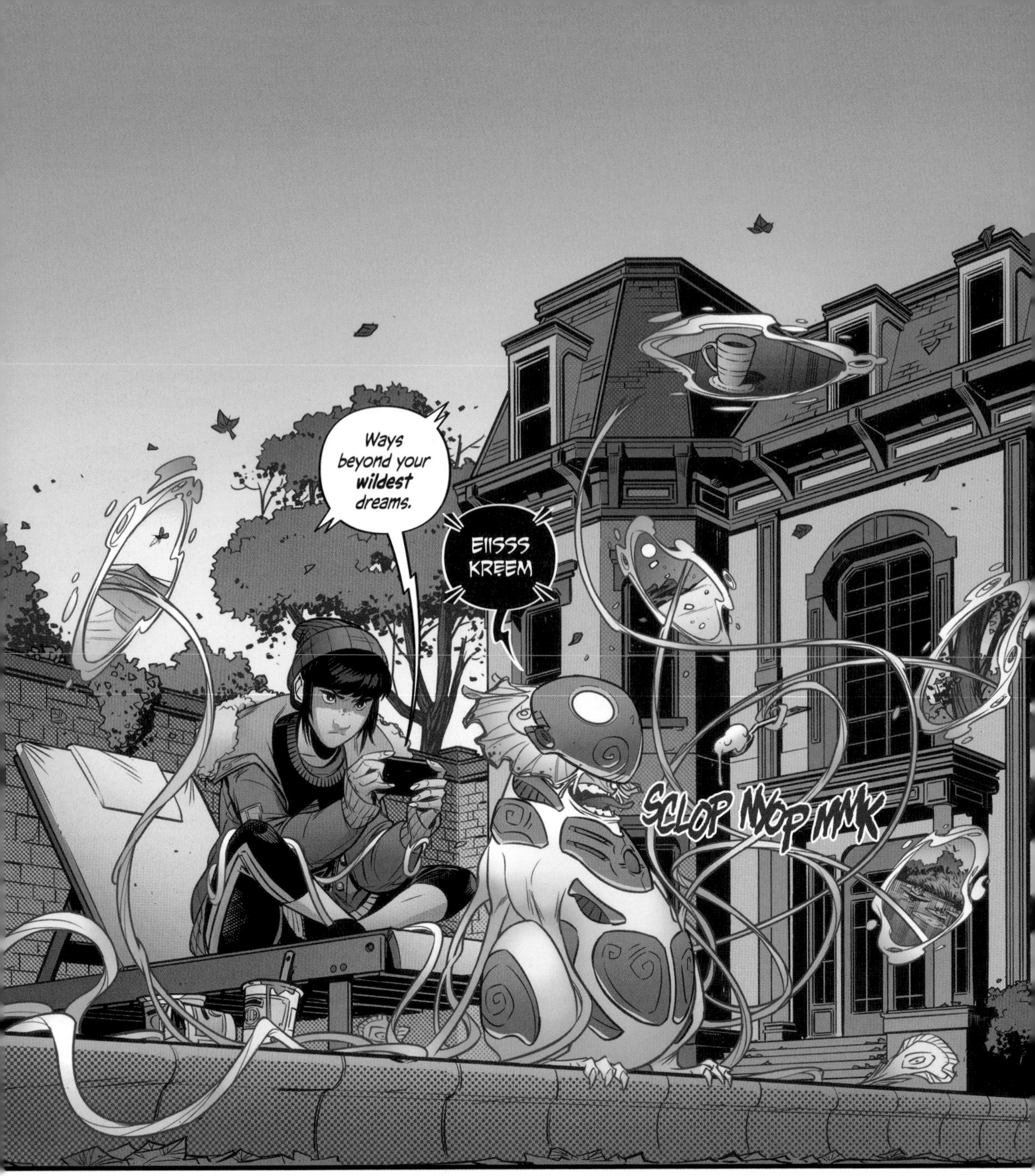
Ways beyond your wildest dreams.
EIISSS KREEM
SCLOP NYOP MNK

Chapter 3:
THINGS TO DO, PEOPLE TO SEE

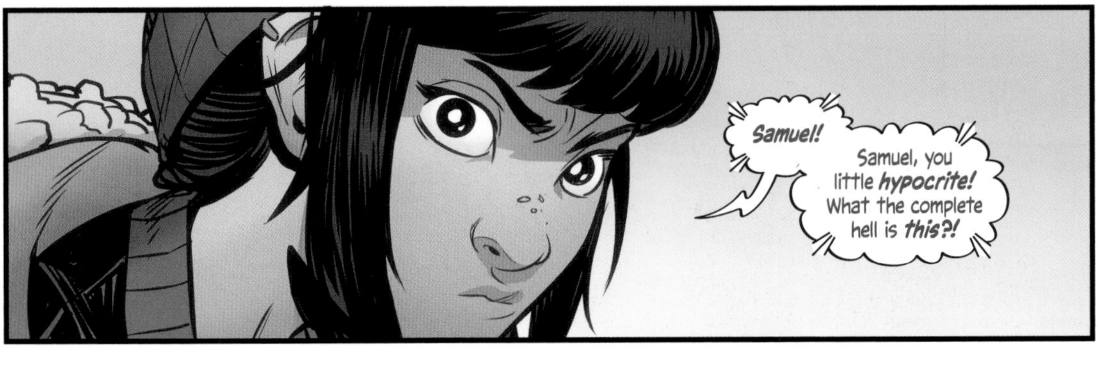
Samuel!
Samuel, you little hypocrite! What the complete hell is this?!

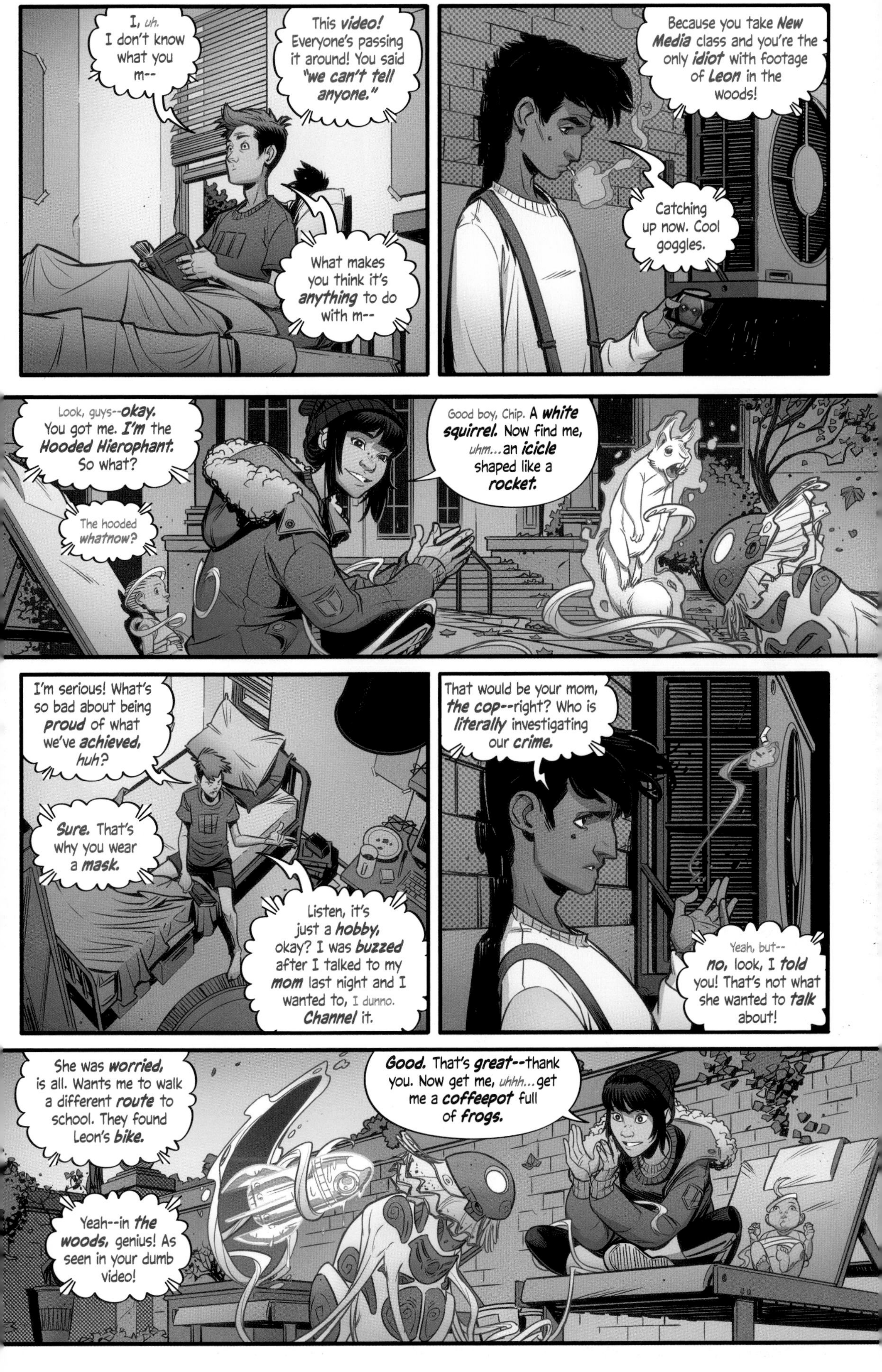
I, uh. I don't know what you m--
This video! Everyone's passing it around! You said "we can't tell anyone."
What makes you think it's anything to do with m--
Because you take New Media class and you're the only idiot with footage of Leon in the woods!
Catching up now. Cool goggles.
Look, guys--okay. You got me. I'm the Hooded Hierophant. So what?
The hooded whatnow?
Good boy, Chip. A white squirrel. Now find me, uhm...an icicle shaped like a rocket.
I'm serious! What's so bad about being proud of what we've achieved, huh?
Sure. That's why you wear a mask.
Listen, it's just a hobby, okay? I was buzzed after I talked to my mom last night and I wanted to, I dunno. Channel it.
That would be your mom, the cop--right? Who is literally investigating our crime.
Yeah, but-- no, look, I told you! That's not what she wanted to talk about!
She was worried, is all. Wants me to walk a different route to school. They found Leon's bike.
Yeah--in the woods, genius! As seen in your dumb video!
Good. That's great--thank you. Now get me, uhhh...get me a coffeepot full of frogs.

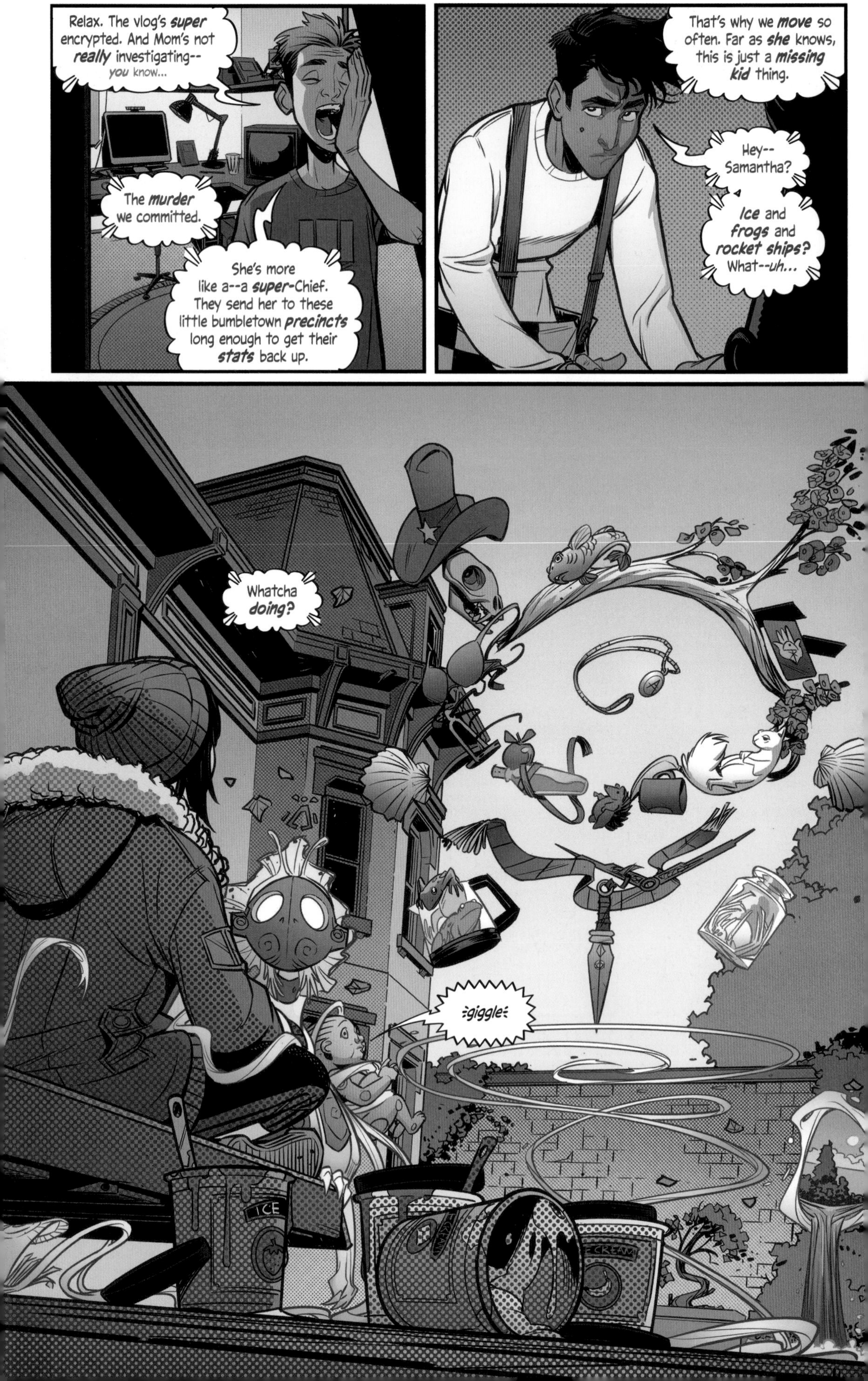

Relax. The vlog's *super* encrypted. And Mom's not *really* investigating--*you* know...
The *murder* we committed.
She's more like a--a *super*-Chief. They send her to these little bumbletown *precincts* long enough to get their *stats* back up.
That's why we *move* so often. Far as *she* knows, this is just a *missing kid* thing.
Hey--Samantha?
Ice and *frogs* and *rocket ships?* What--*uh...*
Whatcha *doing?*
giggle
ICE

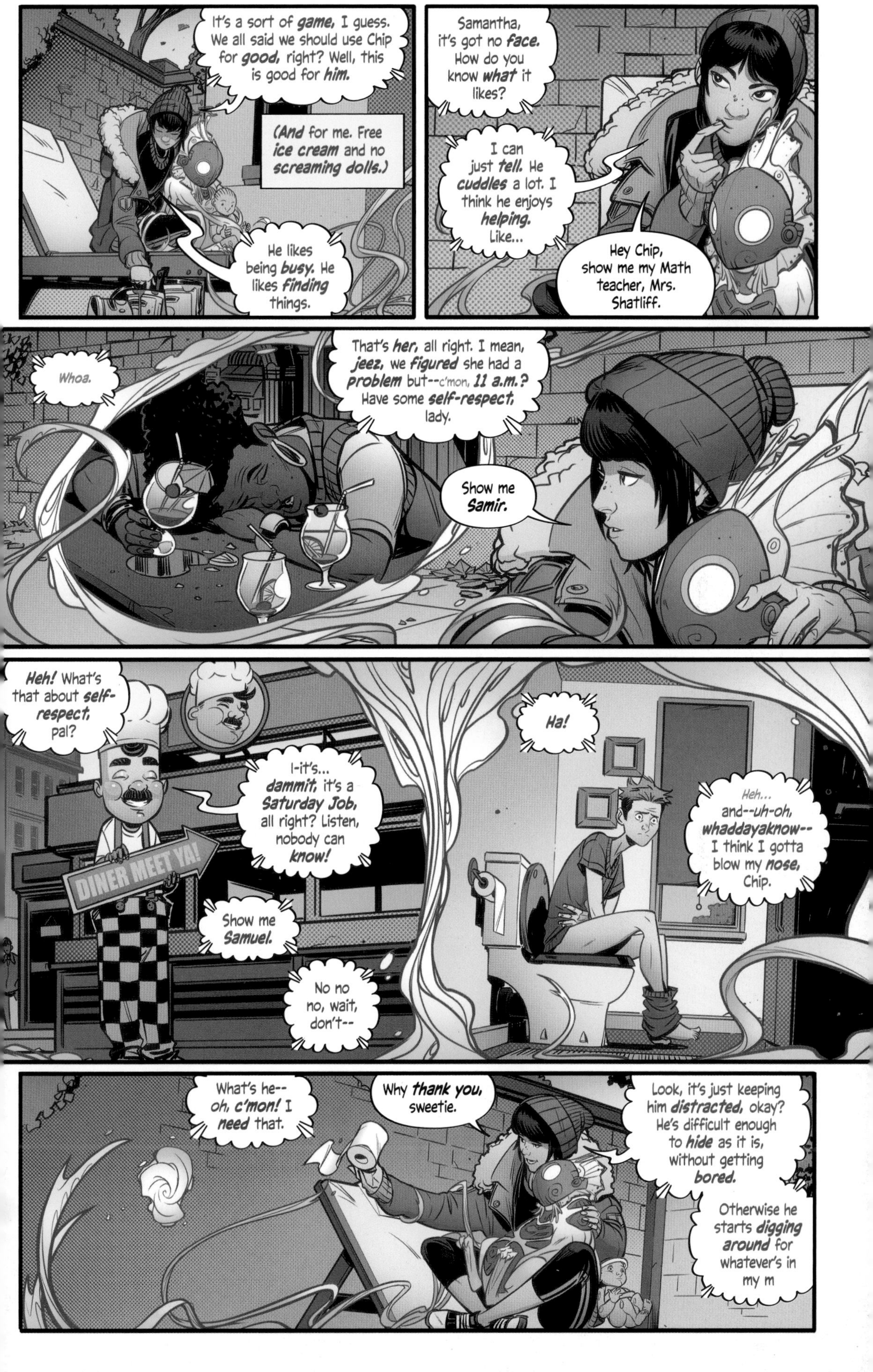
It's a sort of **game,** I guess. We all said we should use Chip for **good,** right? Well, this is good for **him.**
(And for me. Free **ice cream** and no **screaming dolls.)**
He likes being **busy.** He likes **finding** things.
Samantha, it's got no **face.** How do you know **what** it likes?
I can just **tell.** He **cuddles** a lot. I think he enjoys **helping.** Like...
Hey Chip, show me my Math teacher, Mrs. Shatliff.
Whoa.
That's **her,** all right. I mean, **jeez,** we **figured** she had a **problem** but--c'mon, **11 a.m.?** Have some **self-respect,** lady.
Show me **Samir.**
Heh! What's that about **self-respect,** pal?
I-it's... **dammit,** it's a **Saturday Job,** all right? Listen, nobody can **know!**
DINER MEET YA!
Show me **Samuel.**
No no no, wait, don't--
Ha!
Heh... and--**uh-oh, whaddayaknow--** I think I gotta blow my **nose,** Chip.
What's he-- oh, **c'mon!** I **need** that.
Why **thank you,** sweetie.
Look, it's just keeping him **distracted,** okay? He's difficult enough to **hide** as it is, without getting **bored.**
Otherwise he starts **digging around** for whatever's in my m

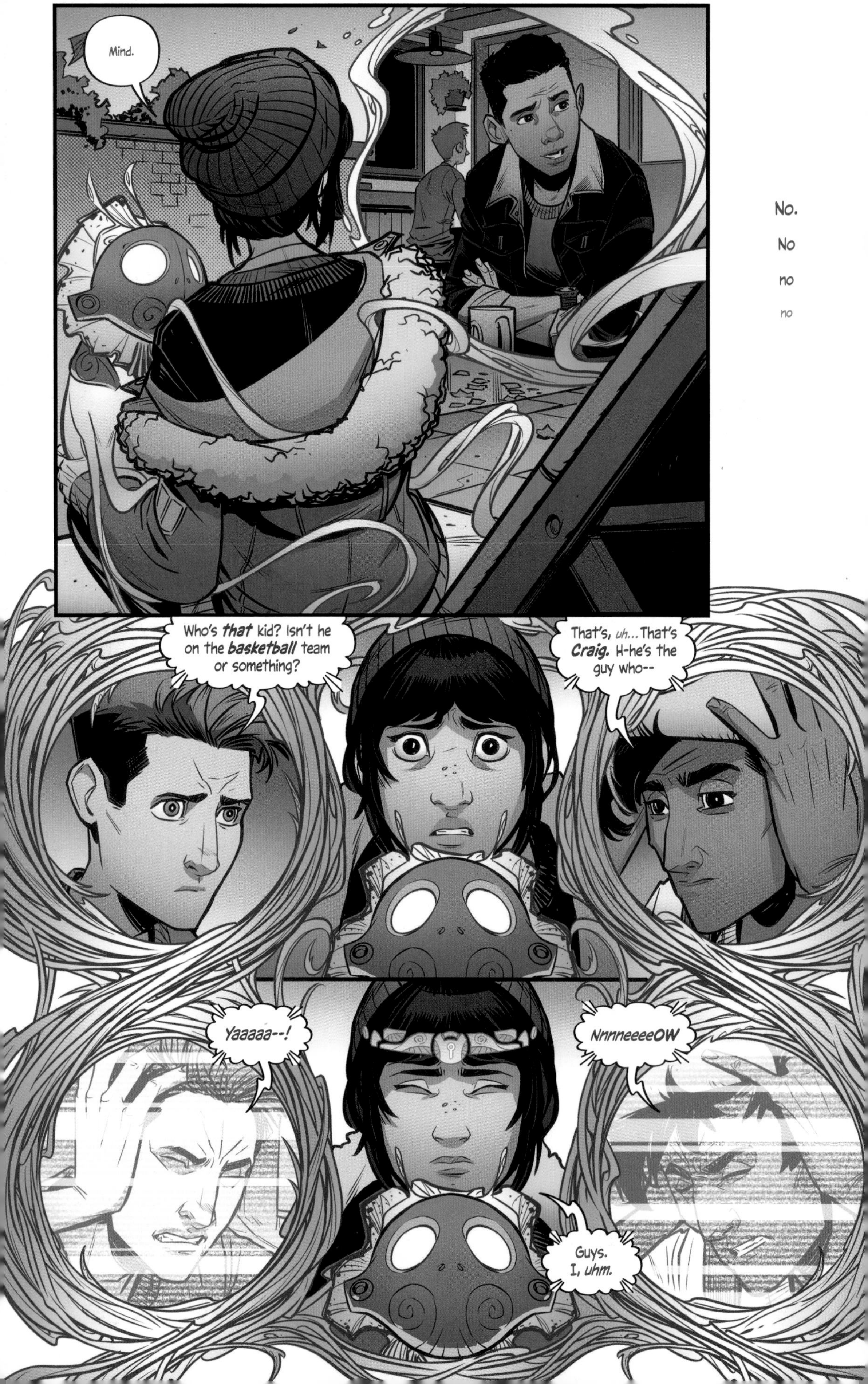
Mind.
No.
No
no
no
Who's *that* kid? Isn't he on the *basketball* team or something?
That's, *uh*... That's *Craig.* H-he's the guy who--
Yaaaaa--!
NnnneeeeOW
Guys. I, *uhm.*

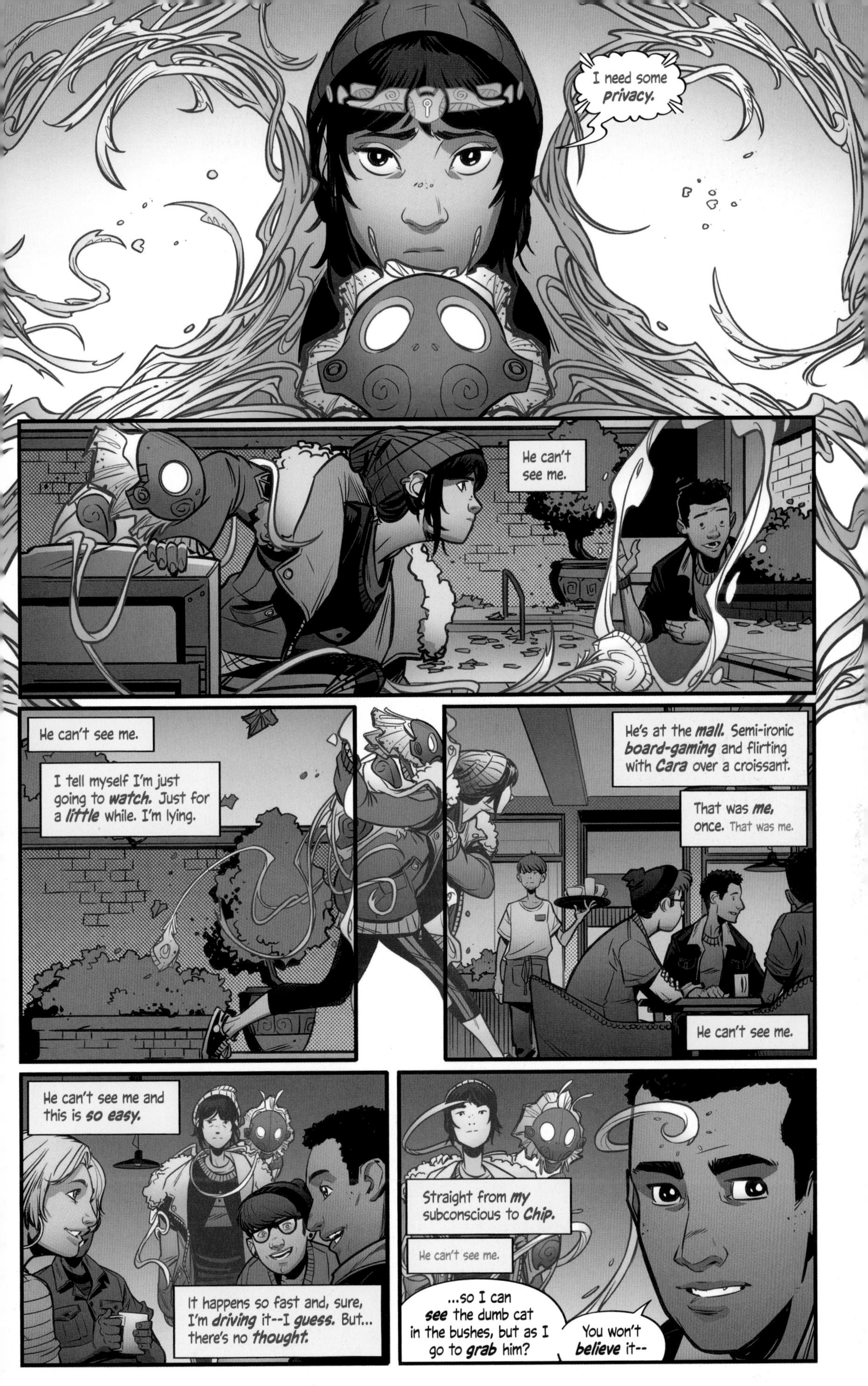
I need some privacy.
He can't see me.
He can't see me.
I tell myself I'm just going to watch. Just for a little while. I'm lying.
He's at the mall. Semi-ironic board-gaming and flirting with Cara over a croissant.
That was me, once. That was me.
He can't see me.
He can't see me and this is so easy.
It happens so fast and, sure, I'm driving it--I guess. But... there's no thought.
Straight from my subconscious to Chip.
He can't see me.
...so I can see the dumb cat in the bushes, but as I go to grab him?
You won't believe it--

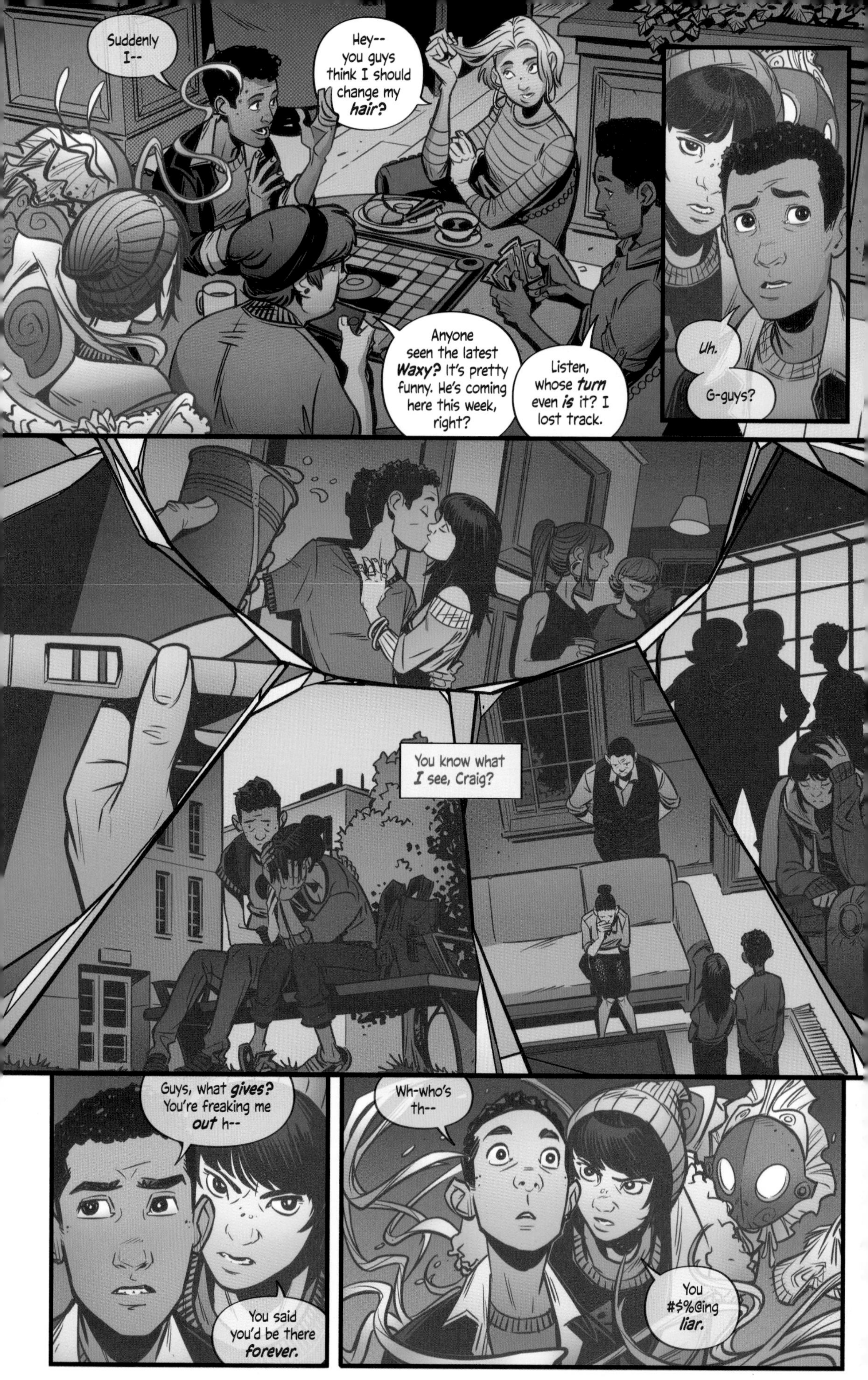
Suddenly I--
Hey-- you guys think I should change my *hair?*
Anyone seen the latest *Waxy?* It's pretty funny. He's coming here this week, right?
Listen, whose *turn* even *is* it? I lost track.
Uh.
G-guys?
You know what *I* see, Craig?
Guys, what *gives?* You're freaking me *out* h--
You said you'd be there *forever.*
Wh-who's th--
You #$%@ing *liar.*

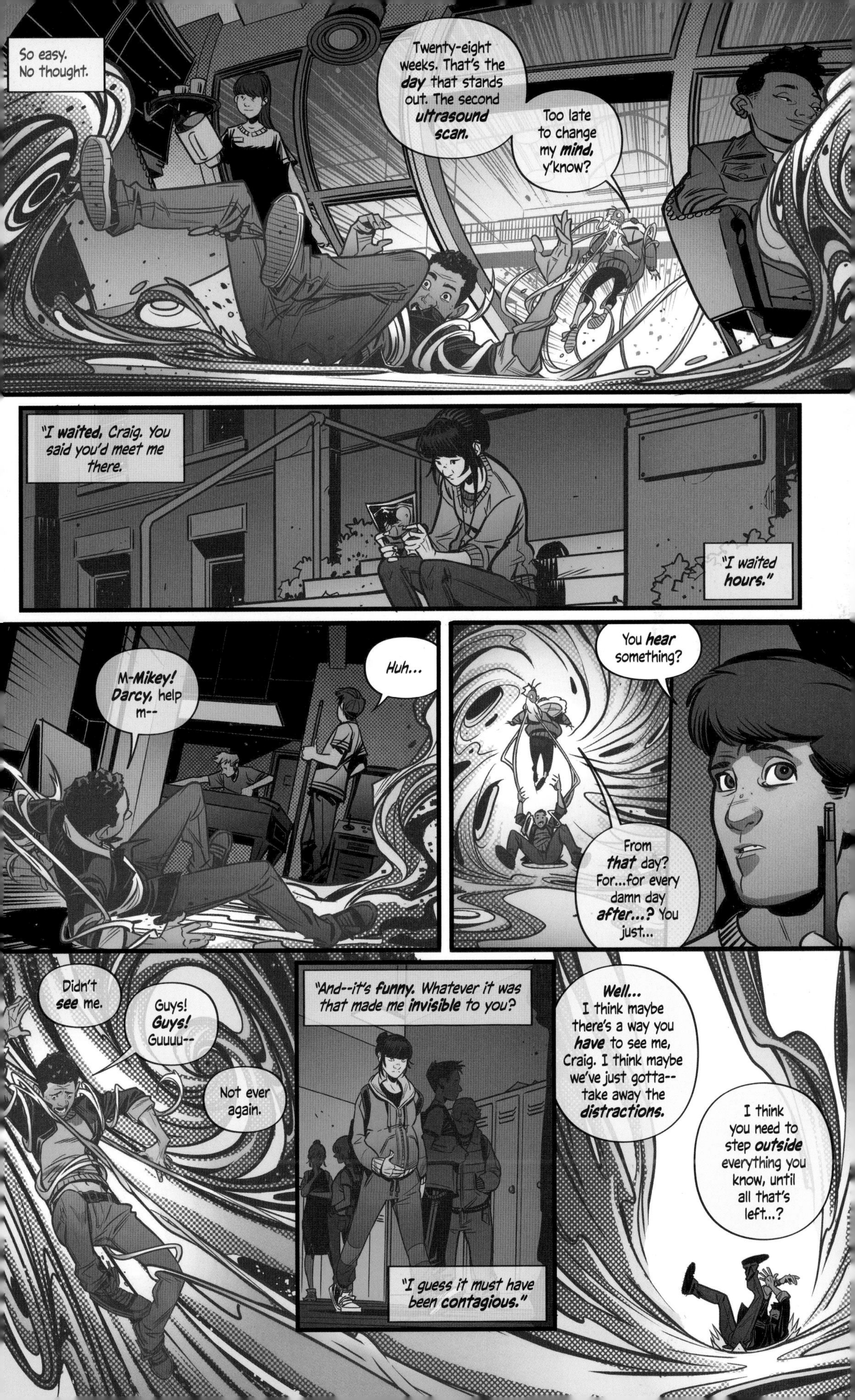
So easy. No thought.
Twenty-eight weeks. That's the day that stands out. The second ultrasound scan.
Too late to change my mind, y'know?
"I waited, Craig. You said you'd meet me there.
"I waited hours."
M-Mikey! Darcy, help m--
Huh...
You hear something?
From that day? For...for every damn day after...? You just...
Didn't see me.
Guys! Guys! Guuuu--
Not ever again.
"And--it's funny. Whatever it was that made me invisible to you?
"I guess it must have been contagious."
Well... I think maybe there's a way you have to see me, Craig. I think maybe we've just gotta-- take away the distractions.
I think you need to step outside everything you know, until all that's left...?

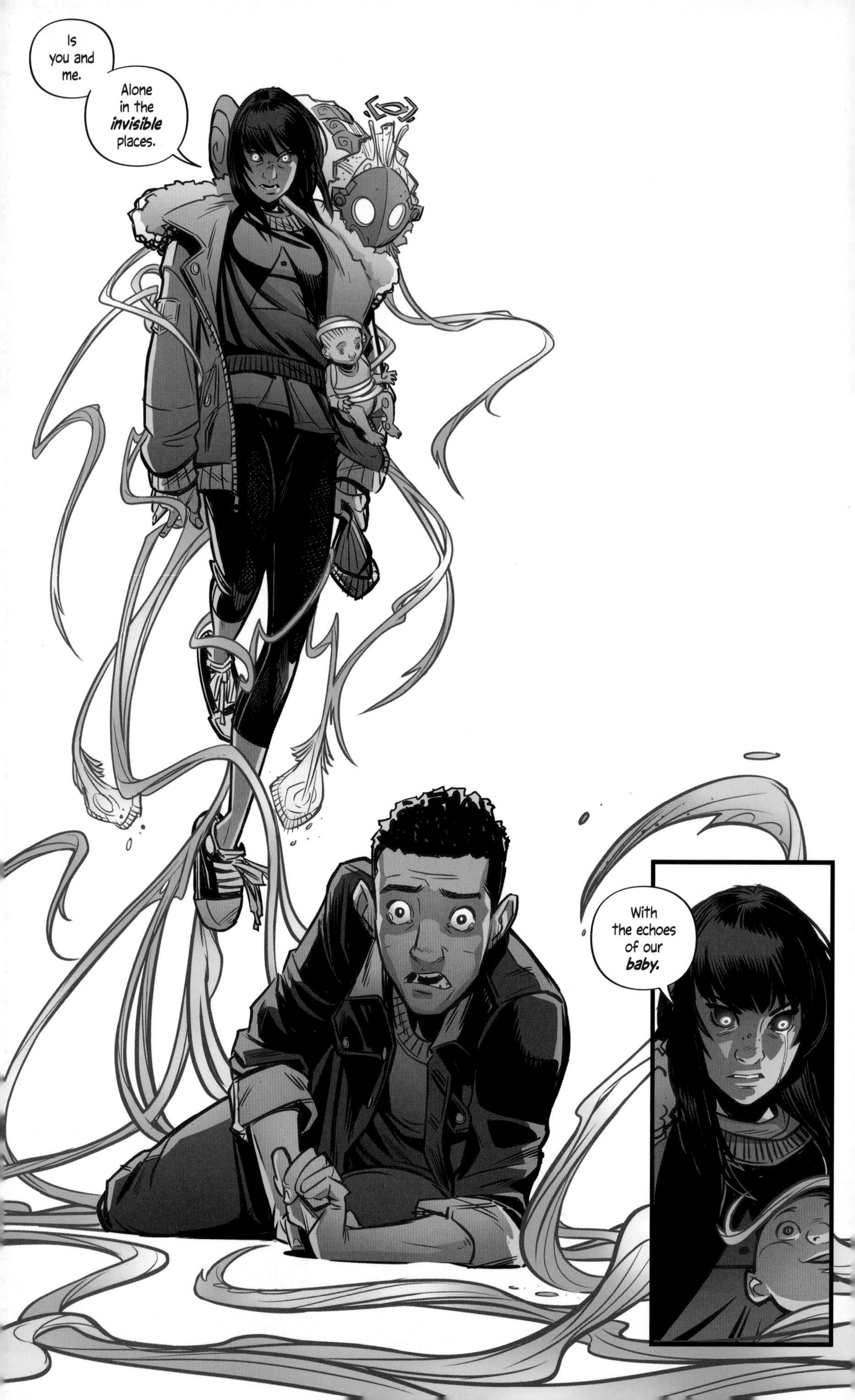
Is you and me.
Alone in the *invisible* places.
With the echoes of our *baby.*

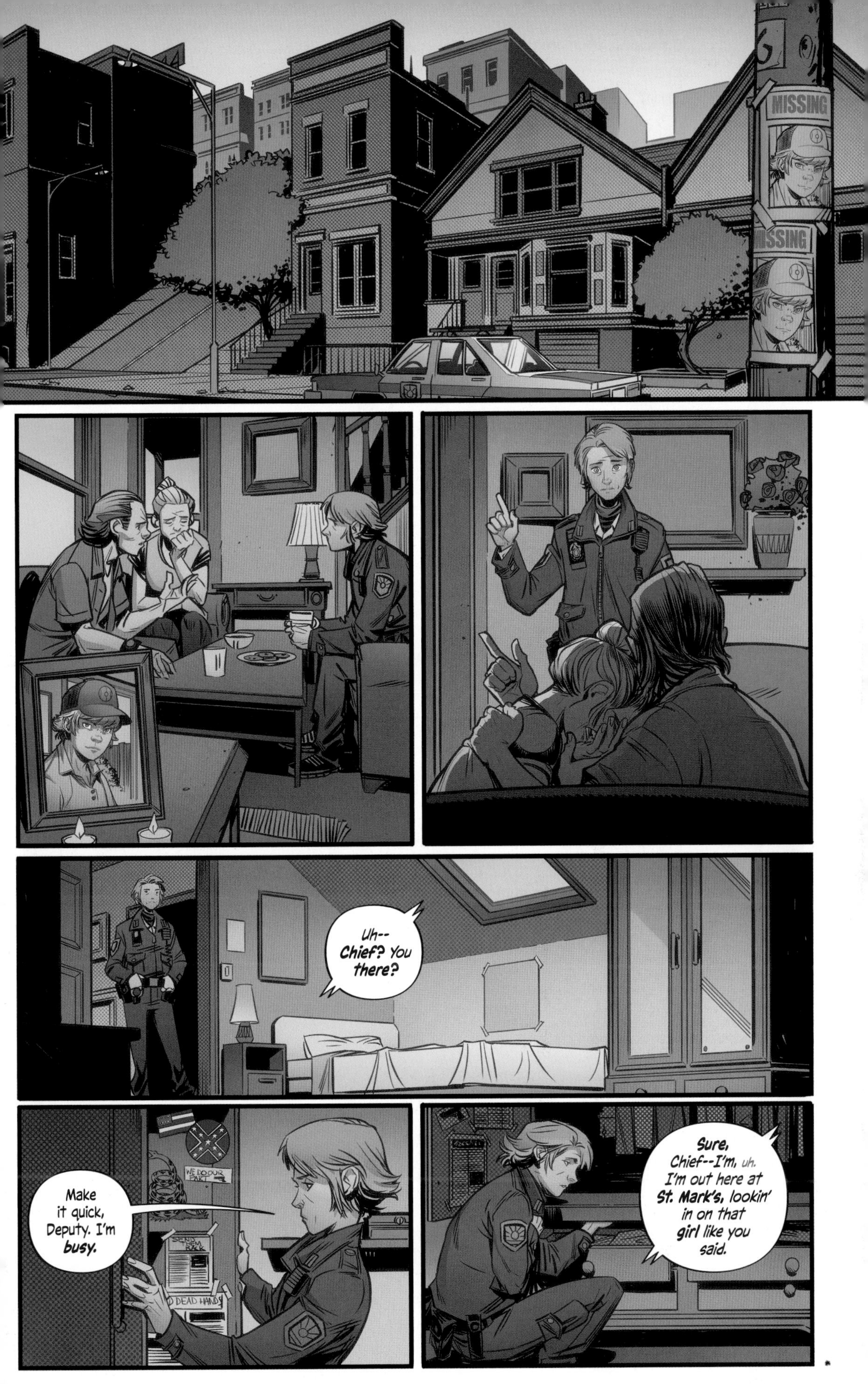
MISSING
MISSING
Uh-- Chief? You there?
Make it quick, Deputy. I'm busy.
Sure, Chief--I'm, uh. I'm out here at St. Mark's, lookin' in on that girl like you said.

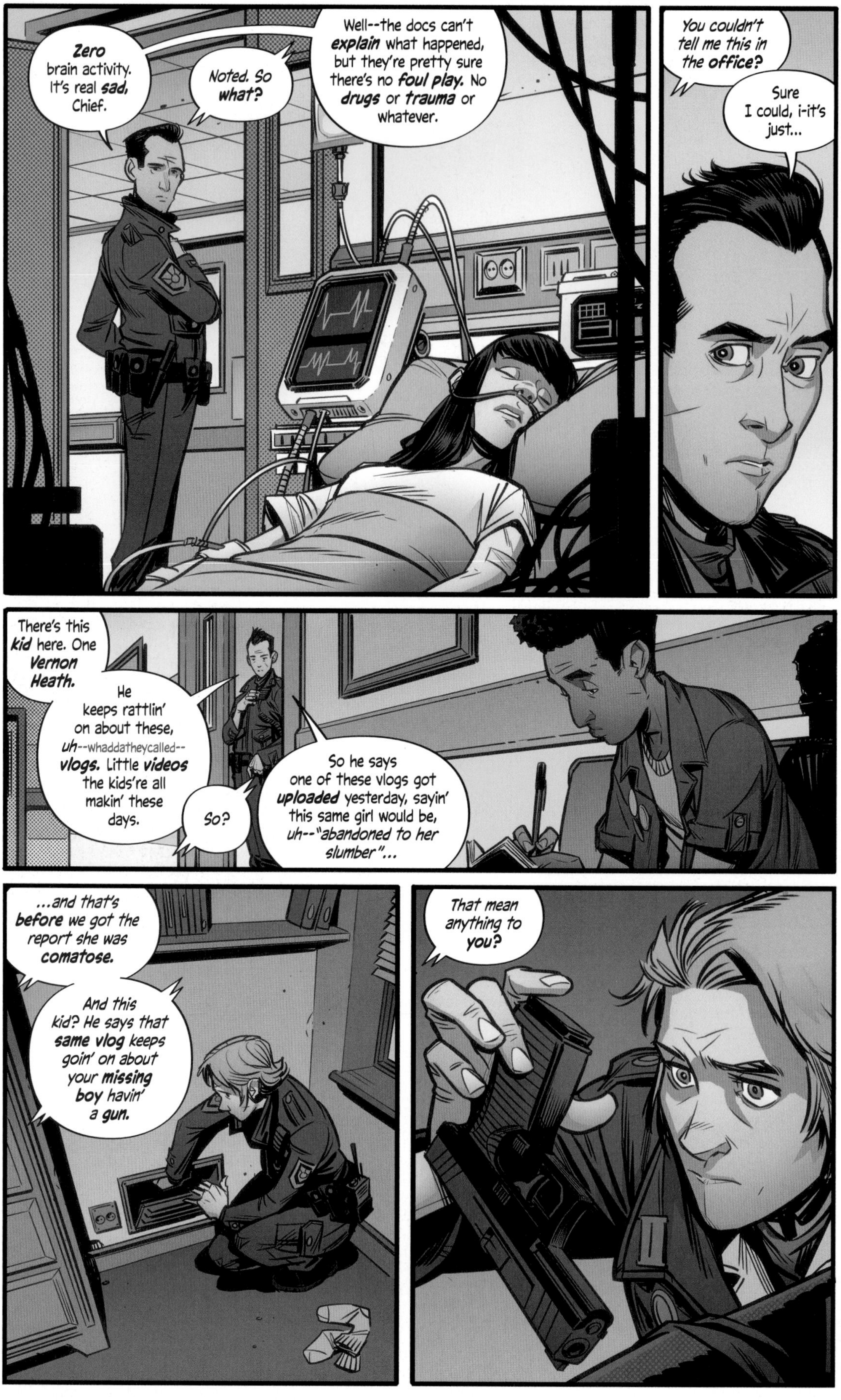

Zero brain activity. It's real sad, Chief.
Noted. So what?
Well--the docs can't explain what happened, but they're pretty sure there's no foul play. No drugs or trauma or whatever.
You couldn't tell me this in the office?
Sure I could, i-it's just...
There's this kid here. One Vernon Heath.
He keeps rattlin' on about these, uh--whaddatheycalled--vlogs. Little videos the kids're all makin' these days.
So?
So he says one of these vlogs got uploaded yesterday, sayin' this same girl would be, uh--"abandoned to her slumber"...
...and that's before we got the report she was comatose.
And this kid? He says that same vlog keeps goin' on about your missing boy havin' a gun.
That mean anything to you?

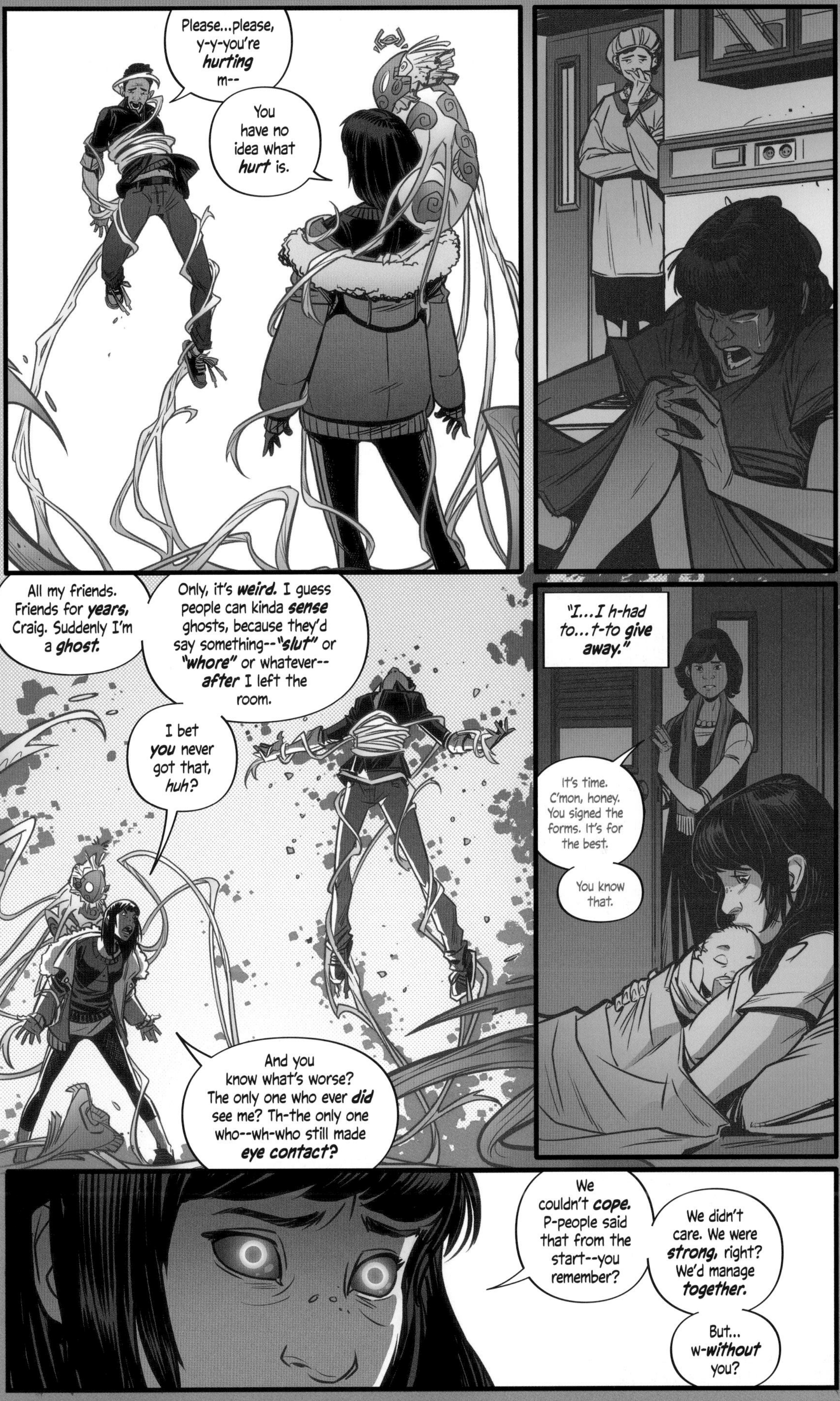
Please...please, y-y-you're *hurting* m--
You have no idea what *hurt* is.
All my friends. Friends for *years,* Craig. Suddenly I'm a *ghost.*
Only, it's *weird.* I guess people can kinda *sense* ghosts, because they'd say something--*"slut"* or *"whore"* or whatever--*after* I left the room.
I bet *you* never got that, *huh?*
And you know what's worse? The only one who ever *did* see me? Th-the only one who--wh-who still made *eye contact?*
"I...I h-had to...t-to *give away.*"
It's time. C'mon, honey. You signed the forms. It's for the best.
You know that.
We couldn't *cope.* P-people said that from the start--you remember?
We didn't care. We were *strong,* right? We'd manage *together.*
But... w-*without* you?

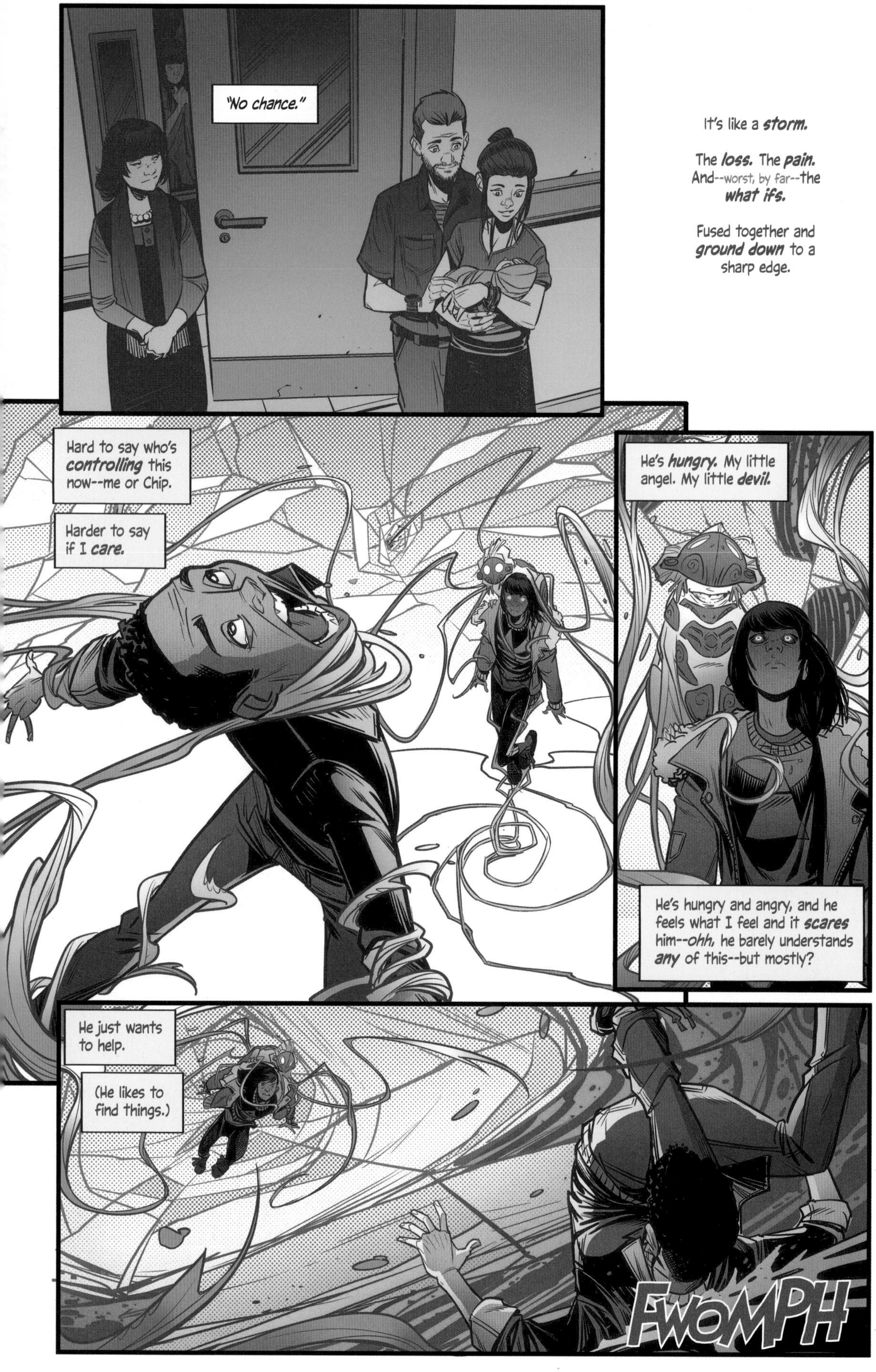
"No chance."
It's like a *storm.*
The *loss.* The *pain.* And--worst, by far--the *what ifs.*
Fused together and *ground down* to a sharp edge.
Hard to say who's *controlling* this now--me or Chip.
Harder to say if I *care.*
He's *hungry.* My little angel. My little *devil.*
He's hungry and angry, and he feels what I feel and it *scares* him--*ohh,* he barely understands *any* of this--but mostly?
He just wants to help.
(He likes to find things.)
FWOMPH

Wh-wh-where's *this*? Where are w--

You *know* where.

Listen.

waaaaa!

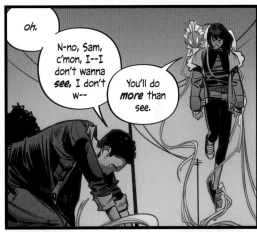

oh.

N-no, Sam, c'mon, I--I don't wanna *see*, I don't w--

You'll do *more* than see.

You will come *with* me into this house.

Y-you'll... you'll *acknowledge* what you *did.* You'll *acknowledge* what you *are* to...to our...

To *him.*

B-because if you *don't?*

I won't just make you *invisible*, Craig. I won't just make everyone *forget* you.

I will make it... so that you...

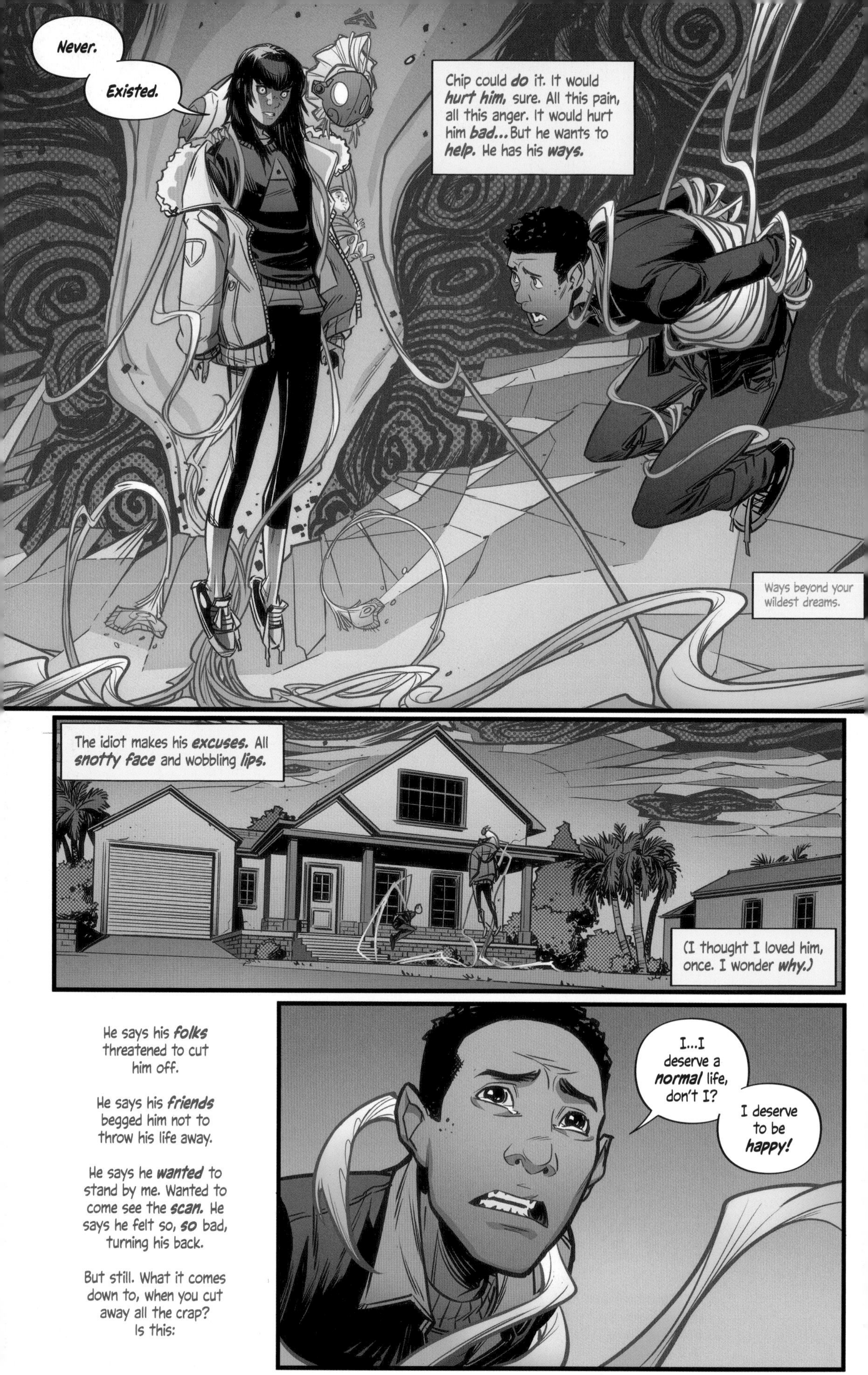
Never.
Existed.
Chip could do it. It would hurt him, sure. All this pain, all this anger. It would hurt him bad...But he wants to help. He has his ways.
Ways beyond your wildest dreams.
The idiot makes his excuses. All snotty face and wobbling lips.
(I thought I loved him, once. I wonder why.)
He says his folks threatened to cut him off.
He says his friends begged him not to throw his life away.
He says he wanted to stand by me. Wanted to come see the scan. He says he felt so, so bad, turning his back.
But still. What it comes down to, when you cut away all the crap? Is this:
I...I deserve a normal life, don't I?
I deserve to be happy!

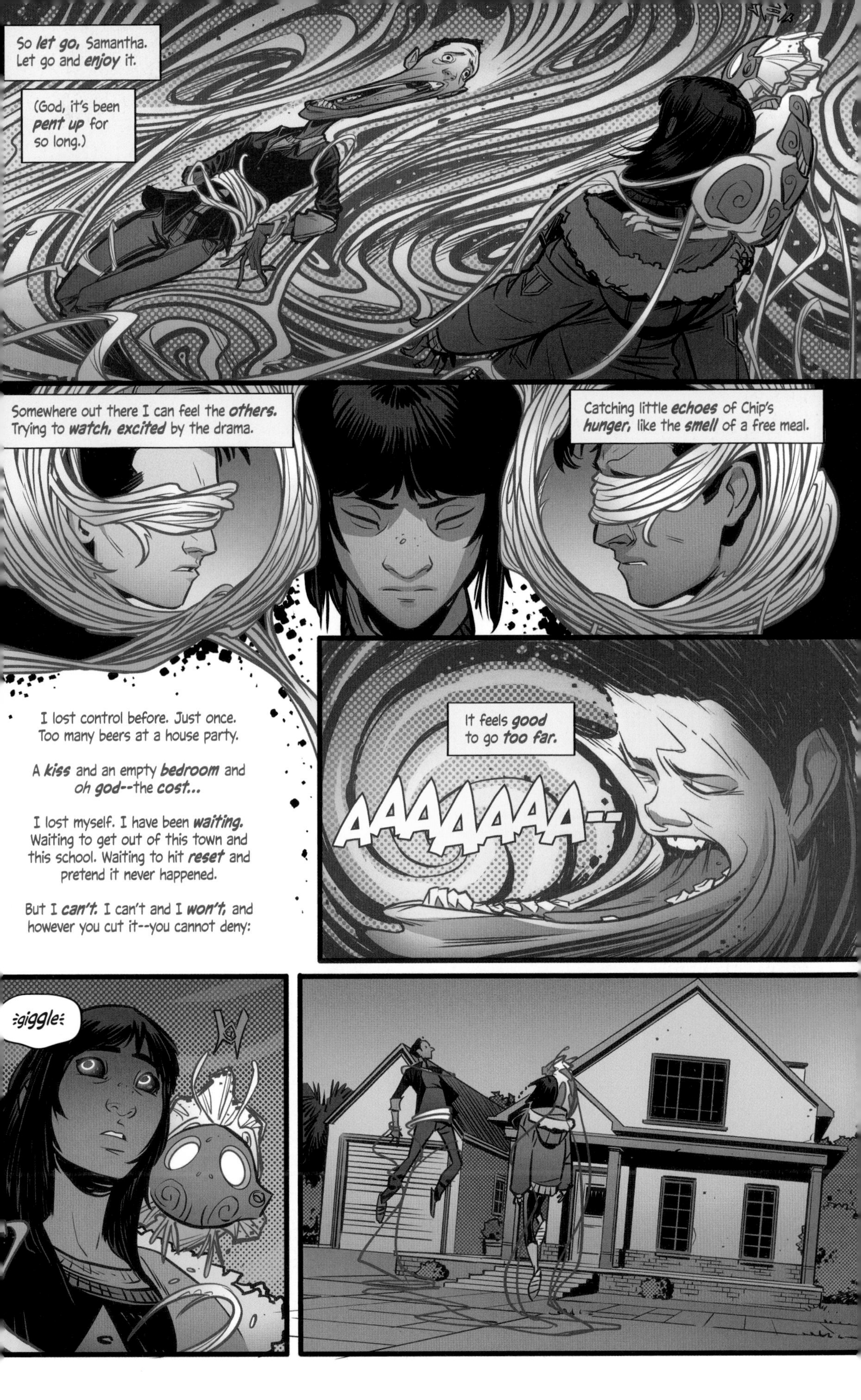

So *let go,* Samantha. Let go and *enjoy* it.
(God, it's been *pent up* for so long.)
Somewhere out there I can feel the *others.* Trying to *watch, excited* by the drama.
Catching little *echoes* of Chip's *hunger,* like the *smell* of a free meal.
I lost control before. Just once. Too many beers at a house party.
A *kiss* and an empty *bedroom* and oh *god*--the *cost...*
I lost myself. I have been *waiting.* Waiting to get out of this town and this school. Waiting to hit *reset* and pretend it never happened.
But I *can't.* I can't and I *won't,* and however you cut it--you cannot deny:
It feels *good* to go *too far.*
AAAAAAA--
:giggle:

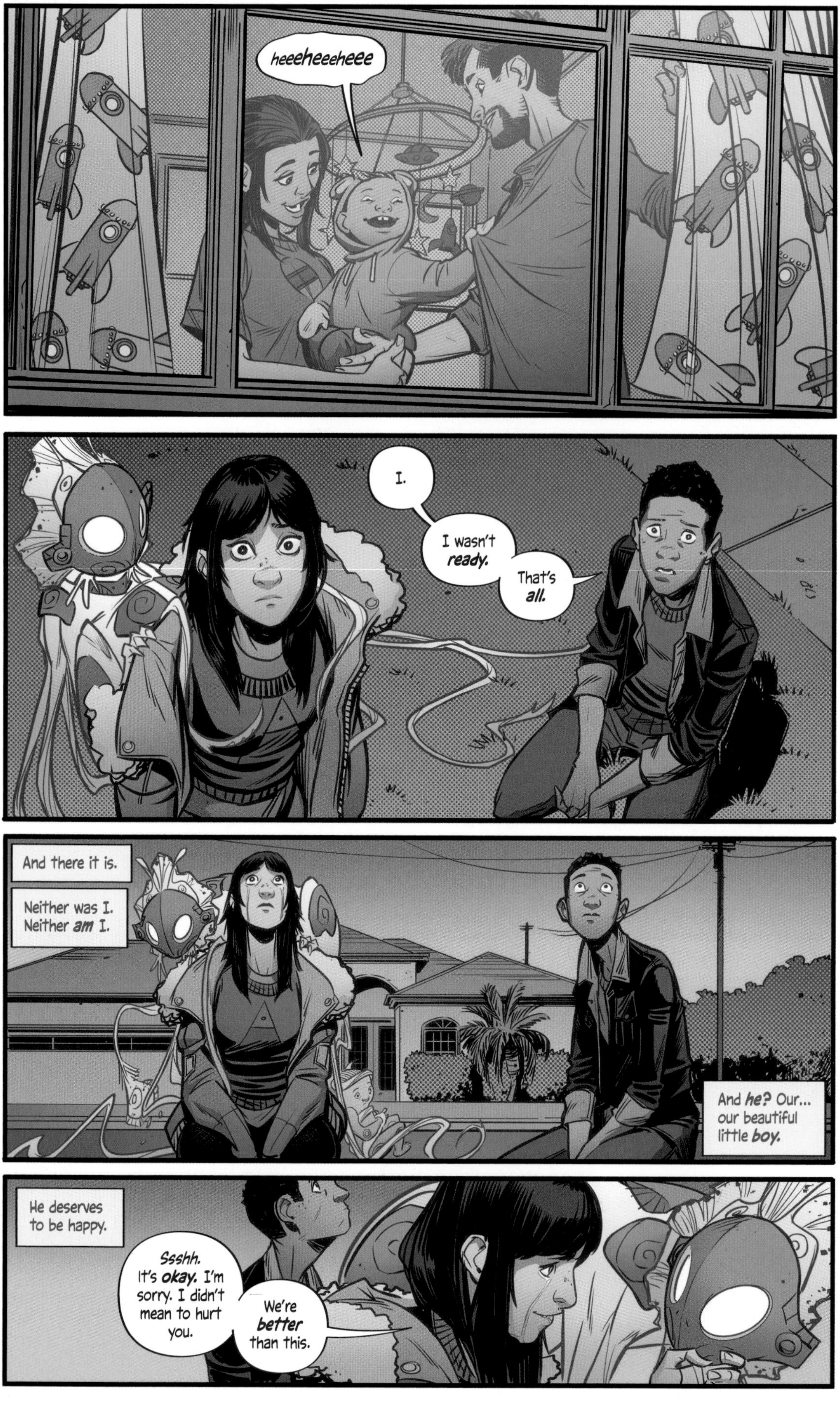

heeeheeeheee
I.
I wasn't *ready.*
That's *all.*
And there it is.
Neither was I. Neither *am* I.
And *he?* Our... our beautiful little *boy.*
He deserves to be happy.
Ssshh. It's *okay.* I'm sorry. I didn't mean to hurt you.
We're *better* than this.

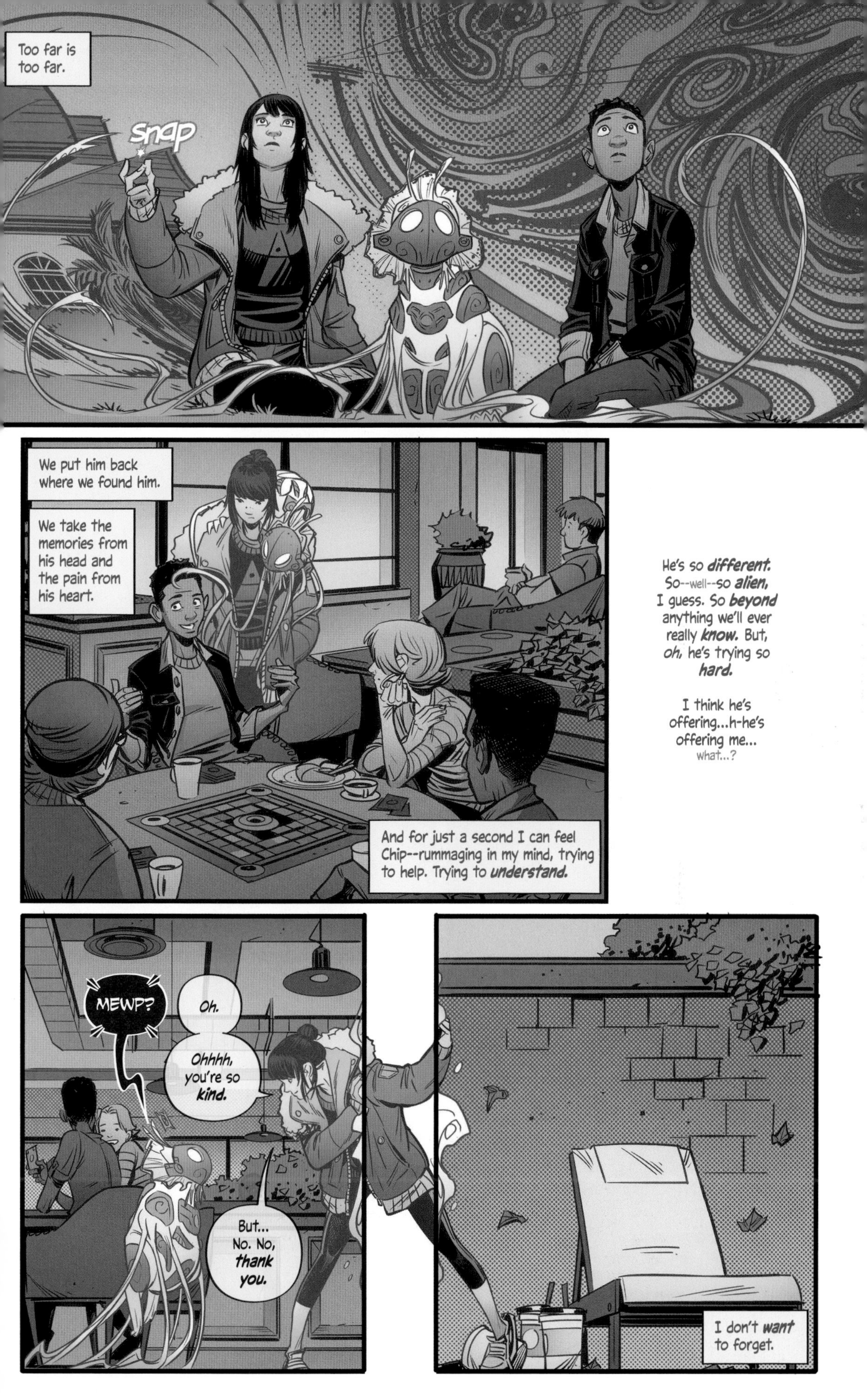
Too far is too far.
SNAP
We put him back where we found him.
We take the memories from his head and the pain from his heart.
He's so ***different.*** So--well--so ***alien,*** I guess. So ***beyond*** anything we'll ever really ***know.*** But, ***oh,*** he's trying so ***hard.***
I think he's offering...h-he's offering me... what...?
And for just a second I can feel Chip--rummaging in my mind, trying to help. Trying to ***understand.***
MEWP?
Oh.
Ohhhh, you're so ***kind.***
But... No. No, ***thank you.***
I don't ***want*** to forget.

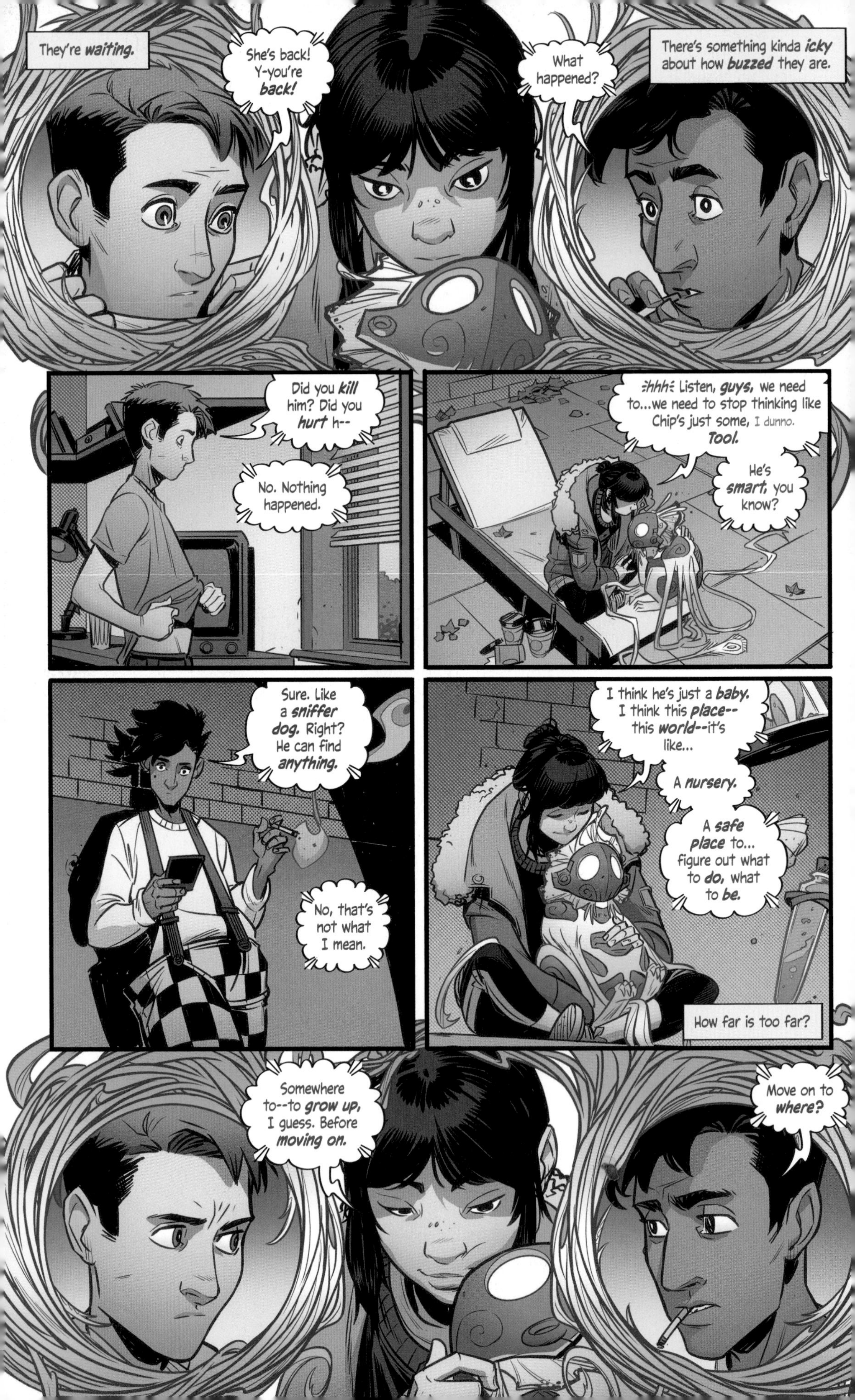
They're *waiting.*
She's back! Y-you're ***back!***
What happened?
There's something kinda ***icky*** about how ***buzzed*** they are.
Did you ***kill*** him? Did you ***hurt*** h--
No. Nothing happened.
hhh Listen, ***guys,*** we need to...we need to stop thinking like Chip's just some, I dunno. ***Tool.***
He's ***smart,*** you know?
Sure. Like a ***sniffer dog.*** Right? He can find ***anything.***
No, that's not what I mean.
I think he's just a ***baby.*** I think this ***place--*** this ***world--***it's like...
A ***nursery.***
A ***safe place*** to... figure out what to ***do,*** what to ***be.***
How far is too far?
Somewhere to--to ***grow up,*** I guess. Before ***moving on.***
Move on to ***where?***

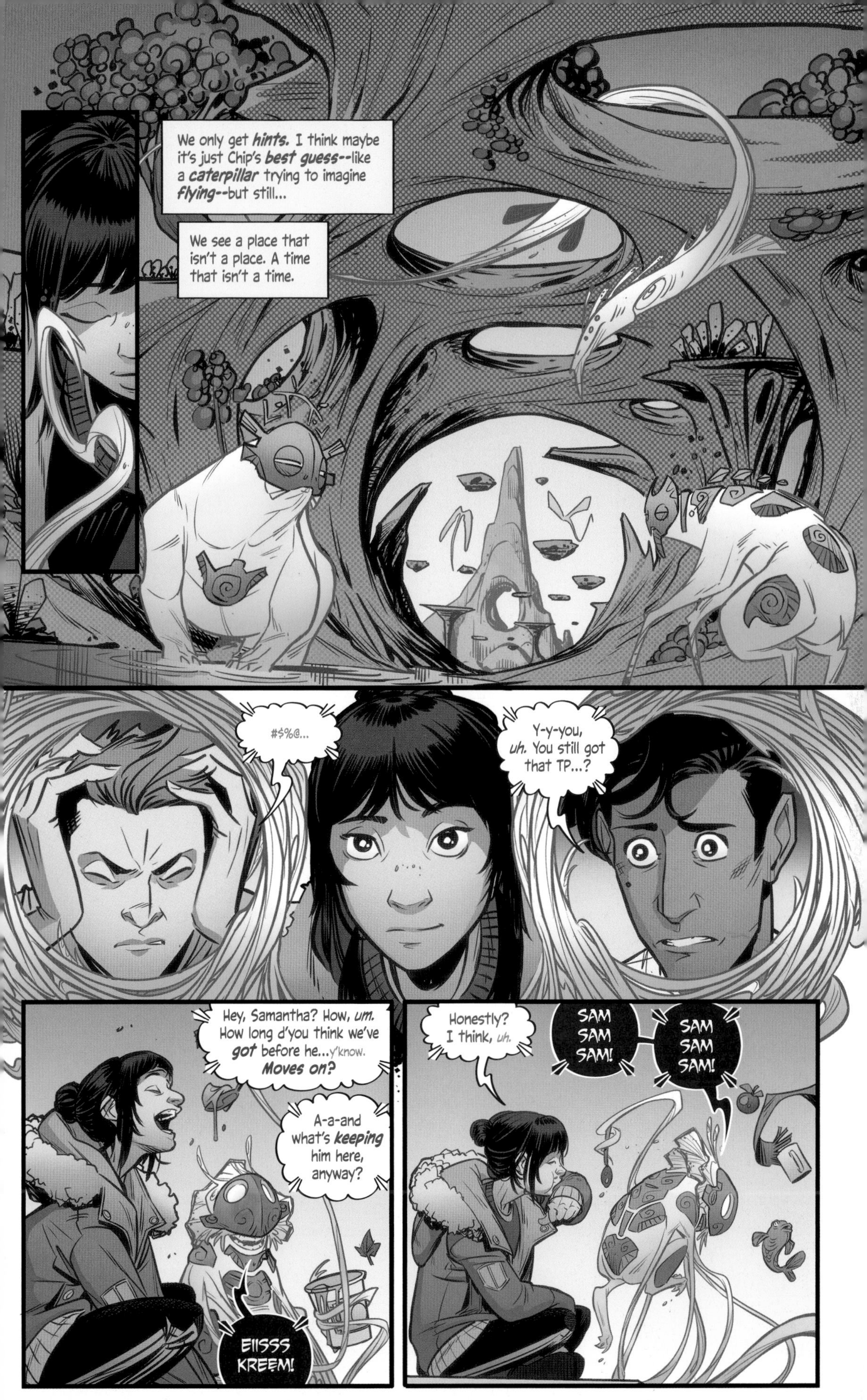

We only get *hints.* I think maybe it's just Chip's *best guess*--like a *caterpillar* trying to imagine *flying*--but still...
We see a place that isn't a place. A time that isn't a time.
#$%@...
Y-y-you, *uh.* You still got that TP...?
Hey, Samantha? How, *um.* How long d'you think we've *got* before he...y'know. *Moves on?*
A-a-and what's *keeping* him here, anyway?
EIISSS KREEM!
Honestly? I think, *uh.*
SAM SAM SAM!
SAM SAM SAM!

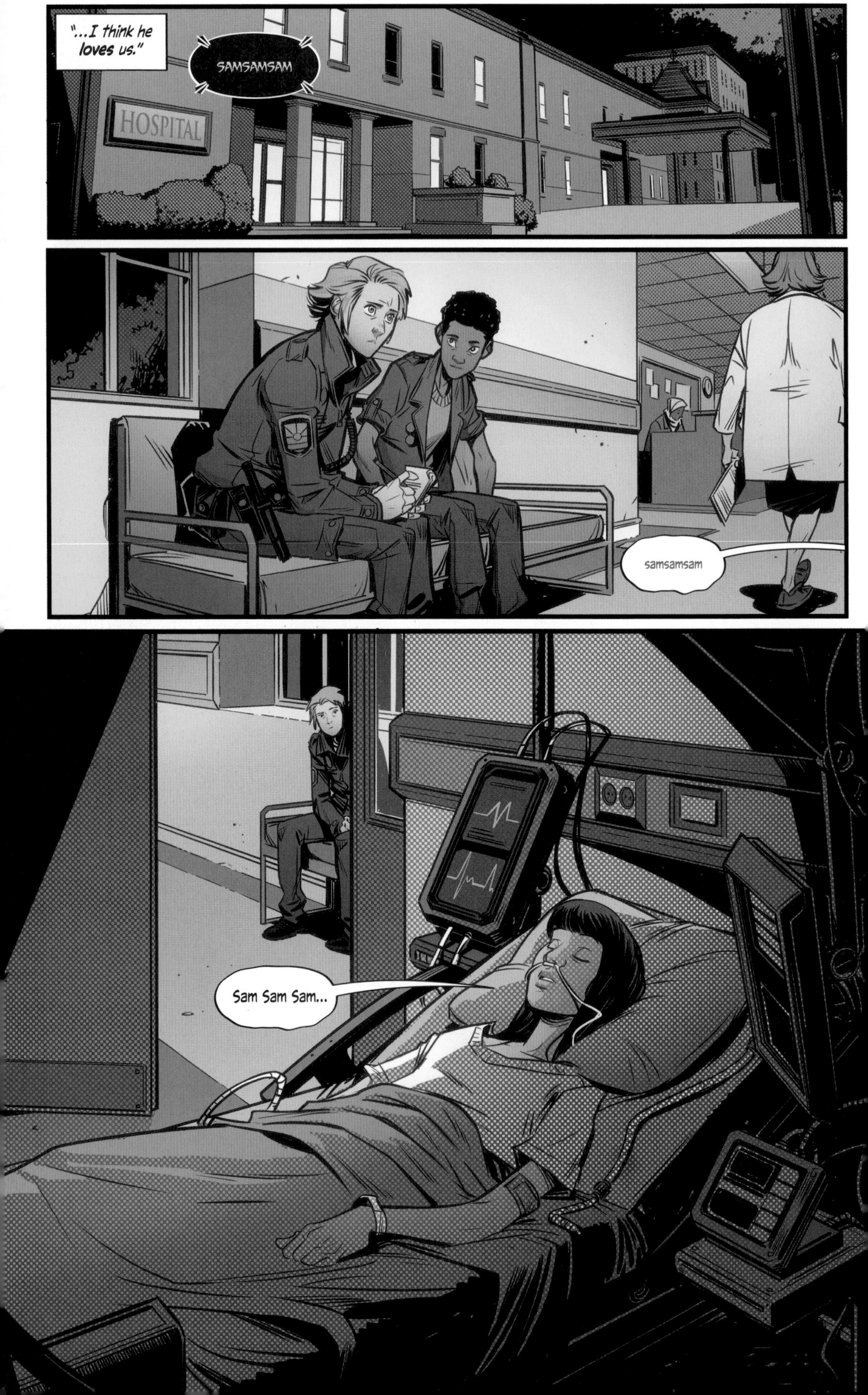
"...I think he loves us."
SAMSAMSAM
HOSPITAL
samsamsam
Sam Sam Sam...

CHAPTER FOUR

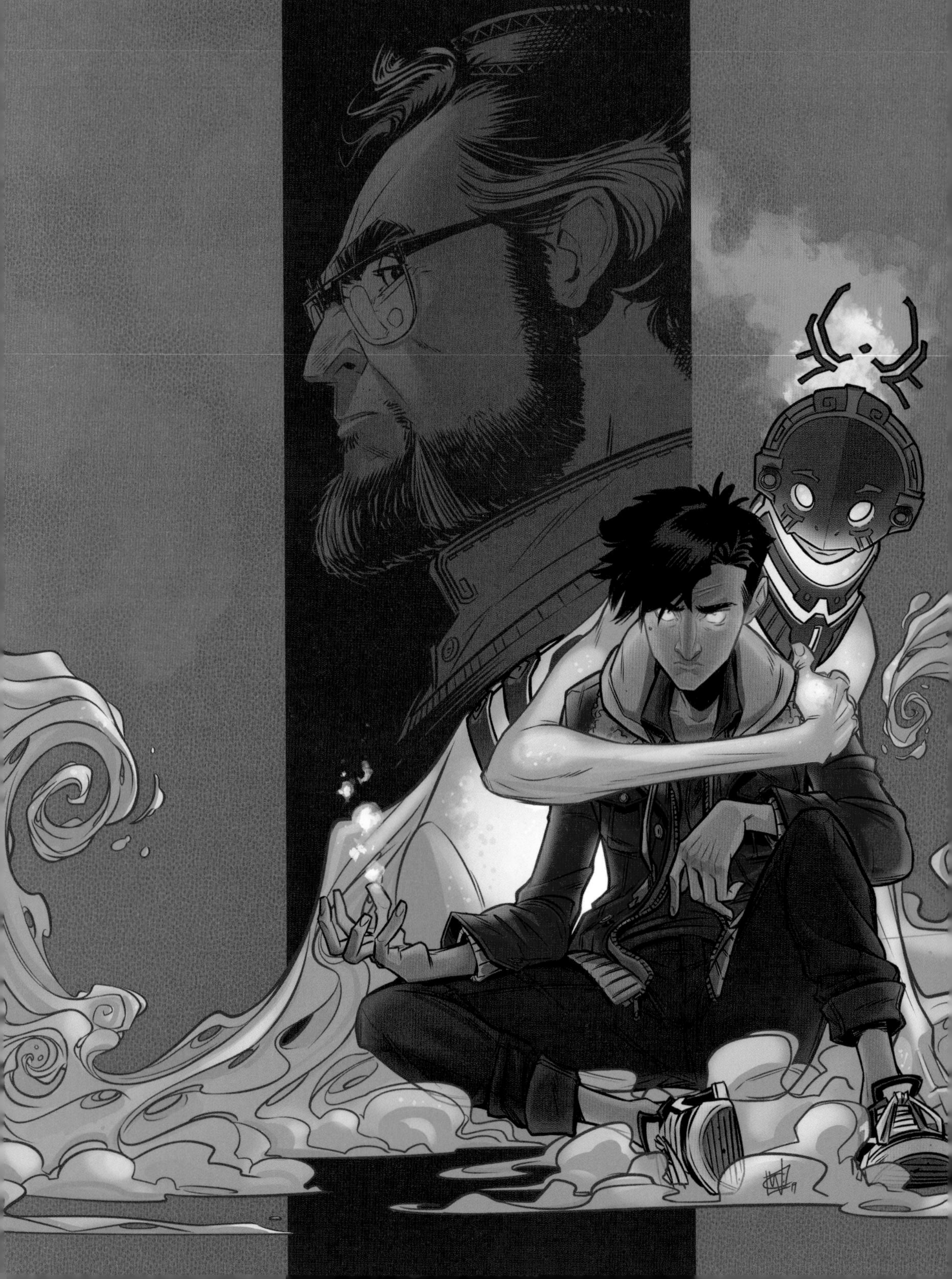

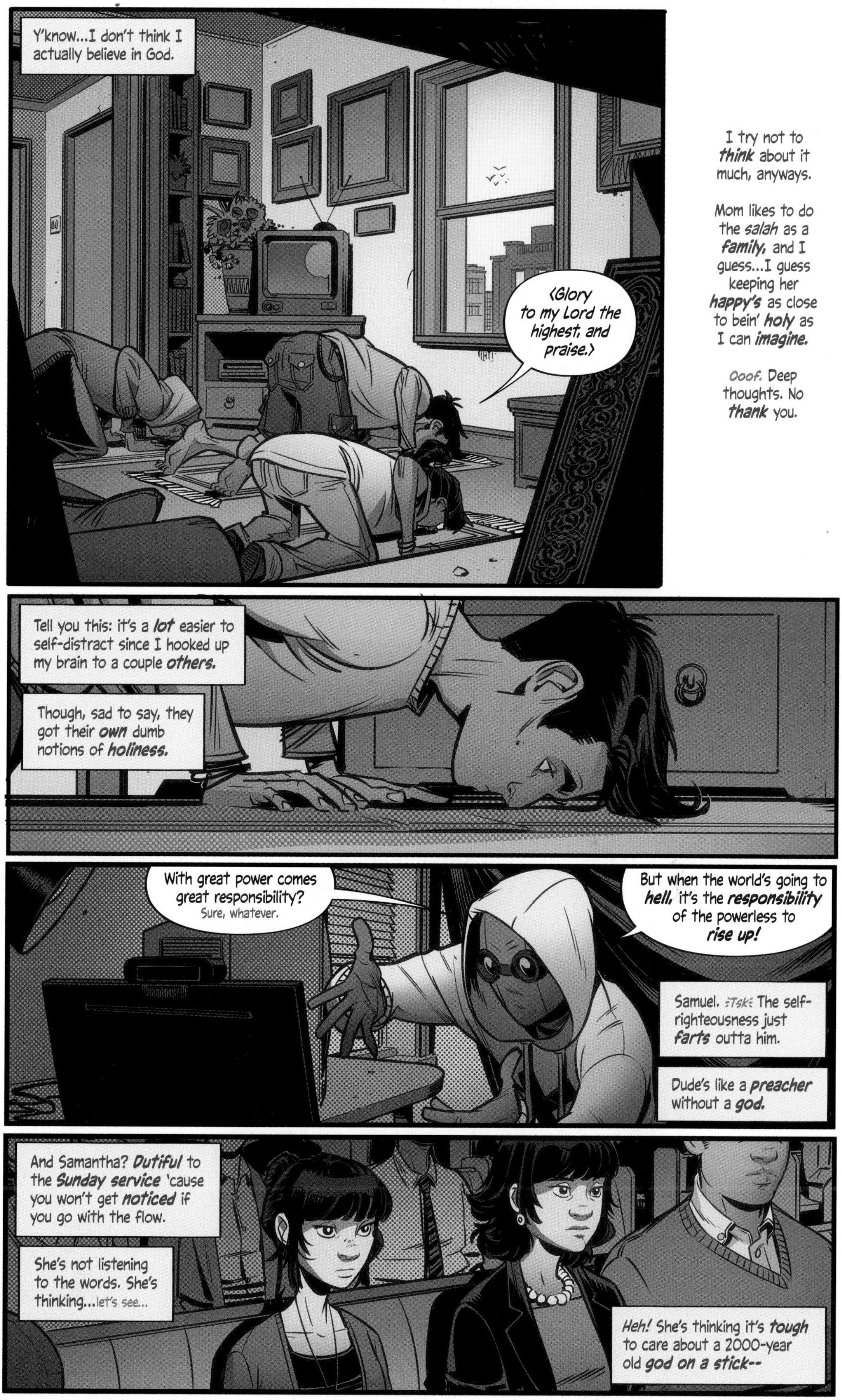
Y'know...I don't think I actually believe in God.
I try not to think about it much, anyways.
Mom likes to do the salah as a family, and I guess...I guess keeping her happy's as close to bein' holy as I can imagine.
Ooof. Deep thoughts. No thank you.
‹Glory to my Lord the highest, and praise.›
Tell you this: it's a lot easier to self-distract since I hooked up my brain to a couple others.
Though, sad to say, they got their own dumb notions of holiness.
With great power comes great responsibility? Sure, whatever.
But when the world's going to hell, it's the responsibility of the powerless to rise up!
Samuel. Tsk. The self-righteousness just farts outta him.
Dude's like a preacher without a god.
And Samantha? Dutiful to the Sunday service 'cause you won't get noticed if you go with the flow.
She's not listening to the words. She's thinking...let's see...
Heh! She's thinking it's tough to care about a 2000-year old god on a stick--

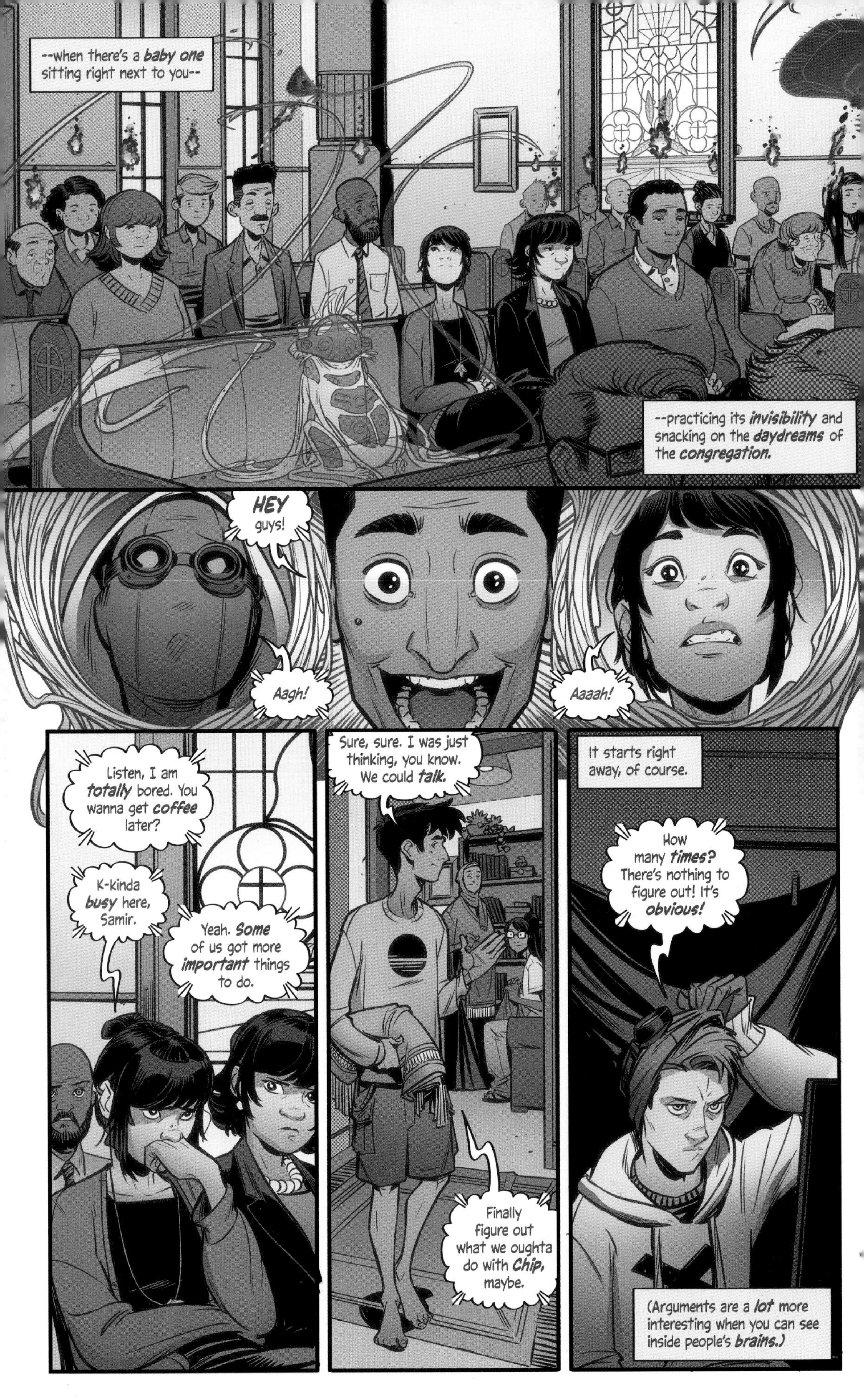
--when there's a baby one sitting right next to you--
--practicing its invisibility and snacking on the daydreams of the congregation.
HEY guys!
Aagh!
Aaaah!
Listen, I am totally bored. You wanna get coffee later?
K-kinda busy here, Samir.
Yeah. Some of us got more important things to do.
Sure, sure. I was just thinking, you know. We could talk.
Finally figure out what we oughta do with Chip, maybe.
It starts right away, of course.
How many times? There's nothing to figure out! It's obvious!
(Arguments are a lot more interesting when you can see inside people's brains.)

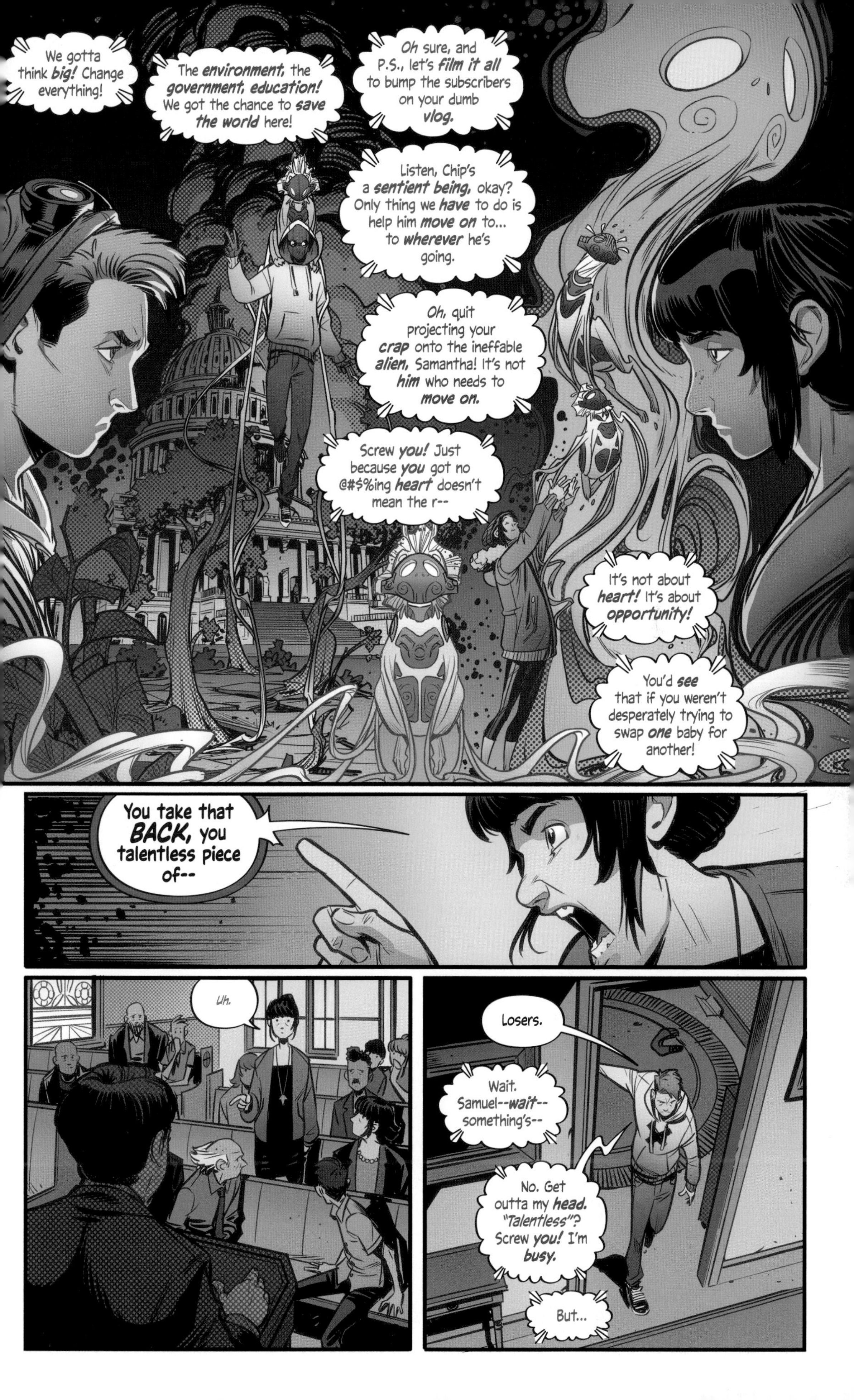
We gotta think big! Change everything!
The environment, the government, education! We got the chance to save the world here!
Oh sure, and P.S., let's film it all to bump the subscribers on your dumb vlog.
Listen, Chip's a sentient being, okay? Only thing we have to do is help him move on to... to wherever he's going.
Oh, quit projecting your crap onto the ineffable alien, Samantha! It's not him who needs to move on.
Screw you! Just because you got no @#$%ing heart doesn't mean the r--
It's not about heart! It's about opportunity!
You'd see that if you weren't desperately trying to swap one baby for another!
You take that BACK, you talentless piece of--
Uh.
Losers.
Wait. Samuel--wait-- something's--
No. Get outta my head. "Talentless"? Screw you! I'm busy.
But...

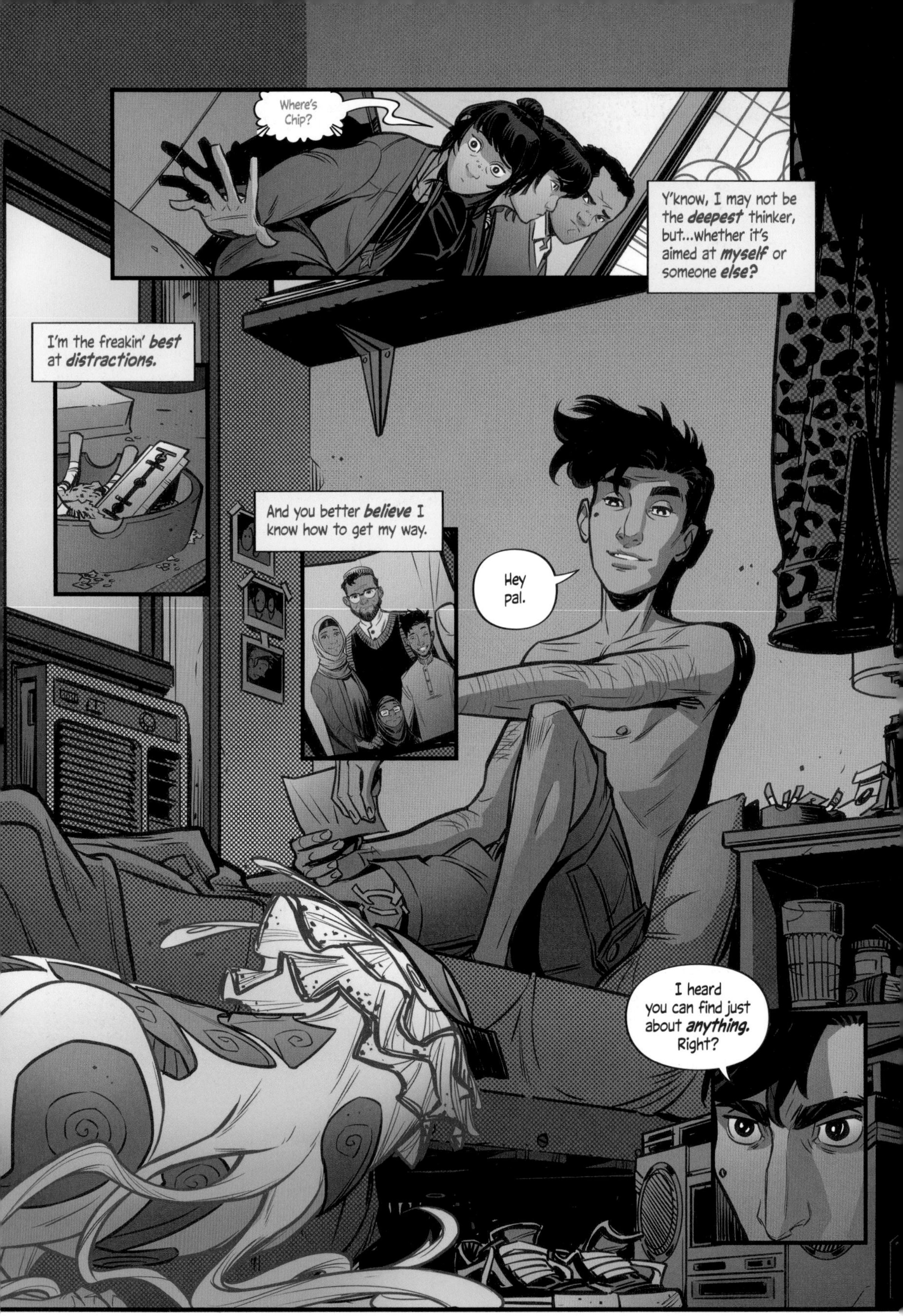
Where's Chip?
Y'know, I may not be the deepest thinker, but...whether it's aimed at myself or someone else?
I'm the freakin' best at distractions.
And you better believe I know how to get my way.
Hey pal.
I heard you can find just about anything. Right?

Chapter 4:
MEET THY MAKER

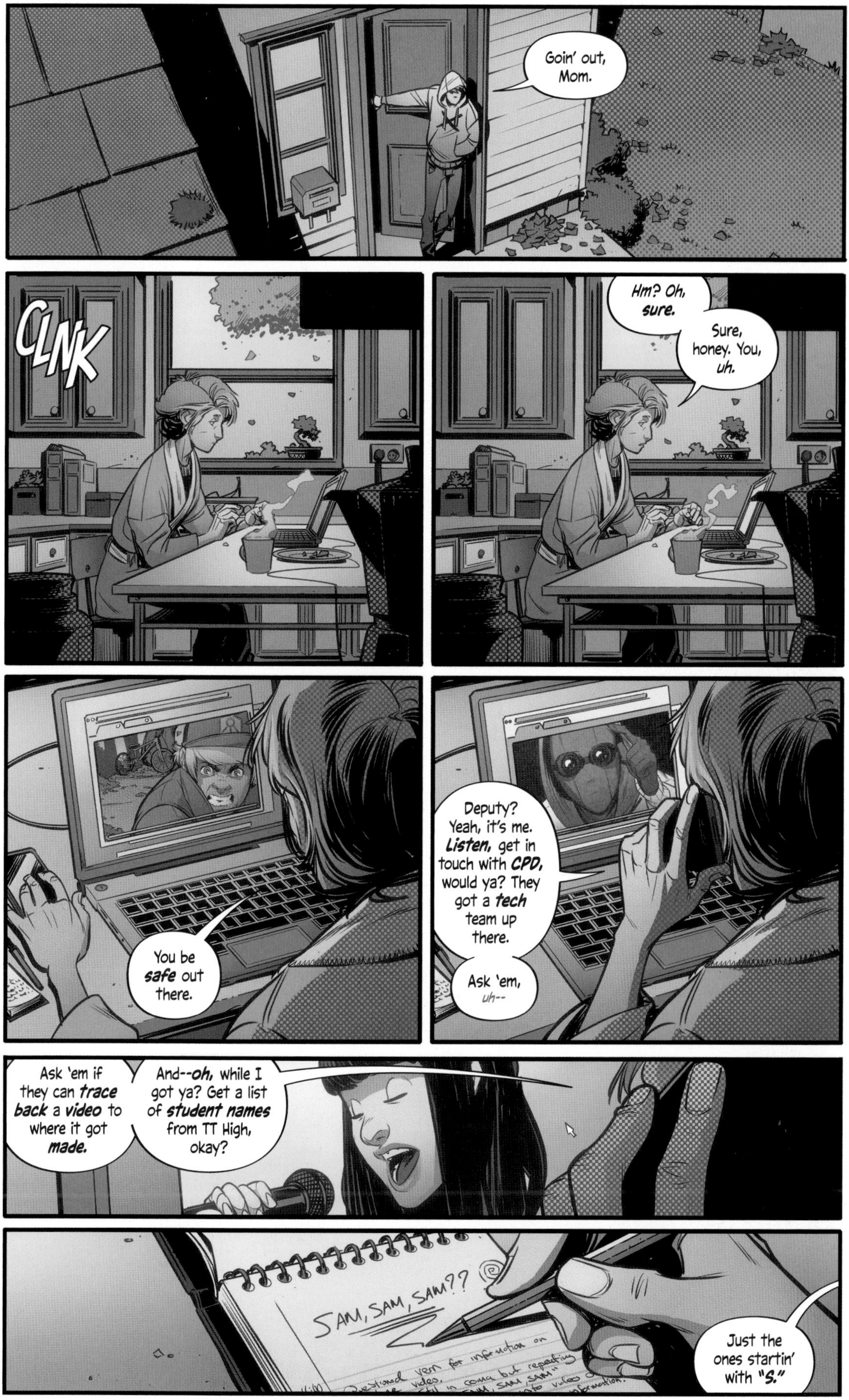
Goin' out, Mom.
CLNK
Hm? Oh, *sure.*
Sure, honey. You, *uh.*
You be *safe* out there.
Deputy? Yeah, it's me. *Listen,* get in touch with *CPD,* would ya? They got a *tech* team up there.
Ask 'em, *uh--*
Ask 'em if they can *trace back* a *video* to where it got *made.*
And--*oh,* while I got ya? Get a list of *student names* from TT High, okay?
SAM, SAM, SAM??
Just the ones startin' with *"S."*

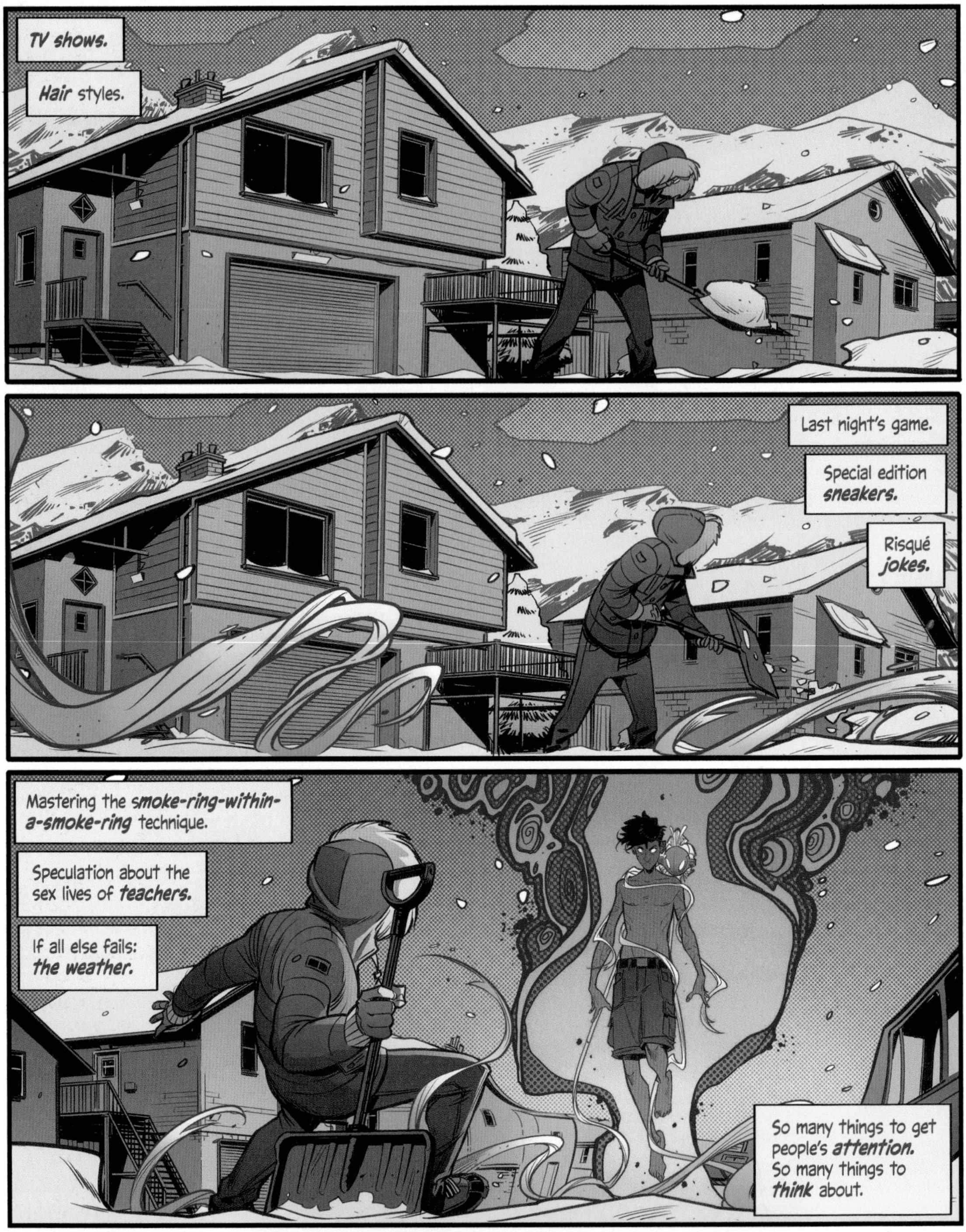
TV shows.
Hair styles.
Last night's game.
Special edition sneakers.
Risqué jokes.
Mastering the smoke-ring-within-a-smoke-ring technique.
Speculation about the sex lives of teachers.
If all else fails: the weather.
So many things to get people's attention. So many things to think about.

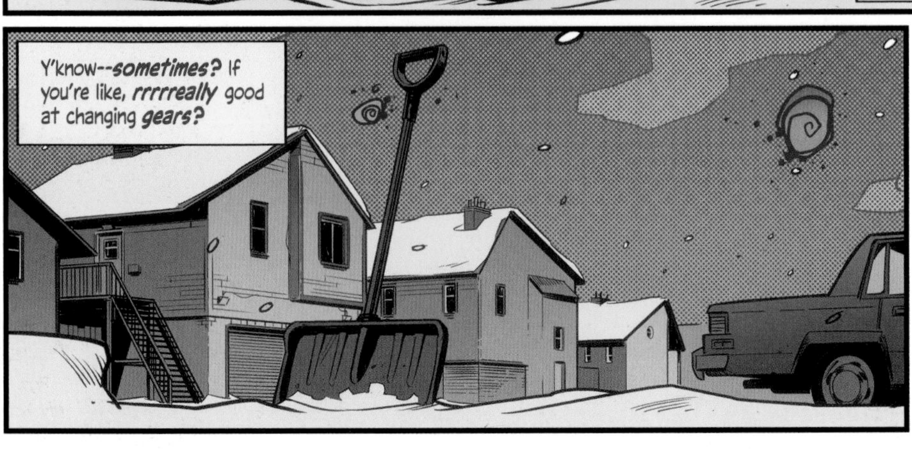
Y'know--sometimes? If you're like, rrrrreally good at changing gears?

Sometimes whole *days* can pass without thinking of ***anything at all.***

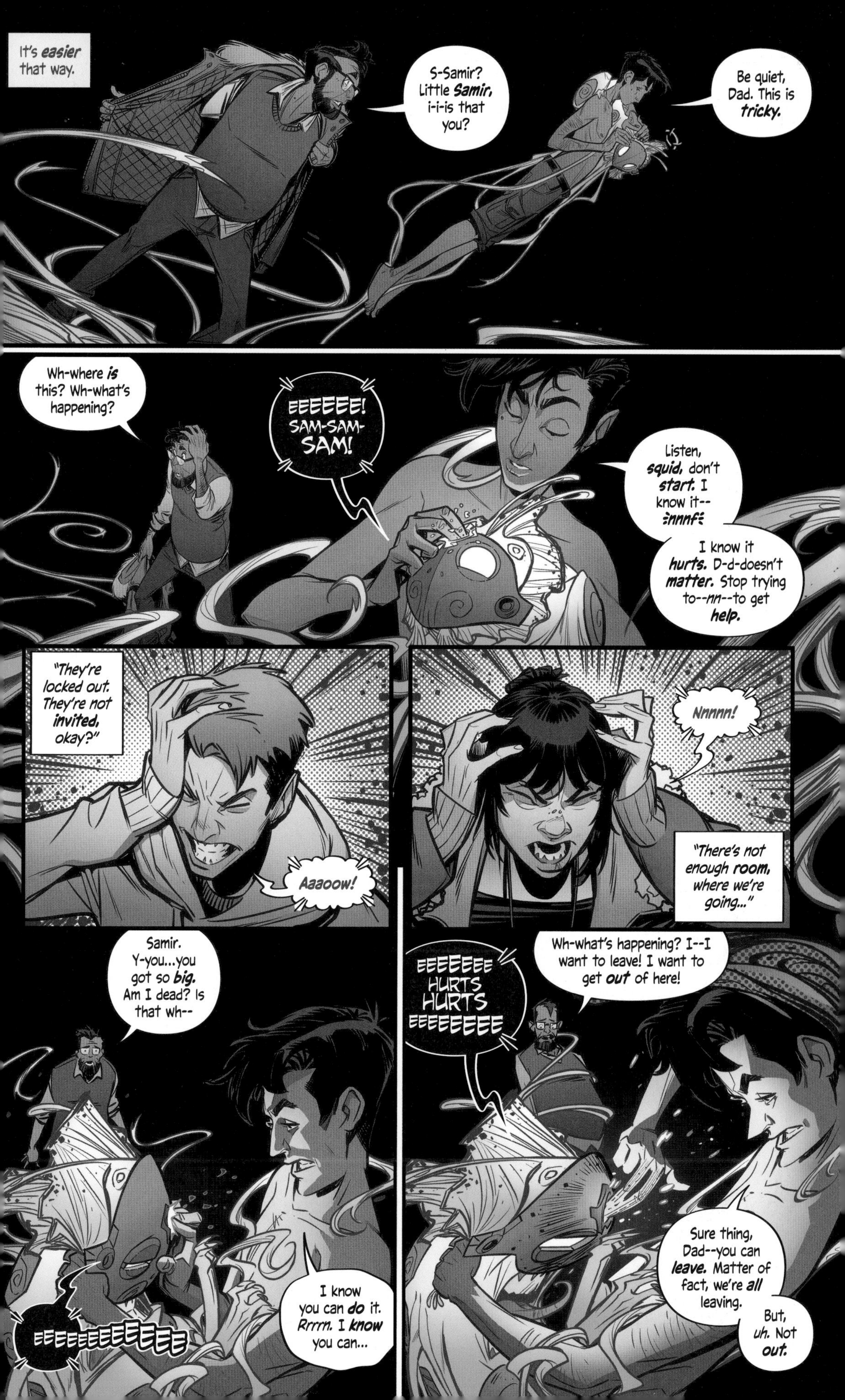
It's easier that way.
S-Samir? Little Samir, i-i-is that you?
Be quiet, Dad. This is tricky.
Wh-where is this? Wh-what's happening?
EEEEEE! SAM-SAM-SAM!
Listen, squid, don't start. I know it-- nnnf
I know it hurts. D-d-doesn't matter. Stop trying to--nn--to get help.
"They're locked out. They're not invited, okay?"
Aaaoow!
Nnnnn!
"There's not enough room, where we're going..."
Samir. Y-you...you got so big. Am I dead? Is that wh--
I know you can do it. Rrrrn. I know you can...
EEEEEEEEEEEE
EEEEEEE HURTS HURTS EEEEEEEE
Wh-what's happening? I--I want to leave! I want to get out of here!
Sure thing, Dad--you can leave. Matter of fact, we're all leaving.
But, uh. Not out.

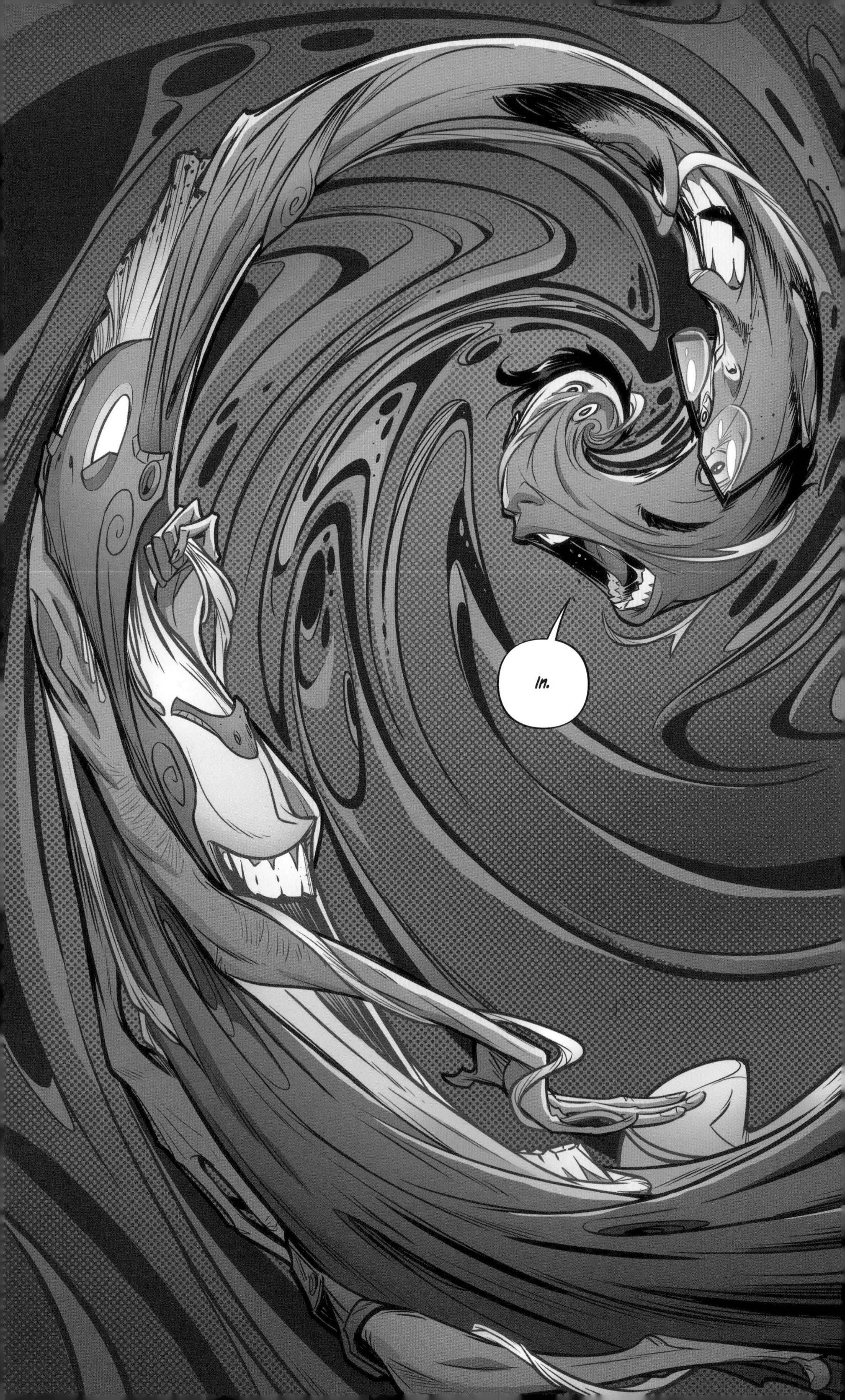
In.

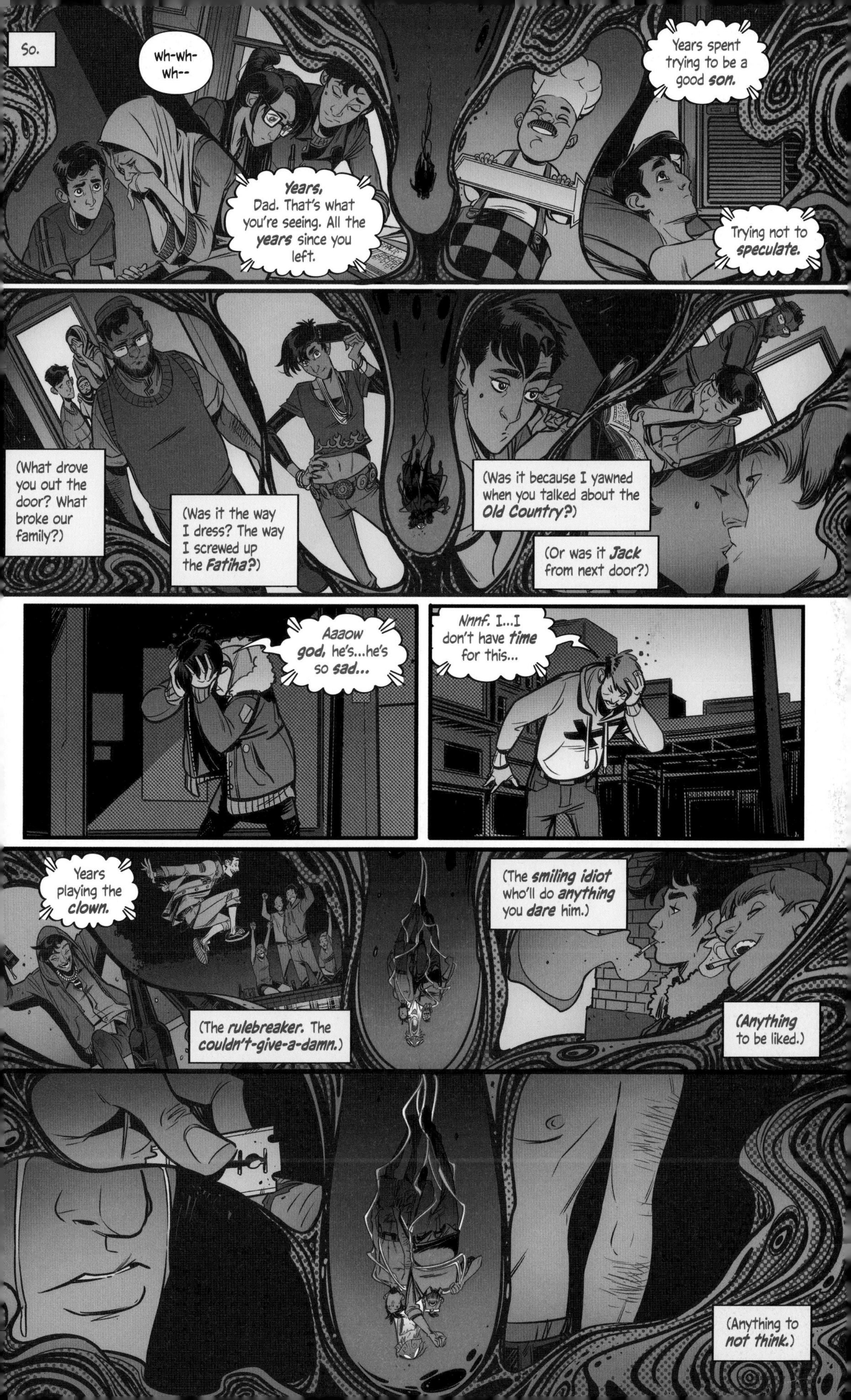
So.
Wh-wh-wh--
Years, Dad. That's what you're seeing. All the years since you left.
Years spent trying to be a good son.
Trying not to speculate.
(What drove you out the door? What broke our family?)
(Was it the way I dress? The way I screwed up the Fatiha?)
(Was it because I yawned when you talked about the Old Country?)
(Or was it Jack from next door?)
Aaaow god, he's...he's so sad...
Nnnf. I...I don't have time for this...
Years playing the clown.
(The rulebreaker. The couldn't-give-a-damn.)
(The smiling idiot who'll do anything you dare him.)
(Anything to be liked.)
(Anything to not think.)

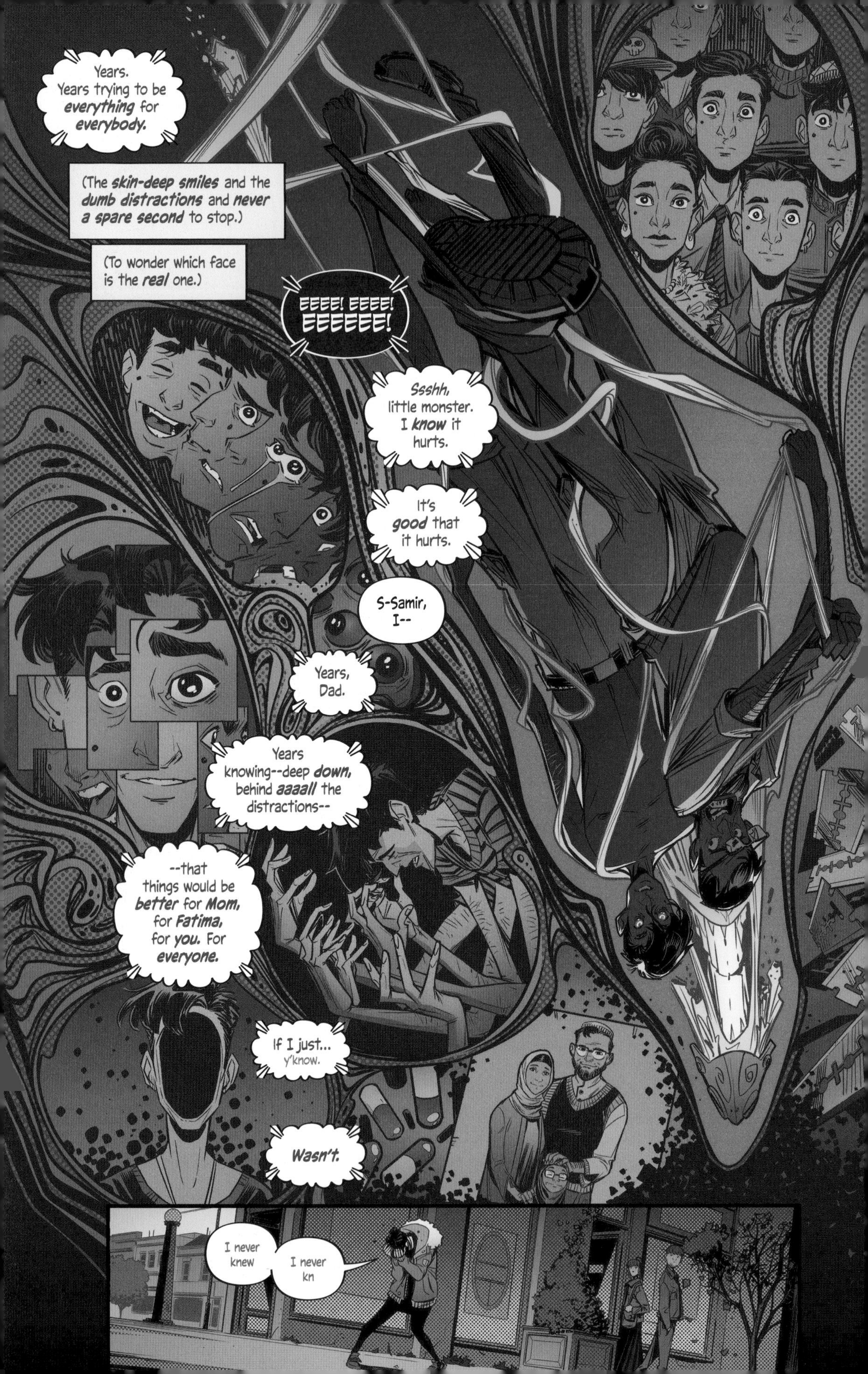

Years. Years trying to be *everything* for *everybody.*
(The ***skin-deep smiles*** and the ***dumb distractions*** and ***never a spare second*** to stop.)
(To wonder which face is the *real* one.)
EEEE! EEEE! EEEEEE!
Ssshh, little monster. I ***know*** it hurts.
It's ***good*** that it hurts.
S-Samir, I--
Years, Dad.
Years knowing--deep ***down,*** behind ***aaaall*** the distractions--
--that things would be ***better*** for ***Mom,*** for ***Fatima,*** for ***you.*** For ***everyone.***
If I just... y'know.
Wasn't.
I never knew
I never kn

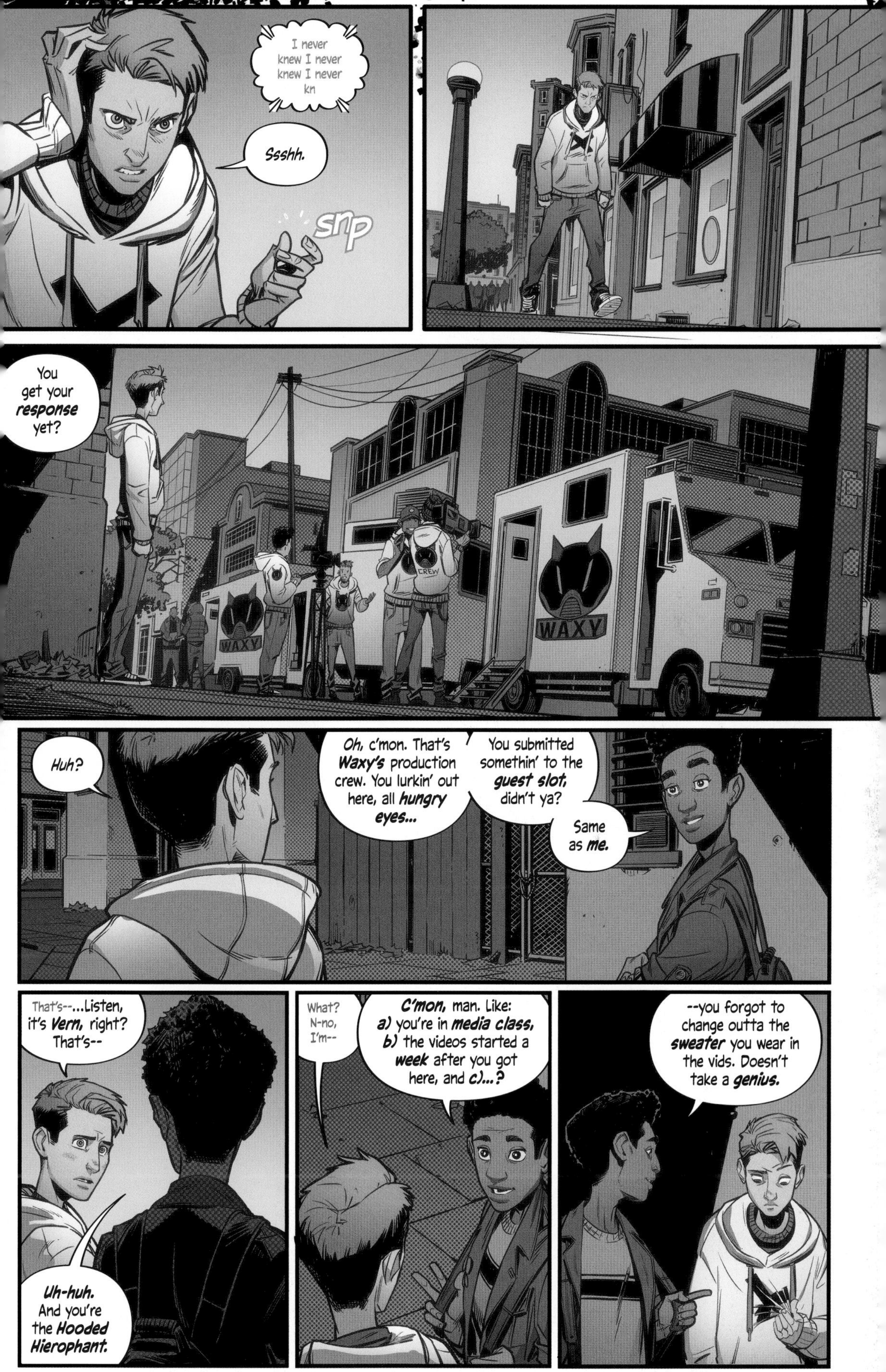
I never knew I never knew I never kn
Ssshh.
snp
You get your response yet?
Huh?
Oh, c'mon. That's Waxy's production crew. You lurkin' out here, all hungry eyes...
You submitted somethin' to the guest slot, didn't ya?
Same as me.
That's--...Listen, it's Vern, right? That's--
Uh-huh. And you're the Hooded Hierophant.
What? N-no, I'm--
C'mon, man. Like: a) you're in media class, b) the videos started a week after you got here, and c)...?
--you forgot to change outta the sweater you wear in the vids. Doesn't take a genius.

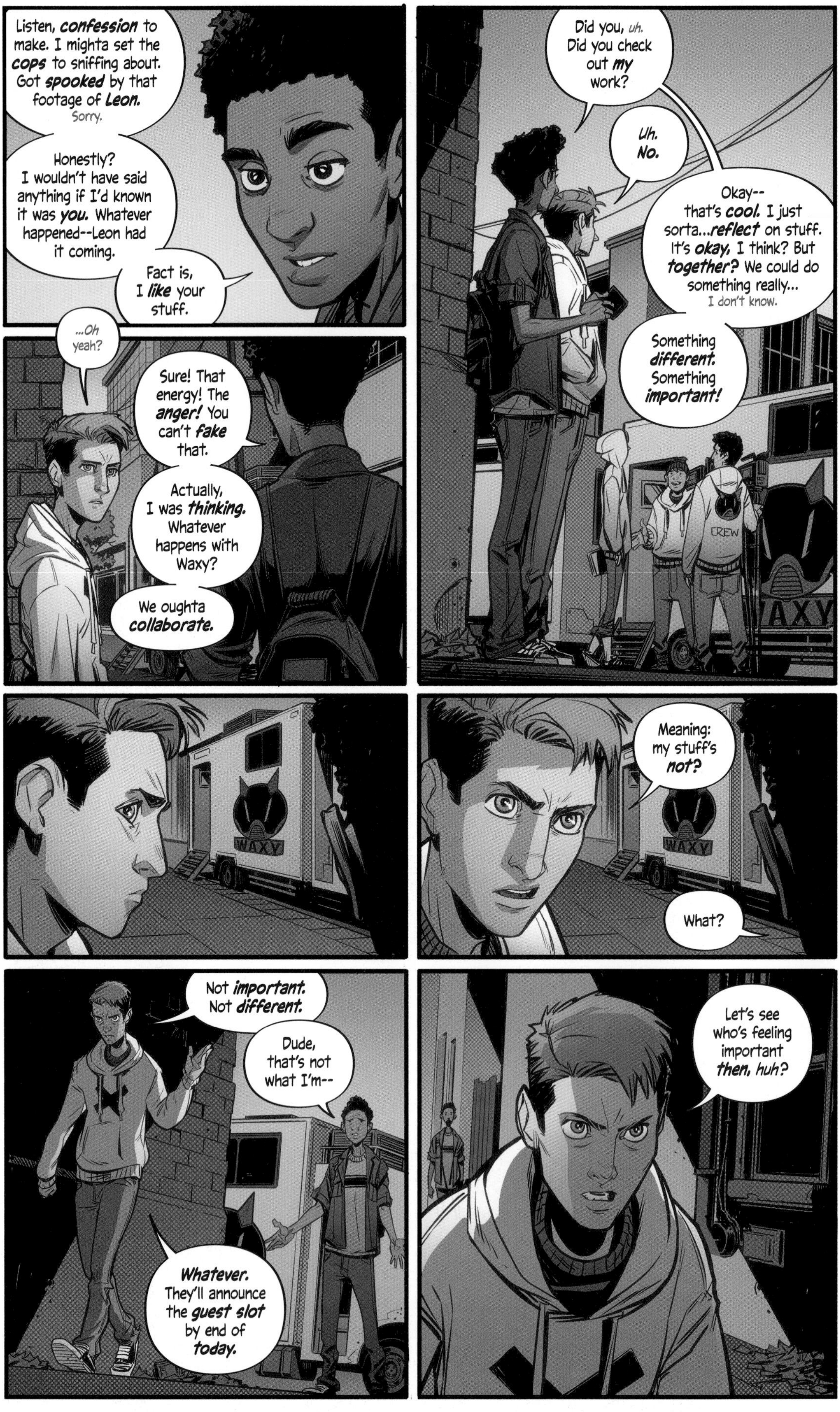
Listen, confession to make. I mighta set the cops to sniffing about. Got spooked by that footage of Leon. Sorry.
Honestly? I wouldn't have said anything if I'd known it was you. Whatever happened--Leon had it coming.
Fact is, I like your stuff.
...Oh yeah?
Sure! That energy! The anger! You can't fake that.
Actually, I was thinking. Whatever happens with Waxy?
We oughta collaborate.
Did you, uh. Did you check out my work?
Uh. No.
Okay-- that's cool. I just sorta...reflect on stuff. It's okay, I think? But together? We could do something really... I don't know.
Something different. Something important!
CREW
WAXY
WAXY
Meaning: my stuff's not?
WAXY
What?
Not important. Not different.
Dude, that's not what I'm--
Whatever. They'll announce the guest slot by end of today.
Let's see who's feeling important then, huh?

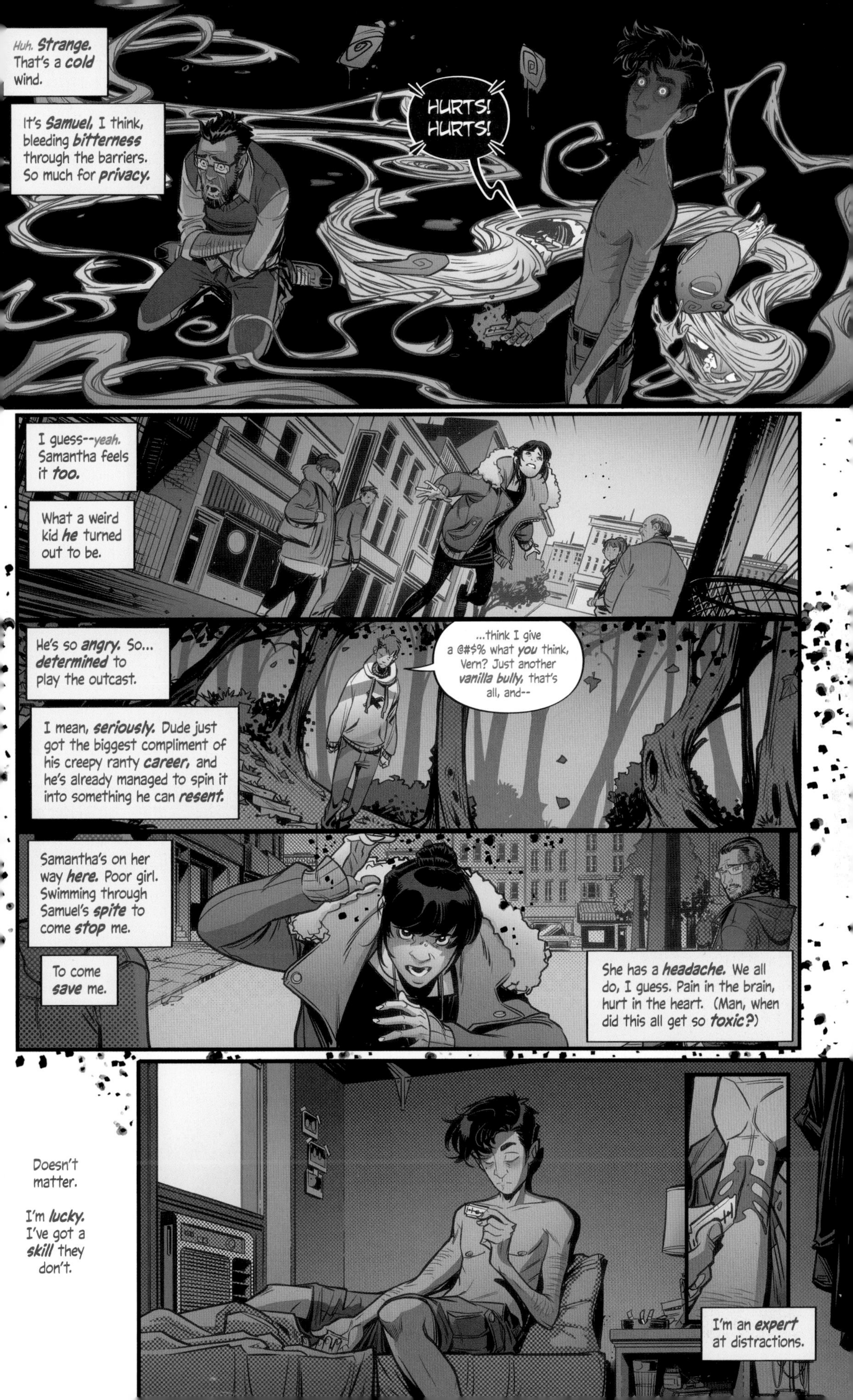
Huh. Strange. That's a cold wind.
It's Samuel, I think, bleeding bitterness through the barriers. So much for privacy.
HURTS! HURTS!
I guess--yeah. Samantha feels it too.
What a weird kid he turned out to be.
He's so angry. So... determined to play the outcast.
I mean, seriously. Dude just got the biggest compliment of his creepy ranty career, and he's already managed to spin it into something he can resent.
...think I give a @#$% what you think, Vern? Just another vanilla bully, that's all, and--
Samantha's on her way here. Poor girl. Swimming through Samuel's spite to come stop me.
To come save me.
She has a headache. We all do, I guess. Pain in the brain, hurt in the heart. (Man, when did this all get so toxic?)
Doesn't matter.
I'm lucky. I've got a skill they don't.
I'm an expert at distractions.

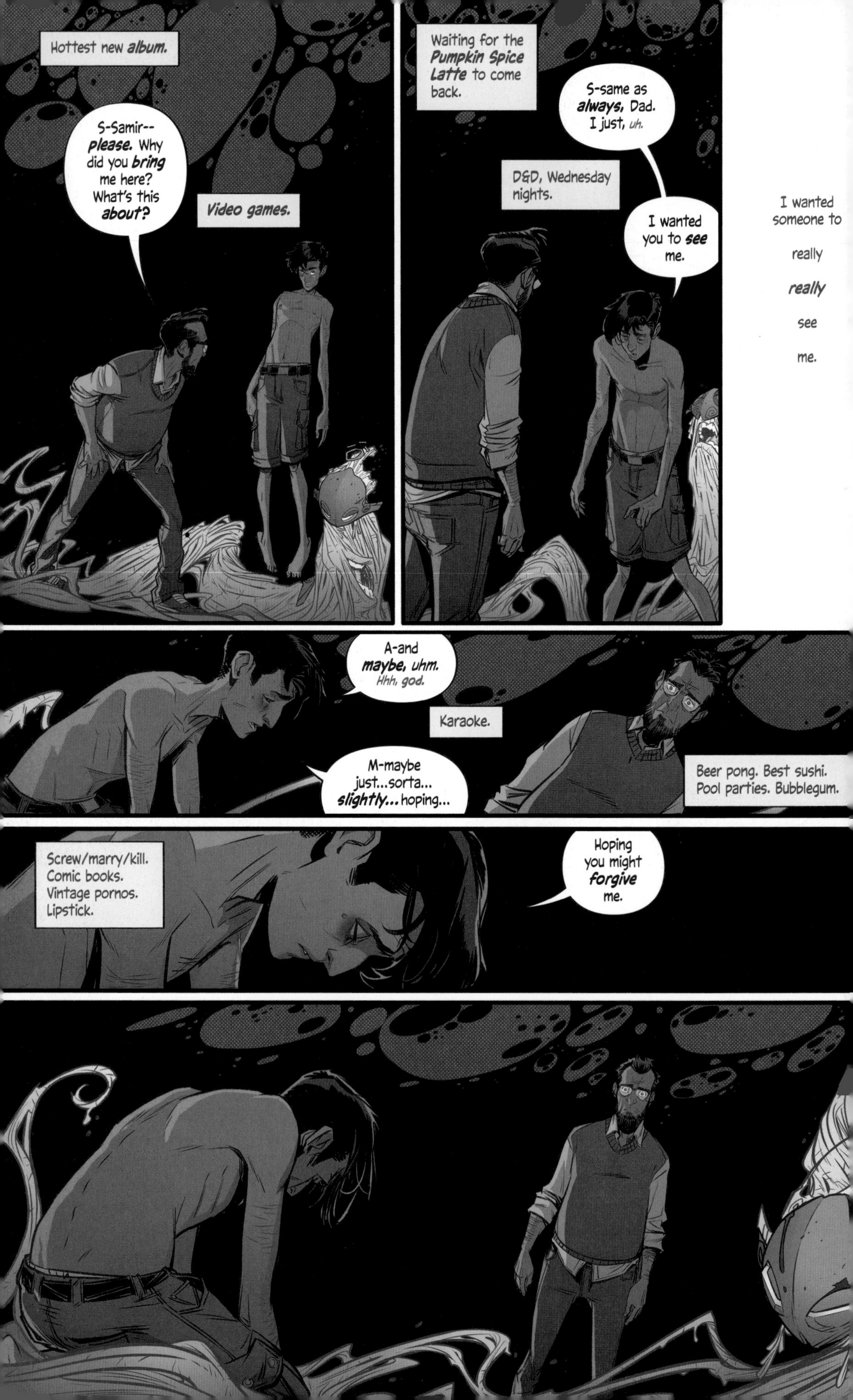
Hottest new **album.**
S-Samir-- **please.** Why did you **bring** me here? What's this **about?**
Video games.
Waiting for the ***Pumpkin Spice Latte*** to come back.
S-same as ***always,*** Dad. I just, *uh.*
D&D, Wednesday nights.
I wanted you to ***see*** me.
I wanted someone to
really
really
see
me.
A-and ***maybe, uhm.*** *Hhh, god.*
Karaoke.
M-maybe just...sorta... ***slightly...*** hoping...
Beer pong. Best sushi. Pool parties. Bubblegum.
Screw/marry/kill. Comic books. Vintage pornos. Lipstick.
Hoping you might ***forgive*** me.

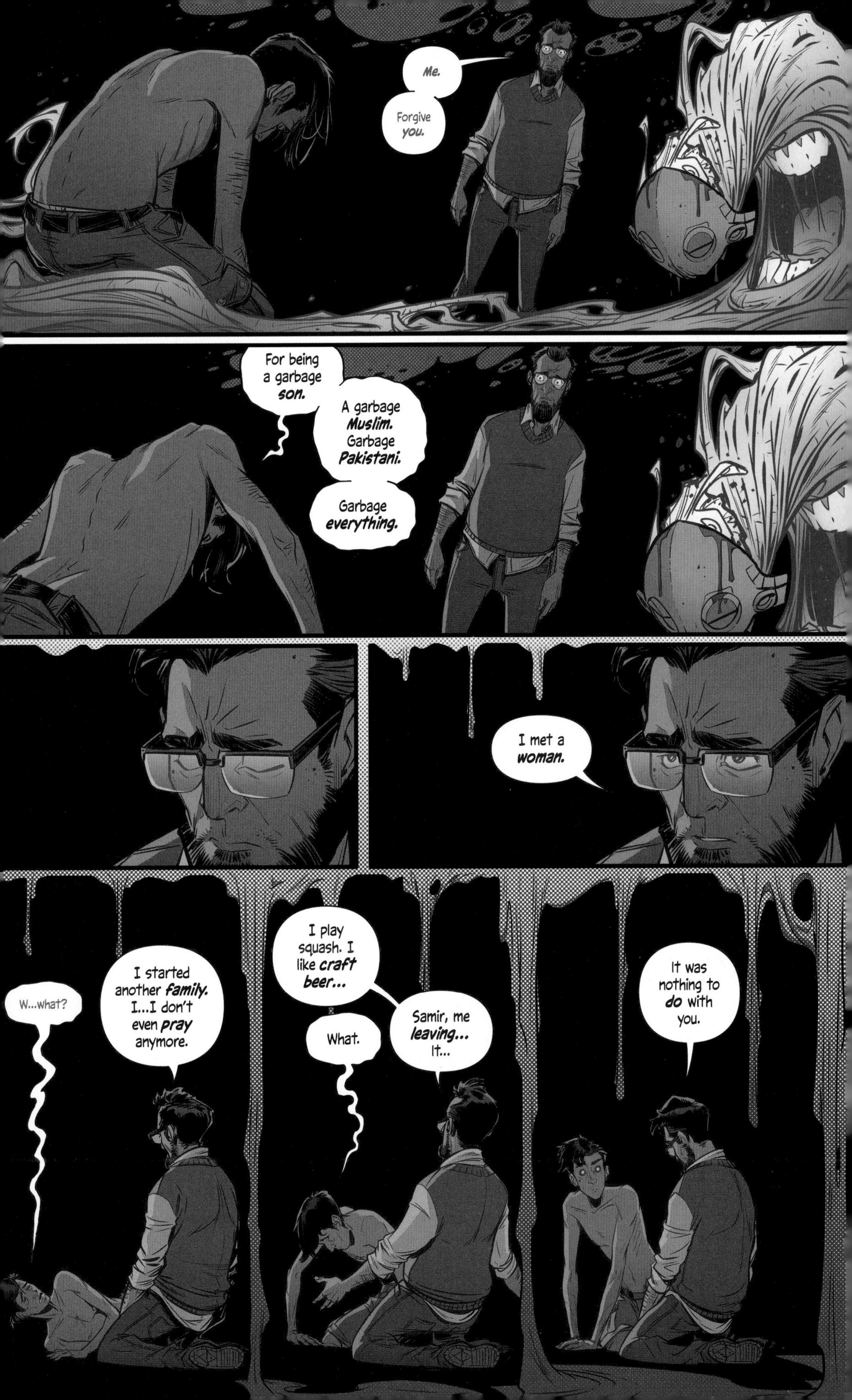
Me.
Forgive you.
For being a garbage son.
A garbage Muslim. Garbage Pakistani.
Garbage everything.
I met a woman.
W...what?
I started another family. I...I don't even pray anymore.
I play squash. I like craft beer...
What.
Samir, me leaving... It...
It was nothing to do with you.

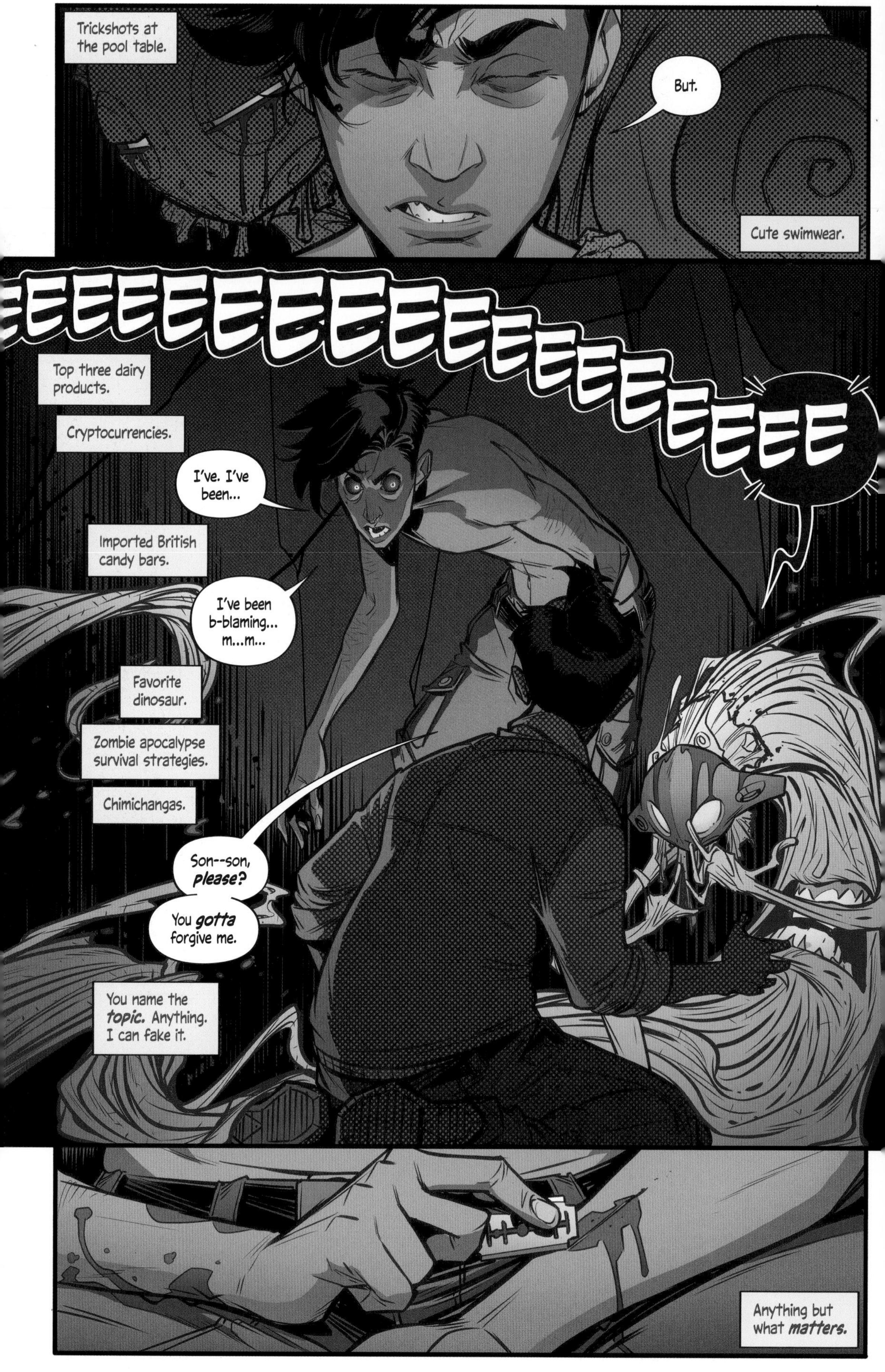
Trickshots at the pool table.
But.
Cute swimwear.
EEEEEEEEEEEEEEEEEEEE
Top three dairy products.
Cryptocurrencies.
I've. I've been...
Imported British candy bars.
I've been b-blaming... m...m...
Favorite dinosaur.
Zombie apocalypse survival strategies.
Chimichangas.
Son--son, *please?*
You *gotta* forgive me.
You name the *topic.* Anything. I can fake it.
Anything but what *matters.*

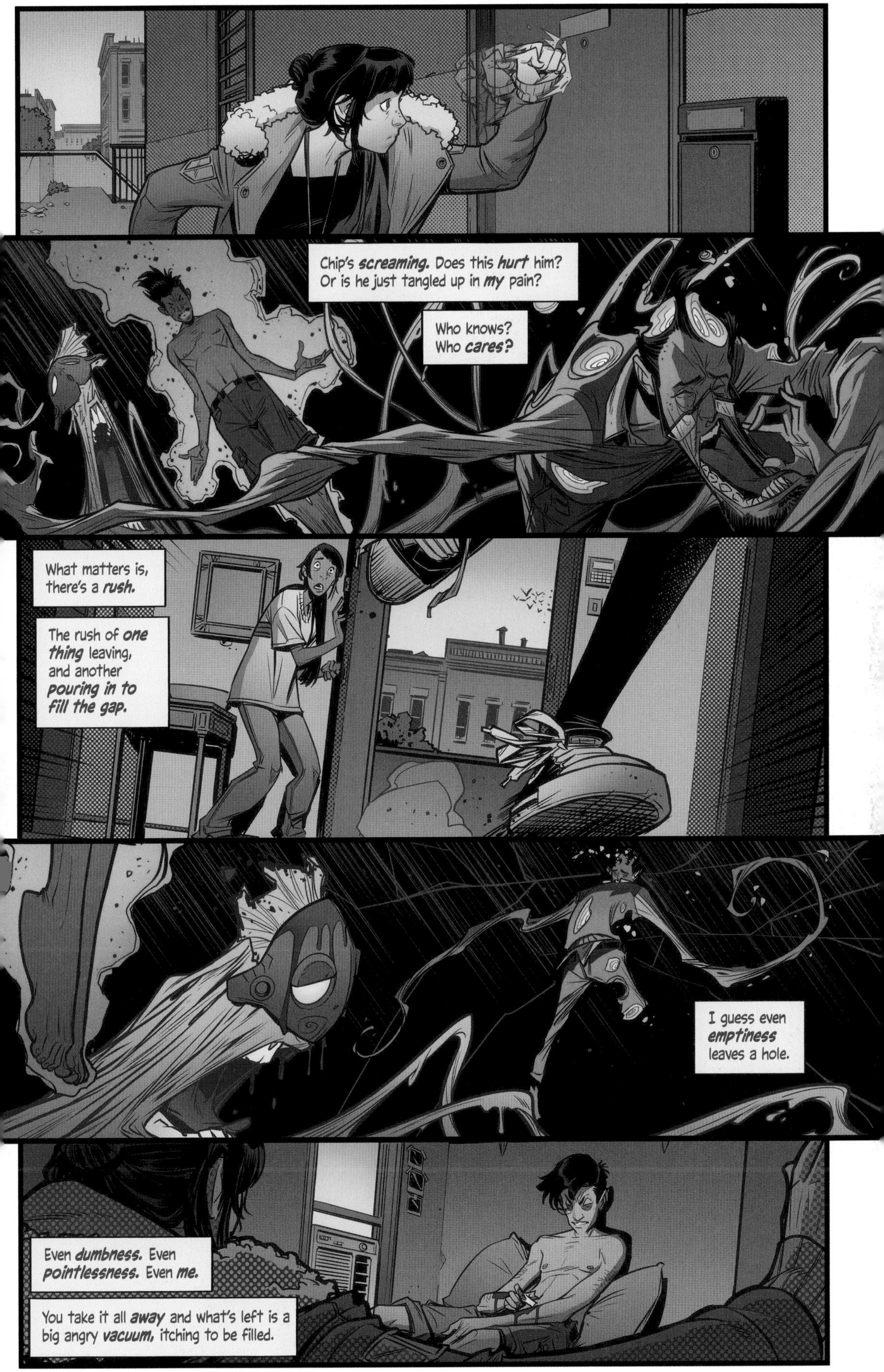
Chip's screaming. Does this hurt him? Or is he just tangled up in my pain?
Who knows? Who cares?
What matters is, there's a rush.
The rush of one thing leaving, and another pouring in to fill the gap.
I guess even emptiness leaves a hole.
Even dumbness. Even pointlessness. Even me.
You take it all away and what's left is a big angry vacuum, itching to be filled.

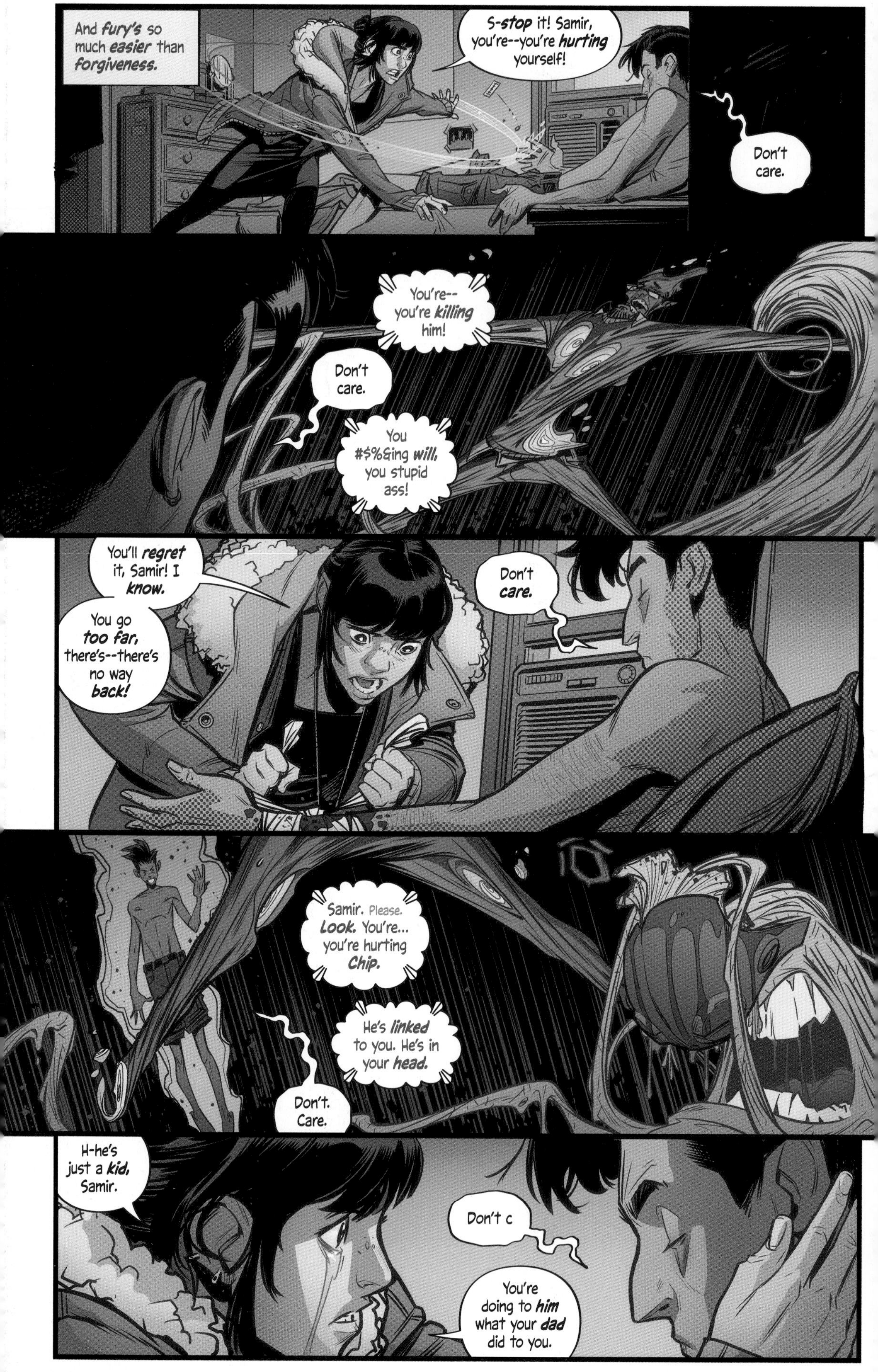
And fury's so much easier than forgiveness.
S-stop it! Samir, you're--you're hurting yourself!
Don't care.
You're-- you're killing him!
Don't care.
You #$%&ing will, you stupid ass!
You'll regret it, Samir! I know.
You go too far, there's--there's no way back!
Don't care.
Samir. Please. Look. You're... you're hurting Chip.
He's linked to you. He's in your head.
Don't. Care.
H-he's just a kid, Samir.
Don't c
You're doing to him what your dad did to you.

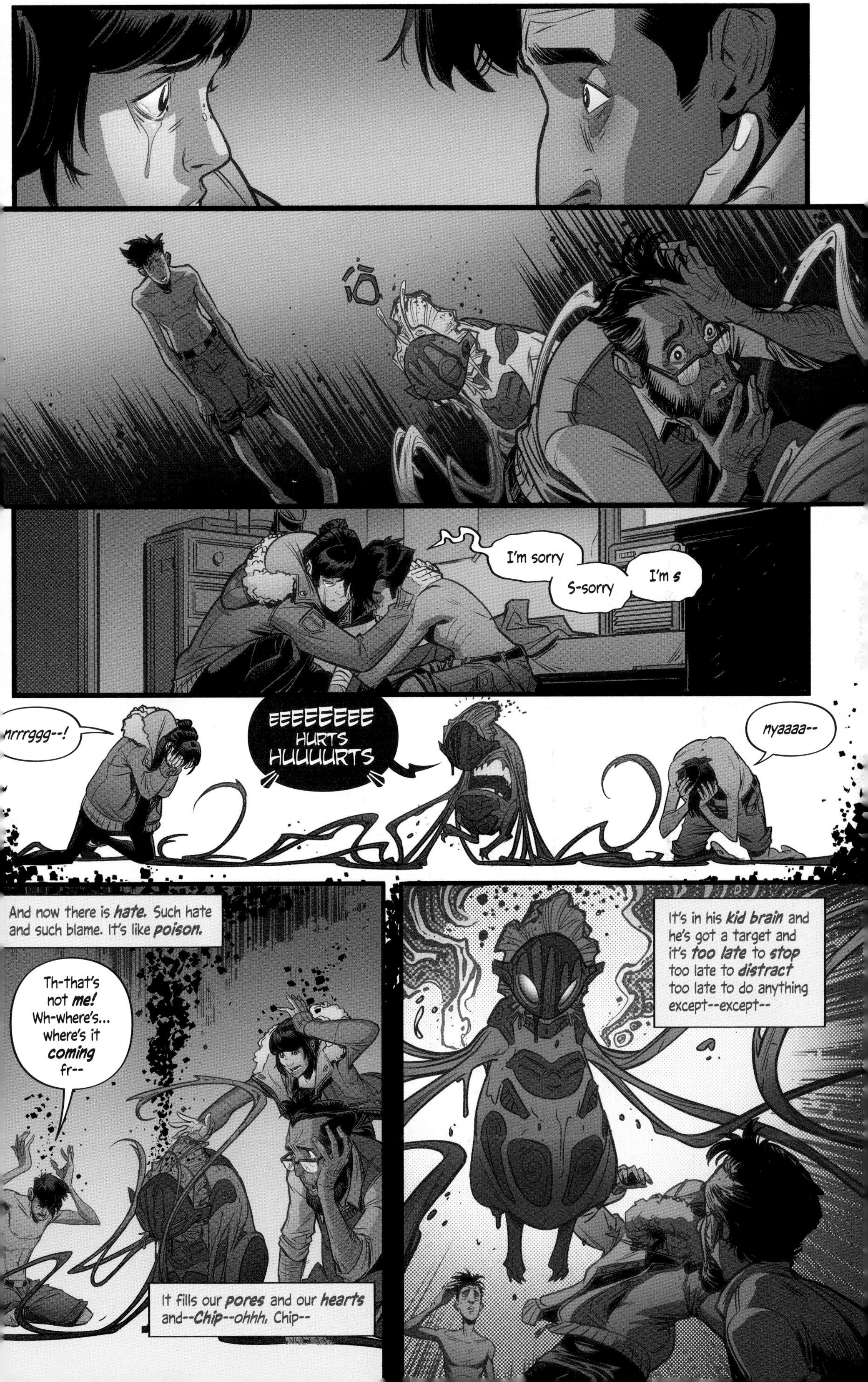
I'm sorry
S-sorry
I'm s
nrrrggg--!
EEEEEEEE HURTS HUUUURTS
nyaaaa--
And now there is *hate.* Such hate and such blame. It's like *poison.*
Th-that's not *me!* Wh-where's... where's it *coming* fr--
It fills our *pores* and our *hearts* and--*Chip*--ohhh, Chip--
It's in his *kid brain* and he's got a target and it's *too late* to *stop* too late to *distract* too late to do anything except--except--

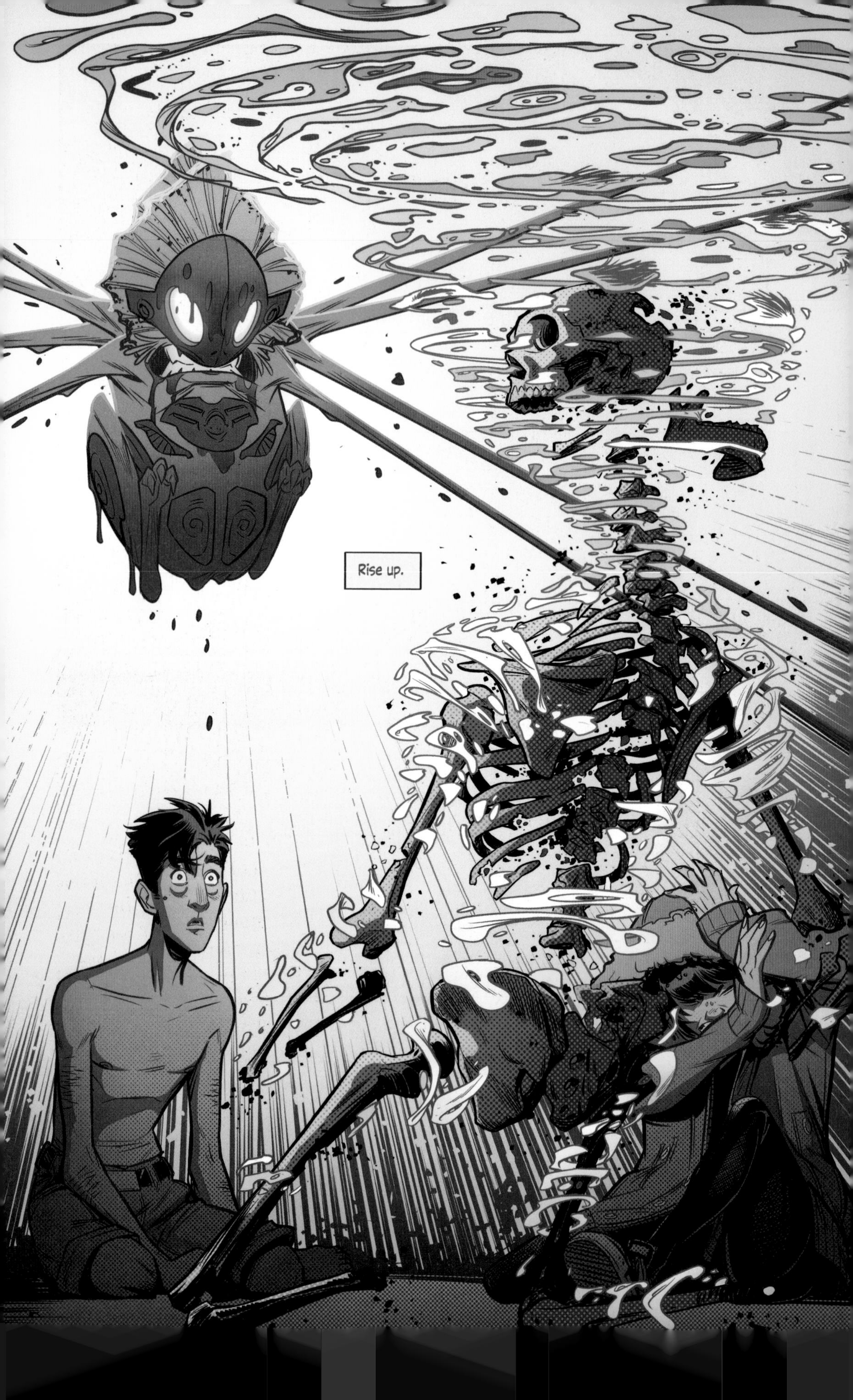
Rise up.

D...d...

d...꙼

Oh no.

Who **did** that?

Wh...where did...where did all that **hate** come from?

Who **DID** this?!

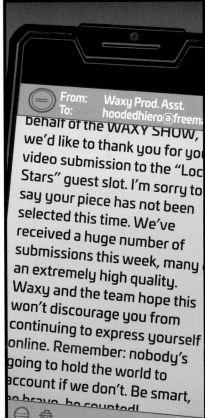
From: Waxy Prod. Asst.
To: hoodedhiero@freem

behalf of the WAXY SHOW, we'd like to thank you for you video submission to the "Loc Stars" guest slot. I'm sorry to say your piece has not been selected this time. We've received a huge number of submissions this week, many an extremely high quality. Waxy and the team hope this won't discourage you from continuing to express yourself online. Remember: nobody's going to hold the world to account if we don't. Be smart, be brave, be counted!

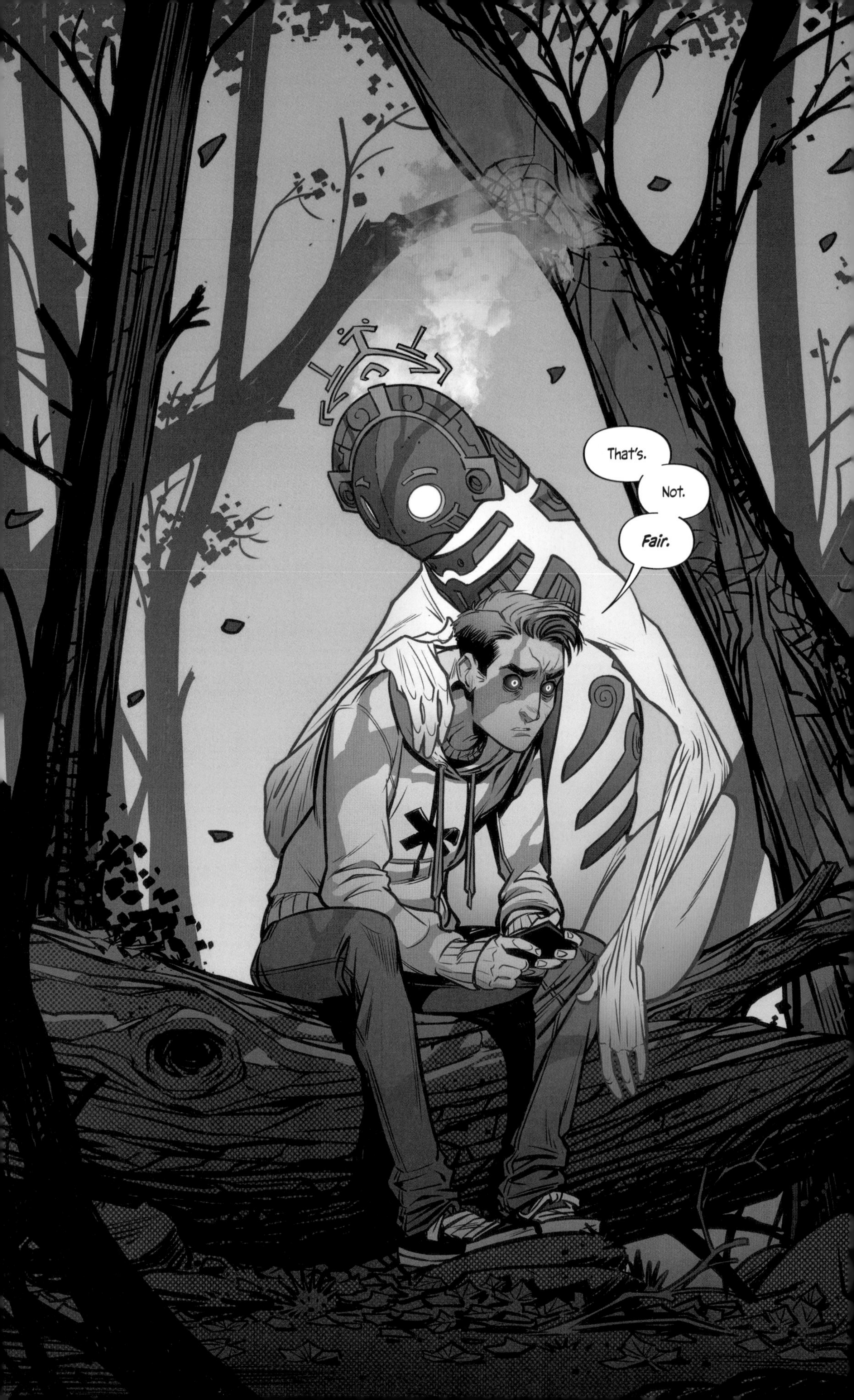
That's.
Not.
Fair.

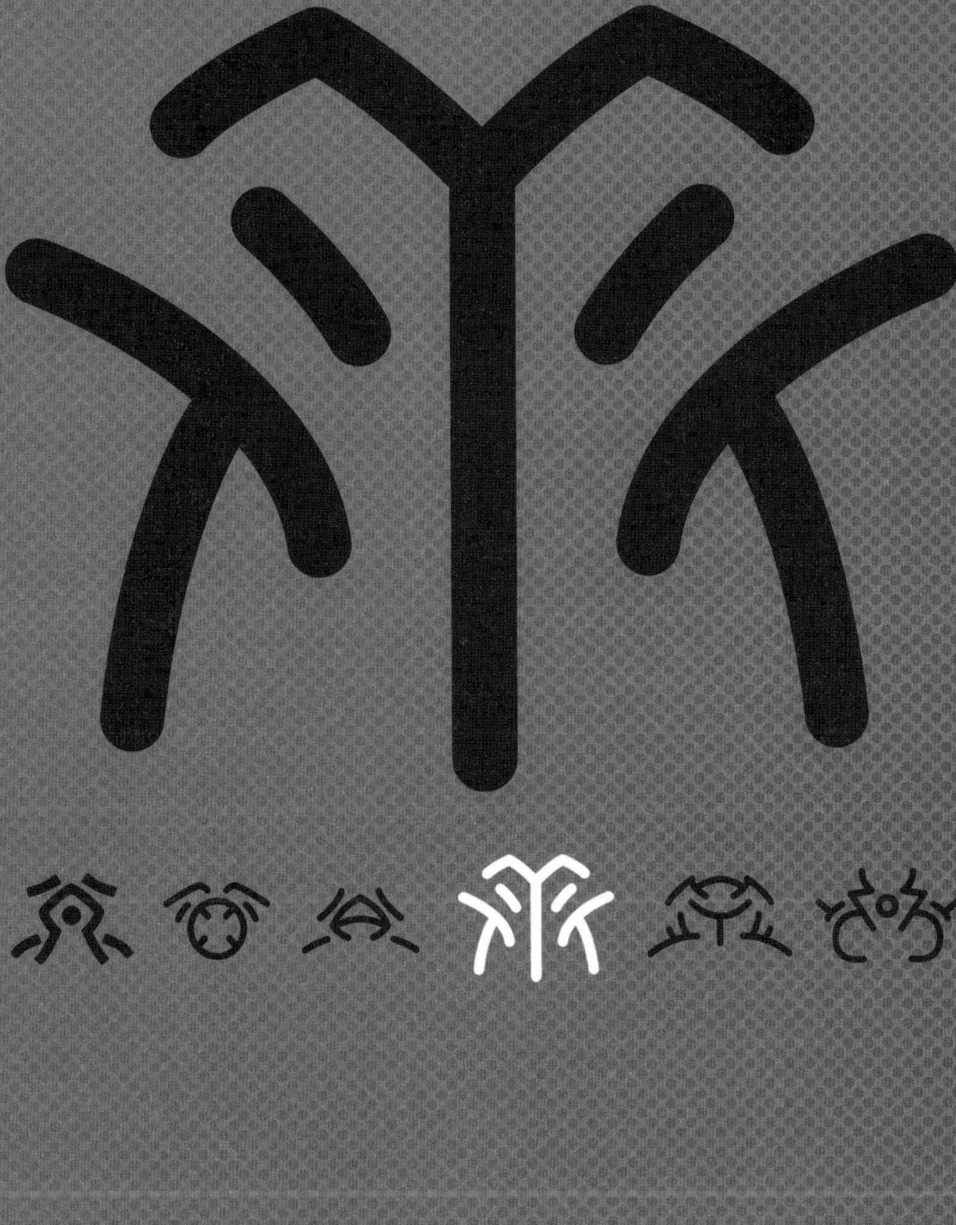

CHAPTER FIVE

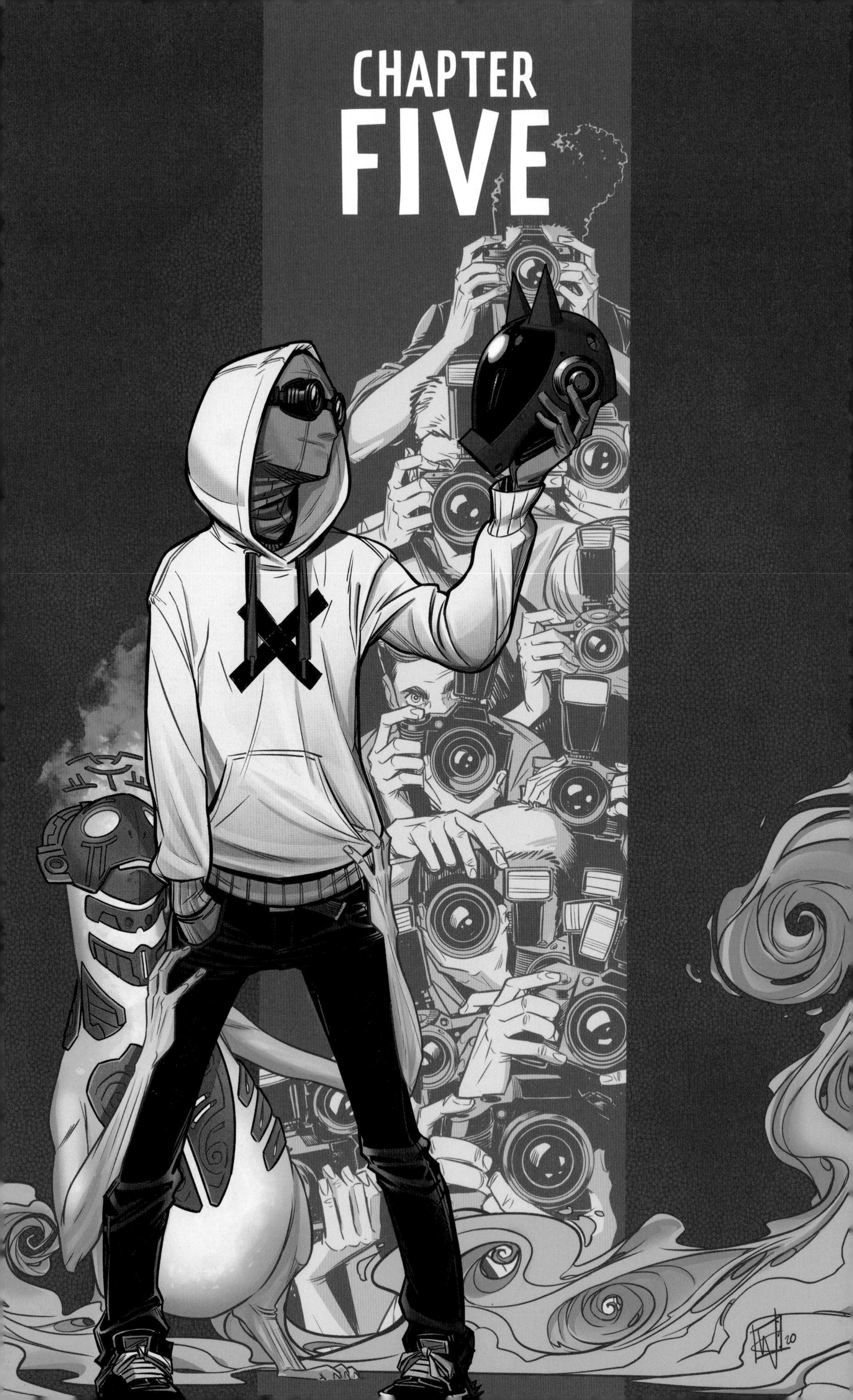

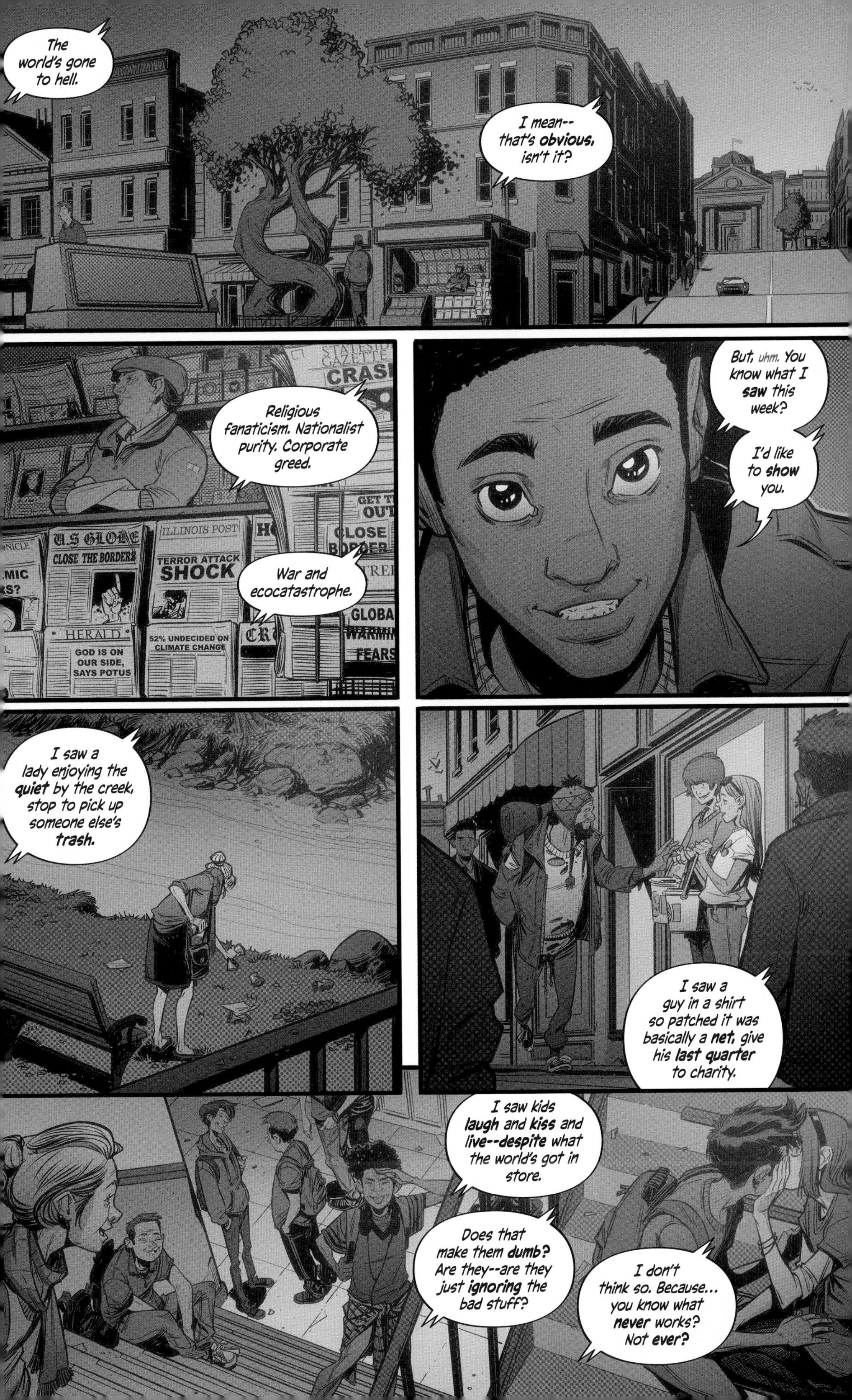
The world's gone to hell.
I mean-- that's obvious, isn't it?
Religious fanaticism. Nationalist purity. Corporate greed.
U.S GLOBE
CLOSE THE BORDERS
ILLINOIS POST
TERROR ATTACK SHOCK
HERALD
GOD IS ON OUR SIDE, SAYS POTUS
52% UNDECIDED ON CLIMATE CHANGE
War and ecocatastrophe.
But, uhm. You know what I saw this week?
I'd like to show you.
I saw a lady enjoying the quiet by the creek, stop to pick up someone else's trash.
I saw a guy in a shirt so patched it was basically a net, give his last quarter to charity.
I saw kids laugh and kiss and live--despite what the world's got in store.
Does that make them dumb? Are they--are they just ignoring the bad stuff?
I don't think so. Because... you know what never works? Not ever?

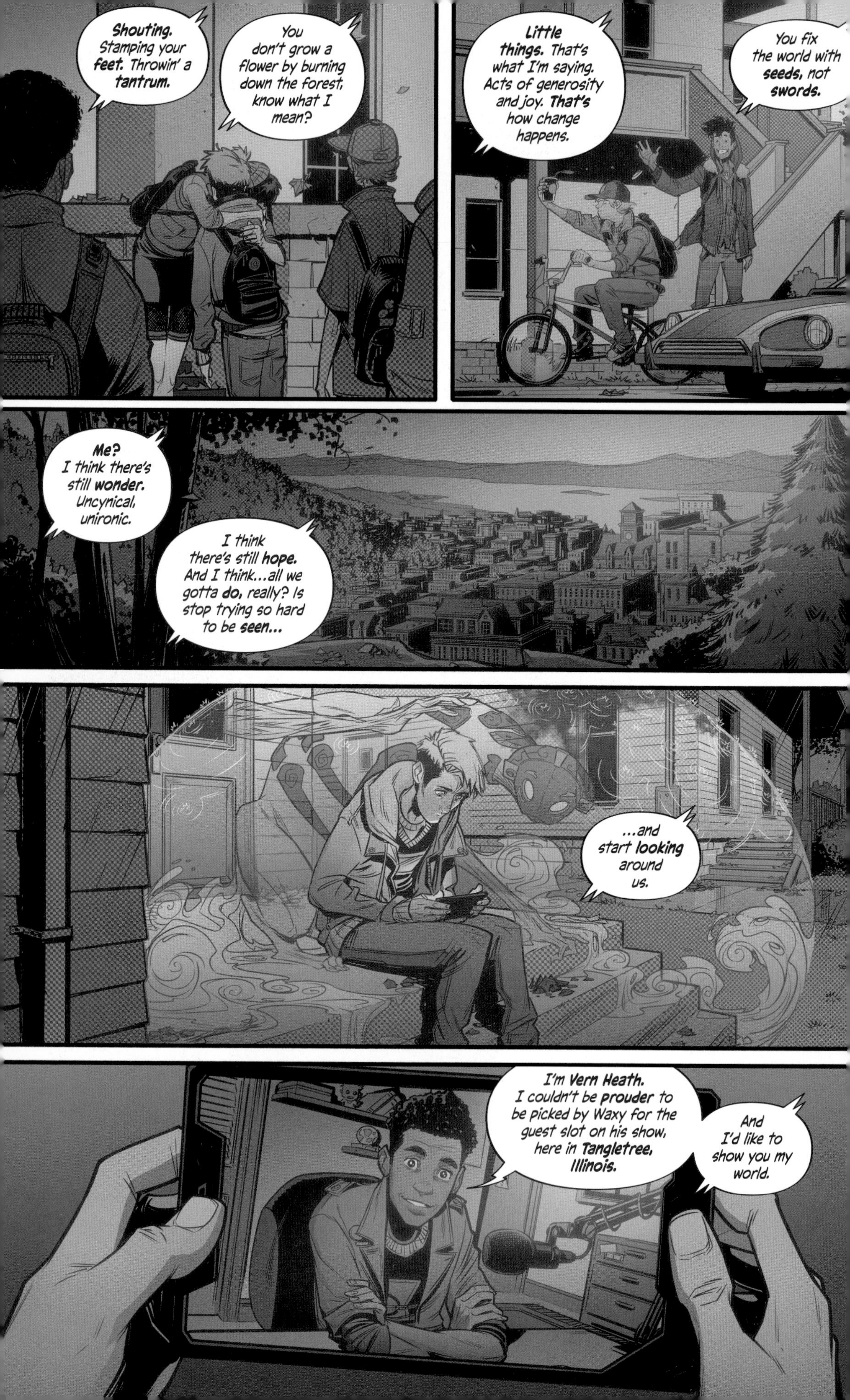
Shouting. Stamping your feet. Throwin' a tantrum.
You don't grow a flower by burning down the forest, know what I mean?
Little things. That's what I'm saying. Acts of generosity and joy. That's how change happens.
You fix the world with seeds, not swords.
Me? I think there's still wonder. Uncynical, unironic.
I think there's still hope. And I think...all we gotta do, really? Is stop trying so hard to be seen...
...and start looking around us.
I'm Vern Heath. I couldn't be prouder to be picked by Waxy for the guest slot on his show, here in Tangletree, Illinois.
And I'd like to show you my world.

This piece is:

Pedestrian.

Unambitious.

Sophomoric.

Sentimental.

Totally #$%&ing pointless.

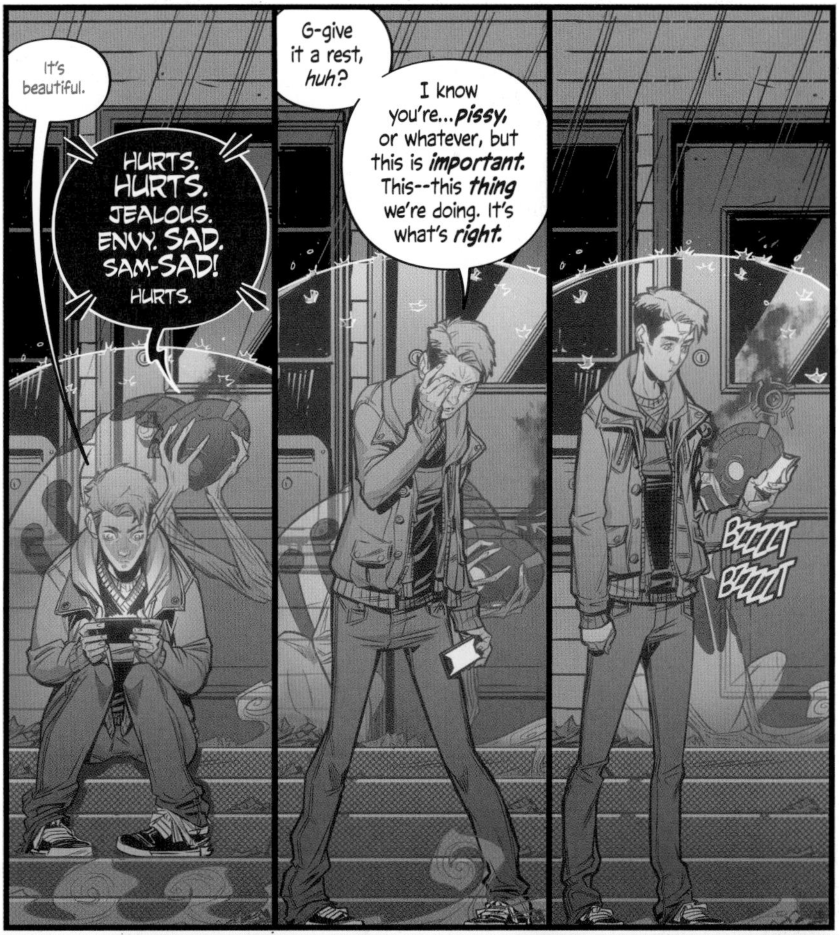
It's beautiful.
HURTS. HURTS. JEALOUS. ENVY. SAD. SAM-SAD! HURTS.
G-give it a rest, *huh?*
I know you're...*pissy,* or whatever, but this is *important.* This--this *thing* we're doing. It's what's *right.*
BZZZT BZZZT

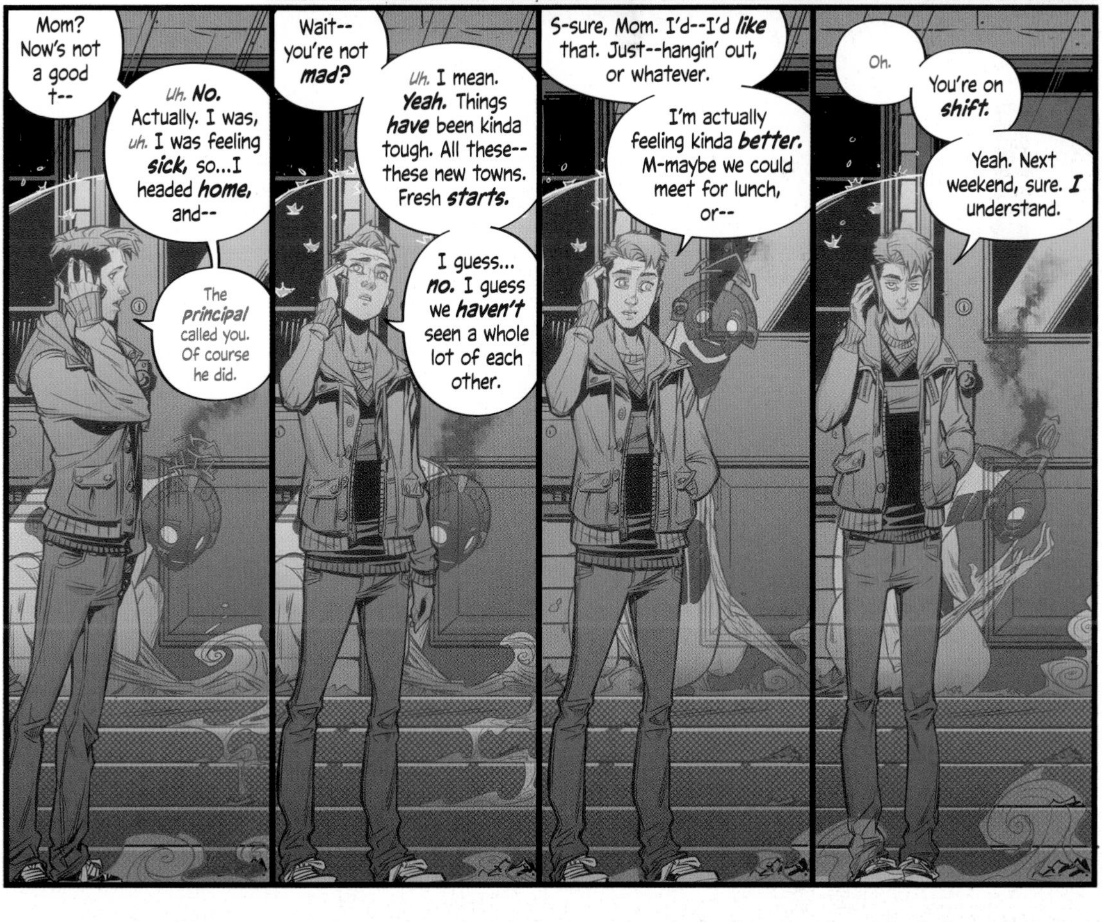
Mom? Now's not a good t--
Uh. **No.** Actually. I was, *uh.* I was feeling ***sick,*** so...I headed ***home,*** and--
The ***principal*** called you. Of course he did.
Wait--you're not ***mad?***
Uh. I mean. ***Yeah.*** Things ***have*** been kinda tough. All these--these new towns. Fresh ***starts.***
I guess... ***no.*** I guess we ***haven't*** seen a whole lot of each other.
S-sure, Mom. I'd--I'd ***like*** that. Just--hangin' out, or whatever.
I'm actually feeling kinda ***better.*** M-maybe we could meet for lunch, or--
Oh.
You're on ***shift.***
Yeah. Next weekend, sure. ***I*** understand.

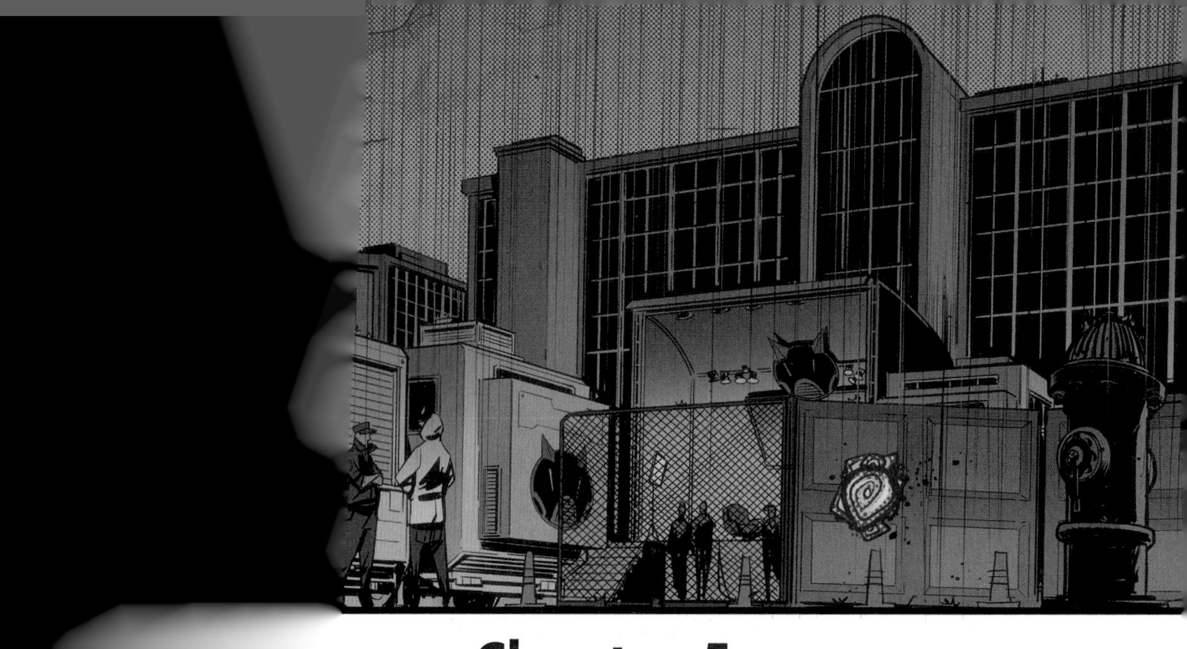

Chapter 5: DUTY FIRST

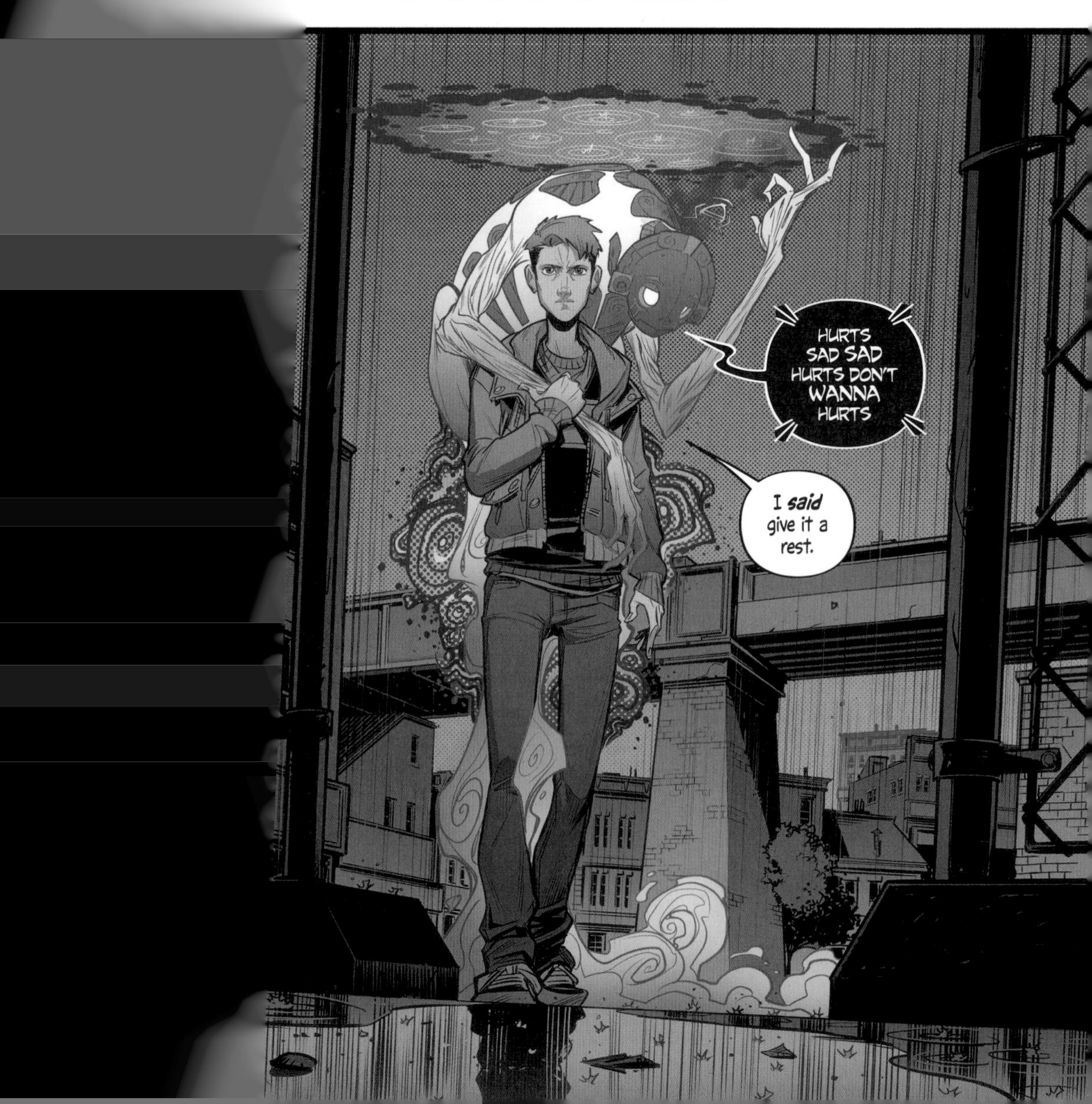
HURTS SAD SAD HURTS DON'T WANNA HURTS
I *said* give it a rest.

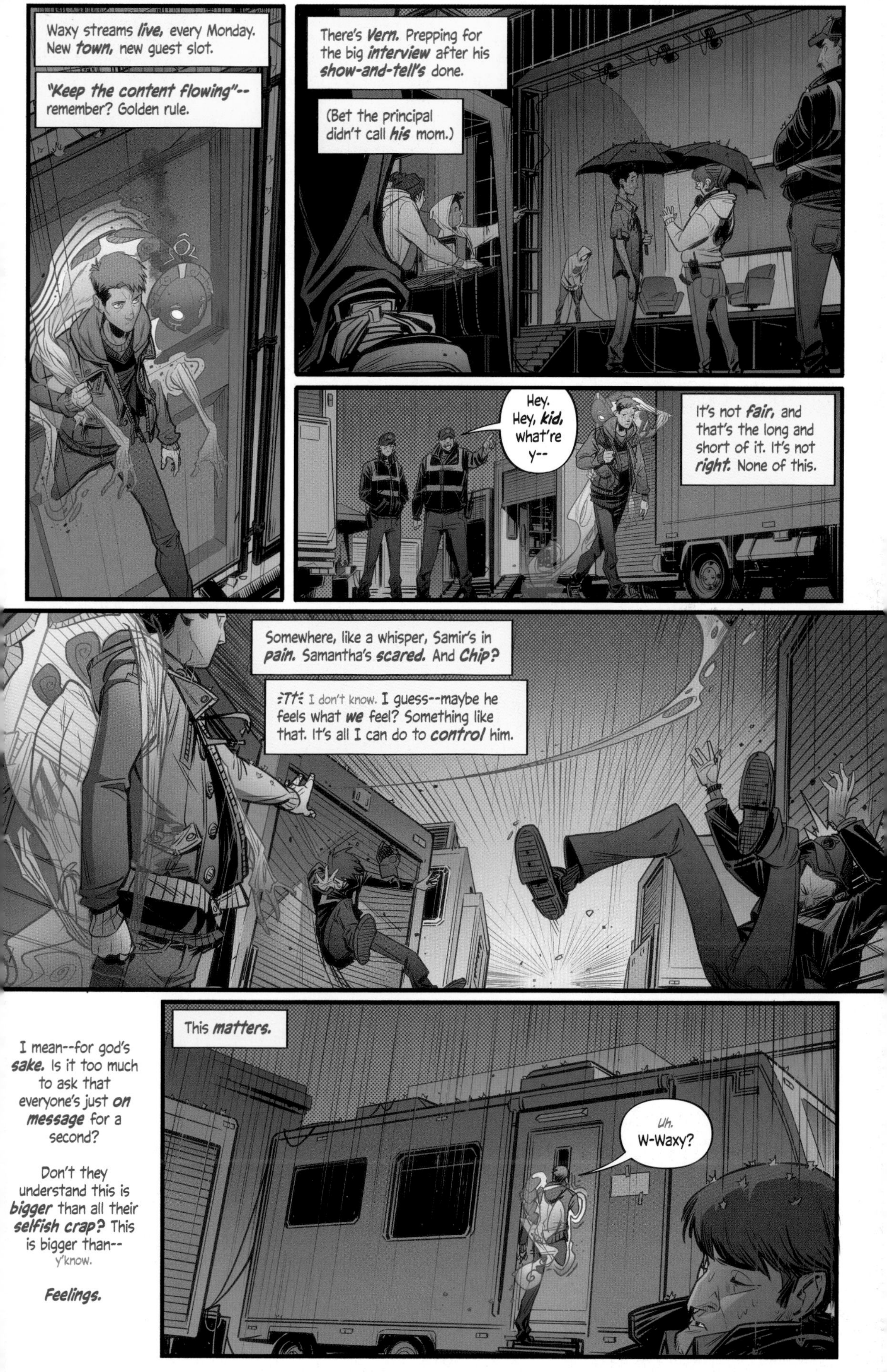
Waxy streams *live,* every Monday. New *town,* new guest slot.
"Keep the content flowing"-- remember? Golden rule.
There's *Vern.* Prepping for the big *interview* after his *show-and-tell's* done.
(Bet the principal didn't call *his* mom.)
Hey. Hey, *kid,* what're y--
It's not *fair,* and that's the long and short of it. It's not *right.* None of this.
Somewhere, like a whisper, Samir's in *pain.* Samantha's *scared.* And *Chip?*
I don't know. I guess--maybe he feels what *we* feel? Something like that. It's all I can do to *control* him.
This *matters.*
I mean--for god's *sake.* Is it too much to ask that everyone's just *on message* for a second?
Don't they understand this is *bigger* than all their *selfish crap?* This is bigger than-- y'know.
Feelings.
Uh. W-Waxy?

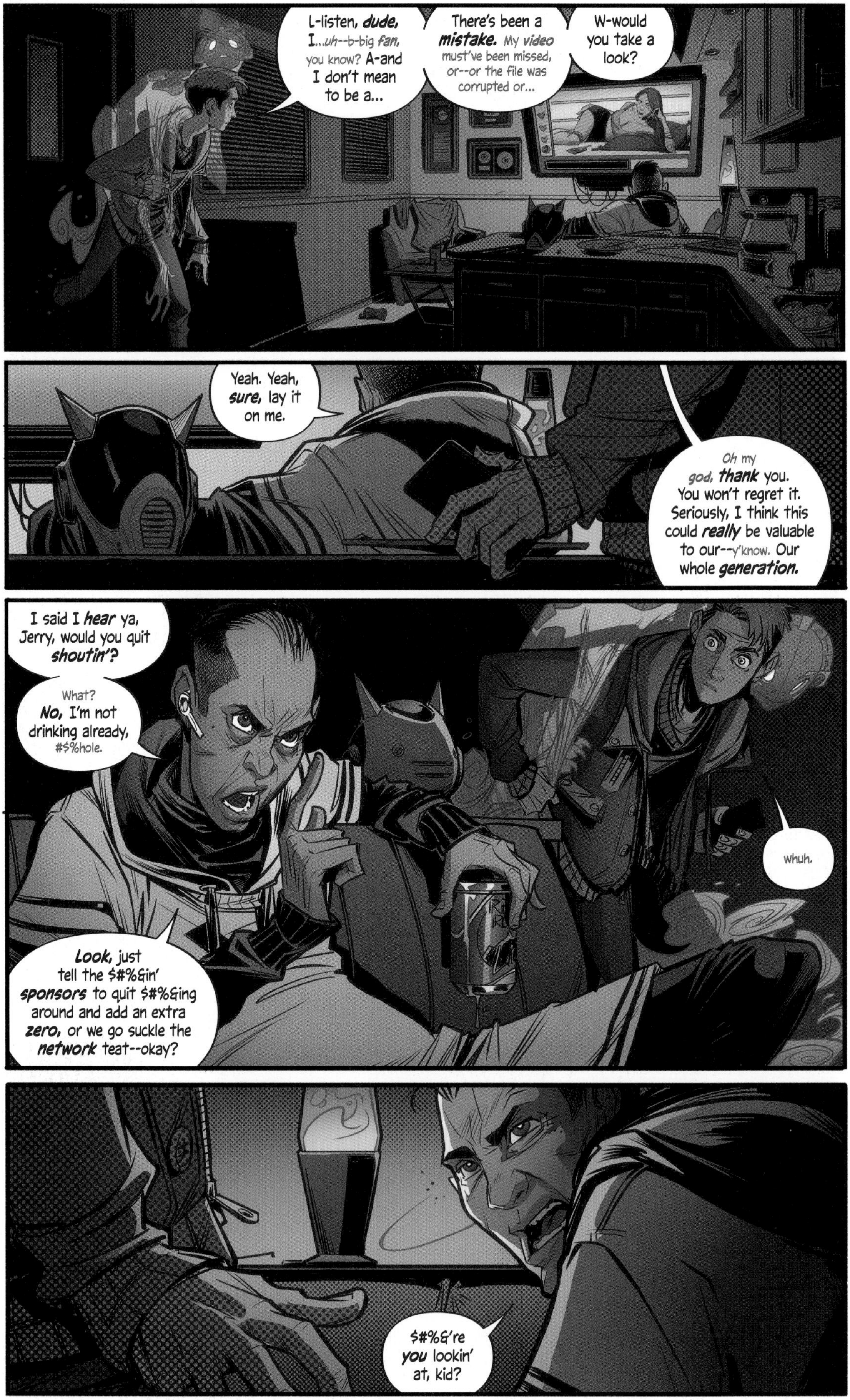
L-listen, dude, I...uh--b-big fan, you know? A-and I don't mean to be a...
There's been a mistake. My video must've been missed, or--or the file was corrupted or...
W-would you take a look?
Yeah. Yeah, sure, lay it on me.
Oh my god, thank you. You won't regret it. Seriously, I think this could really be valuable to our--y'know. Our whole generation.
I said I hear ya, Jerry, would you quit shoutin'?
What? No, I'm not drinking already, #$%hole.
whuh.
Look, just tell the $#%&in' sponsors to quit $#%&ing around and add an extra zero, or we go suckle the network teat--okay?
$#%&'re you lookin' at, kid?

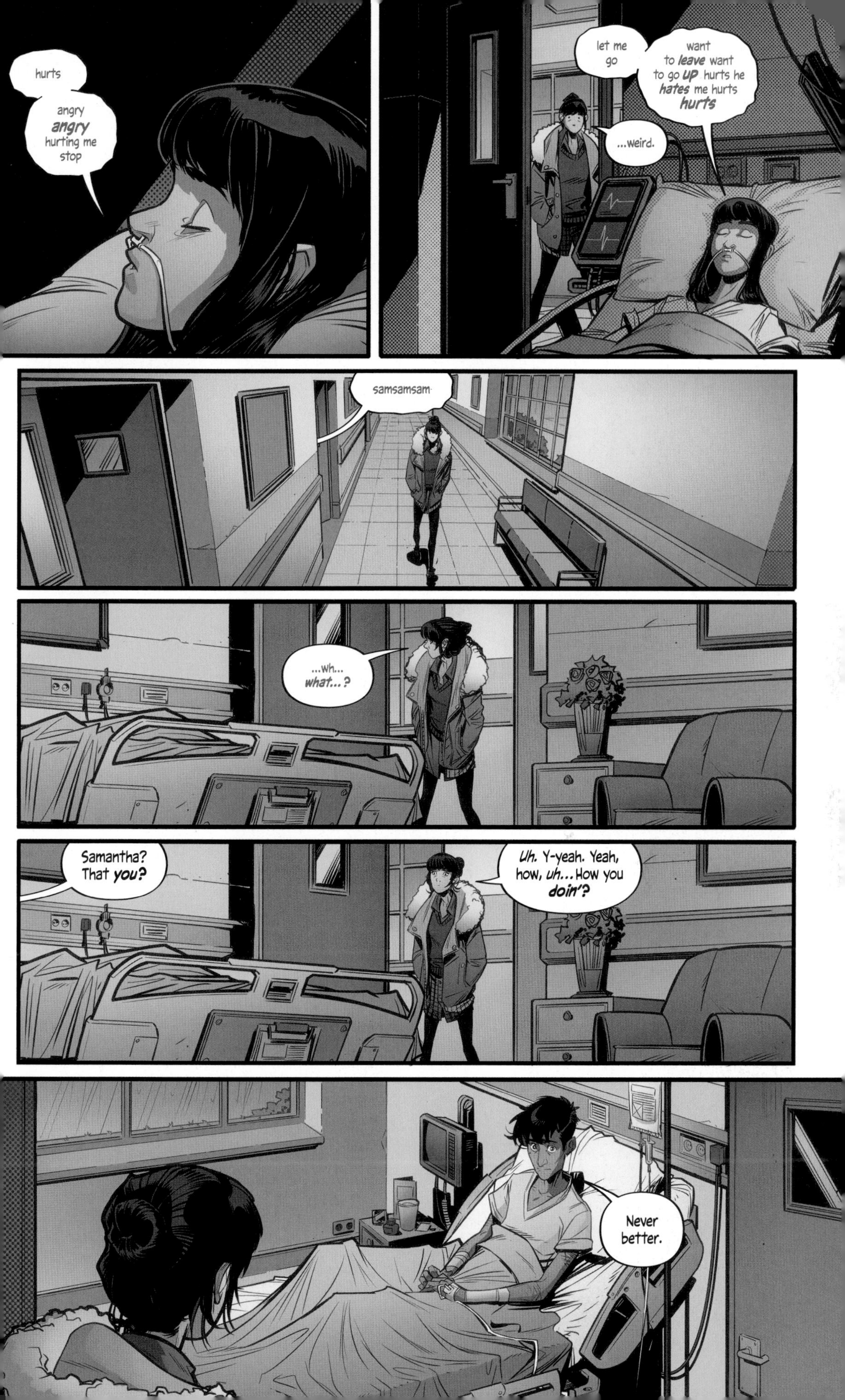
hurts
angry **angry** hurting me stop
let me go
want to **leave** want to go **up** hurts he **hates** me hurts **hurts**
...weird.
samsamsam
...wh... **what...?**
Samantha? That **you?**
Uh. Y-yeah. Yeah, how, **uh...** How you **doin'?**
Never better.

Listen, *Samir*...what happened yesterday. With your...your *dad*. It's not your f--

It is.

Nuh-uh. Something got--mixed up. *Anger*, or... I dunno. I think we gotta talk to *Samuel* and figure out wh--

I wanted to hurt *Dad.* I wanted to hurt *me.* Didn't *care* about hurting *Chip.* It got taken outta my hands, sure, but...

...I knew what I was doing.

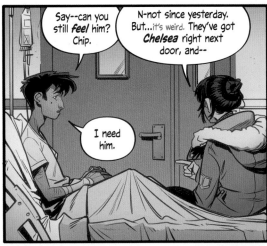

Say--can you still *feel* him? Chip.

N-not since yesterday. But...it's weird. They've got *Chelsea* right next door, and--

I need him.

I gotta set things *right.* I gotta *own* this, Samantha. I gotta *fix* it.

Samir.

We can't keep--clicking our fingers. Doing spooky alien *magic* to make *everything better.* It doesn't *work.*

Not what I mean.

I want to tell him I'm *sorry.*

S-sorry Mr. Waxy, I, *uh*--

I *said,* whaddaya*want?*

I-it's just... I make these-- these *vlogs,* and--

Oh for $#%&'s sake. *This* again.

Gimme a sec here, wouldja Jerry?

You're. You're *old.* I thought...I mean, everyone thinks you're... you're...

Young. Angry. *Trickster God* of the *dispossessed generation...*

Yeahyeahyeah, youth's a state of mind. *Listen.*

I dunno how you got *in* here, but we got *procedures.* I'm sorry your little *video* didn't make the cut, but--it ain't because we didn't *see* it.

I got *dozens* of folks wadin' through the *slush pile* every day, y'know?

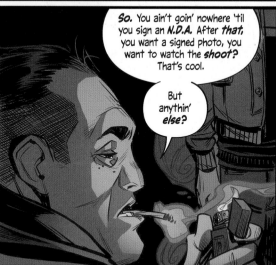

So. You ain't goin' nowhere 'til you sign an *N.D.A.* After *that,* you want a signed photo, you want to watch the *shoot?* That's cool.

But anythin' *else?*

Come back when you're something *special,* huh?

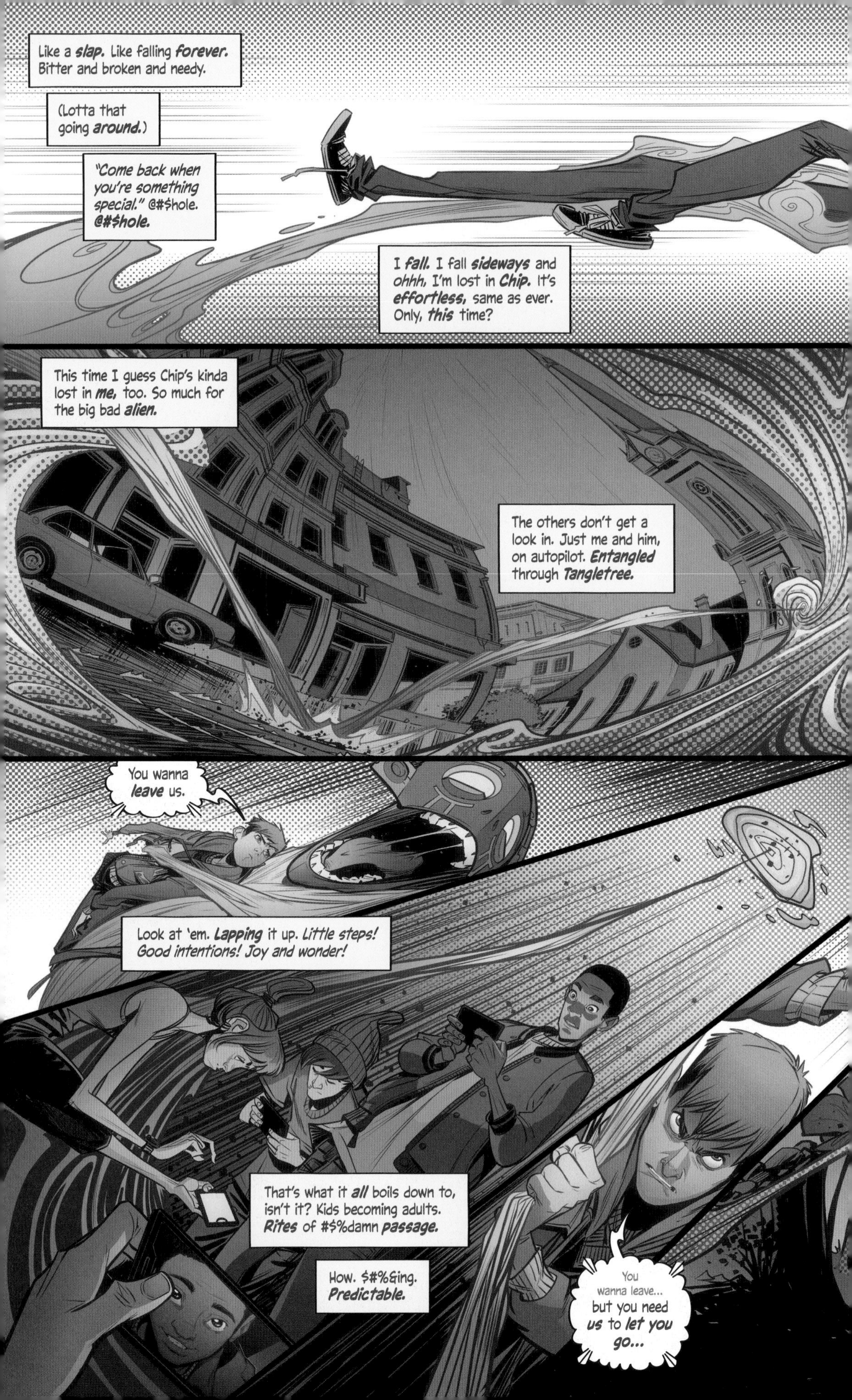
Like a *slap.* Like falling *forever.* Bitter and broken and needy.
(Lotta that going *around.*)
"Come back when you're something special." @#$hole. ***@#$hole.***
I *fall.* I fall *sideways* and *ohhh,* I'm lost in *Chip.* It's *effortless,* same as ever. Only, *this* time?
This time I guess Chip's kinda lost in *me,* too. So much for the big bad *alien.*
The others don't get a look in. Just me and him, on autopilot. *Entangled* through *Tangletree.*
You wanna *leave* us.
Look at 'em. *Lapping* it up. *Little steps! Good intentions! Joy and wonder!*
That's what it *all* boils down to, isn't it? Kids becoming adults. *Rites* of #$%damn *passage.*
How. $#%&ing. *Predictable.*
You wanna leave... but you need *us* to *let you go...*

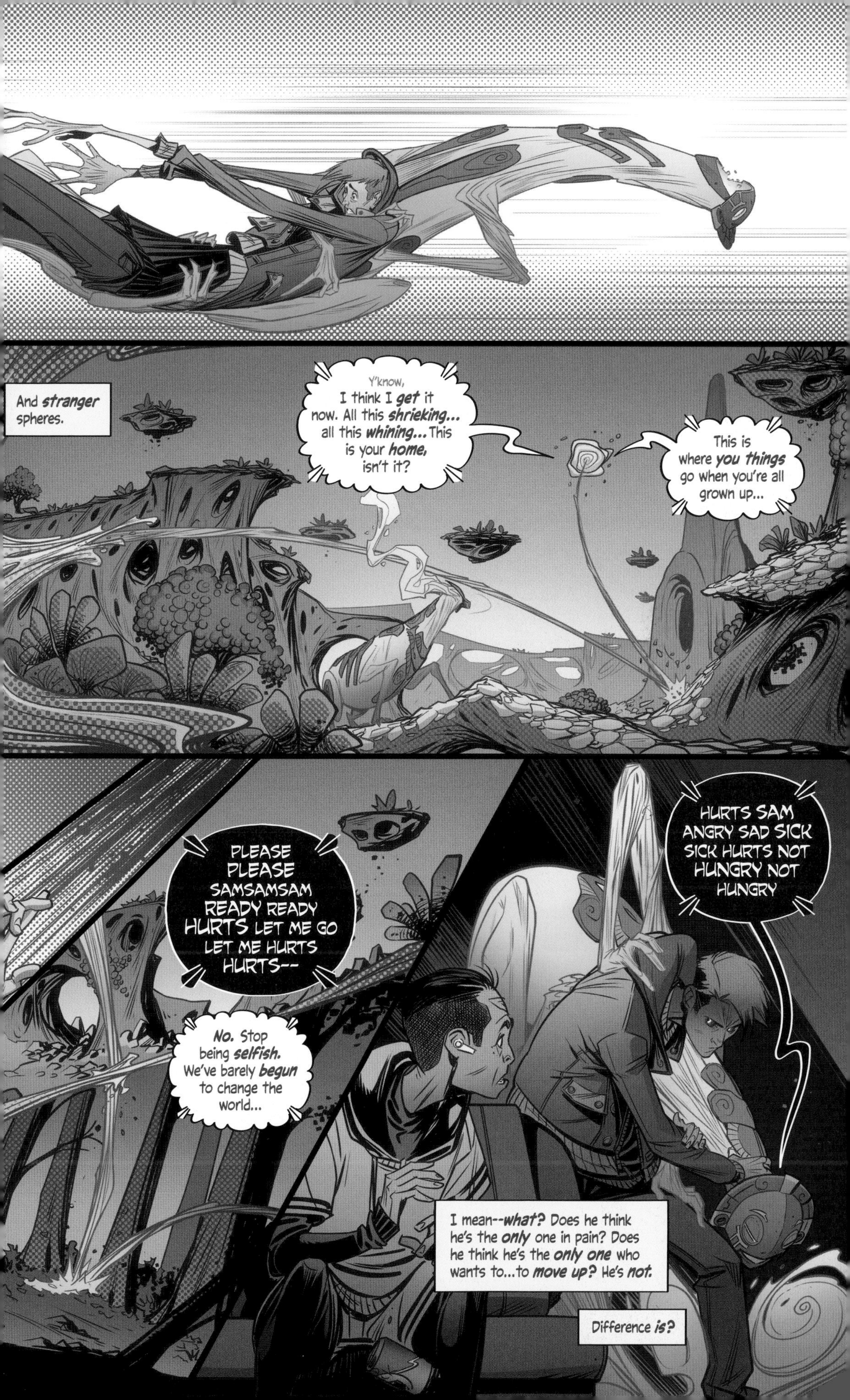
And stranger spheres.
Y'know, I think I get it now. All this shrieking... all this whining... This is your home, isn't it?
This is where you things go when you're all grown up...
PLEASE PLEASE SAMSAMSAM READY READY HURTS LET ME GO LET ME HURTS HURTS--
No. Stop being selfish. We've barely begun to change the world...
HURTS SAM ANGRY SAD SICK SICK HURTS NOT HUNGRY NOT HUNGRY
I mean--what? Does he think he's the only one in pain? Does he think he's the only one who wants to...to move up? He's not.
Difference is?

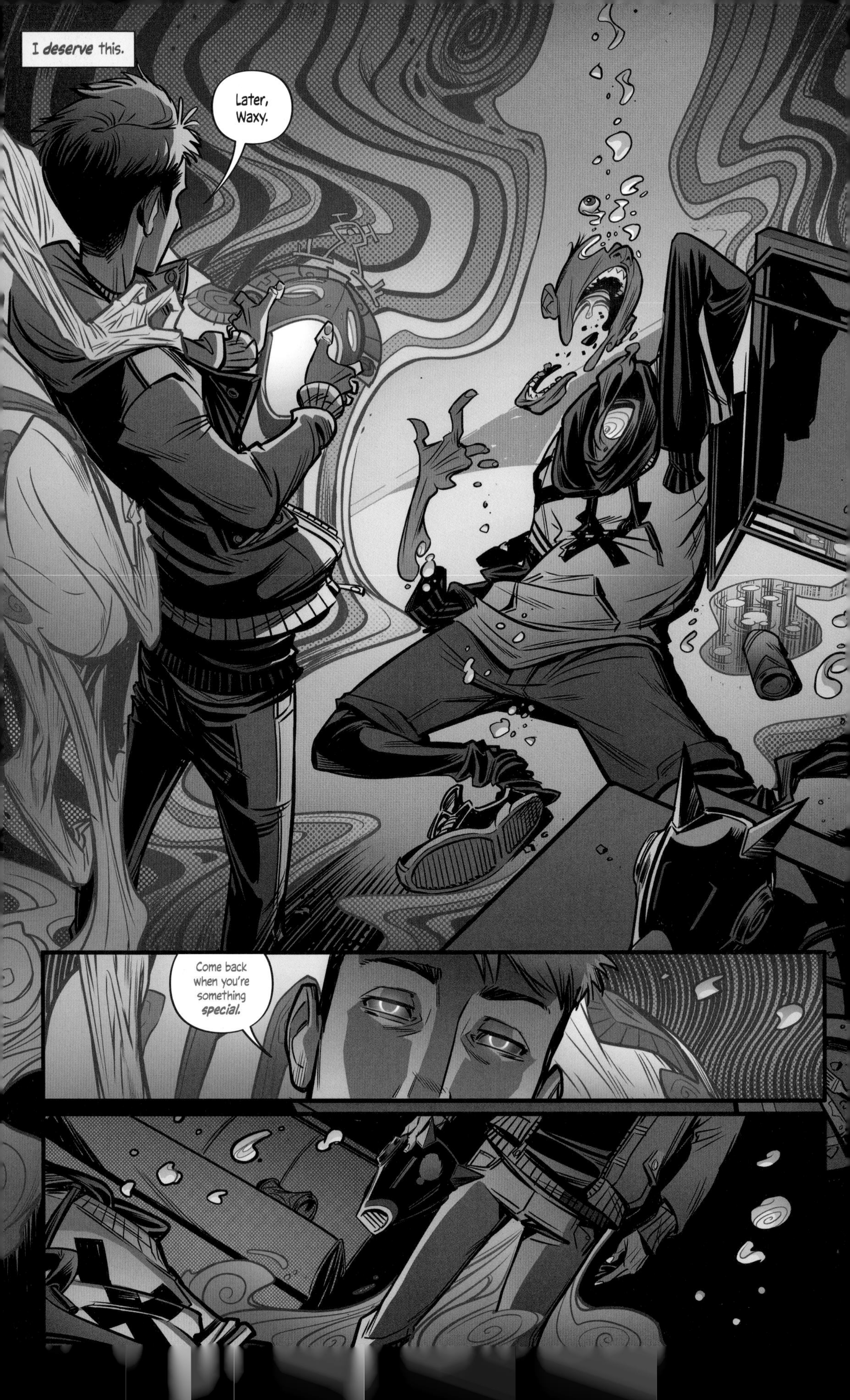
I *deserve* this.
Later, Waxy.
Come back when you're something *special.*

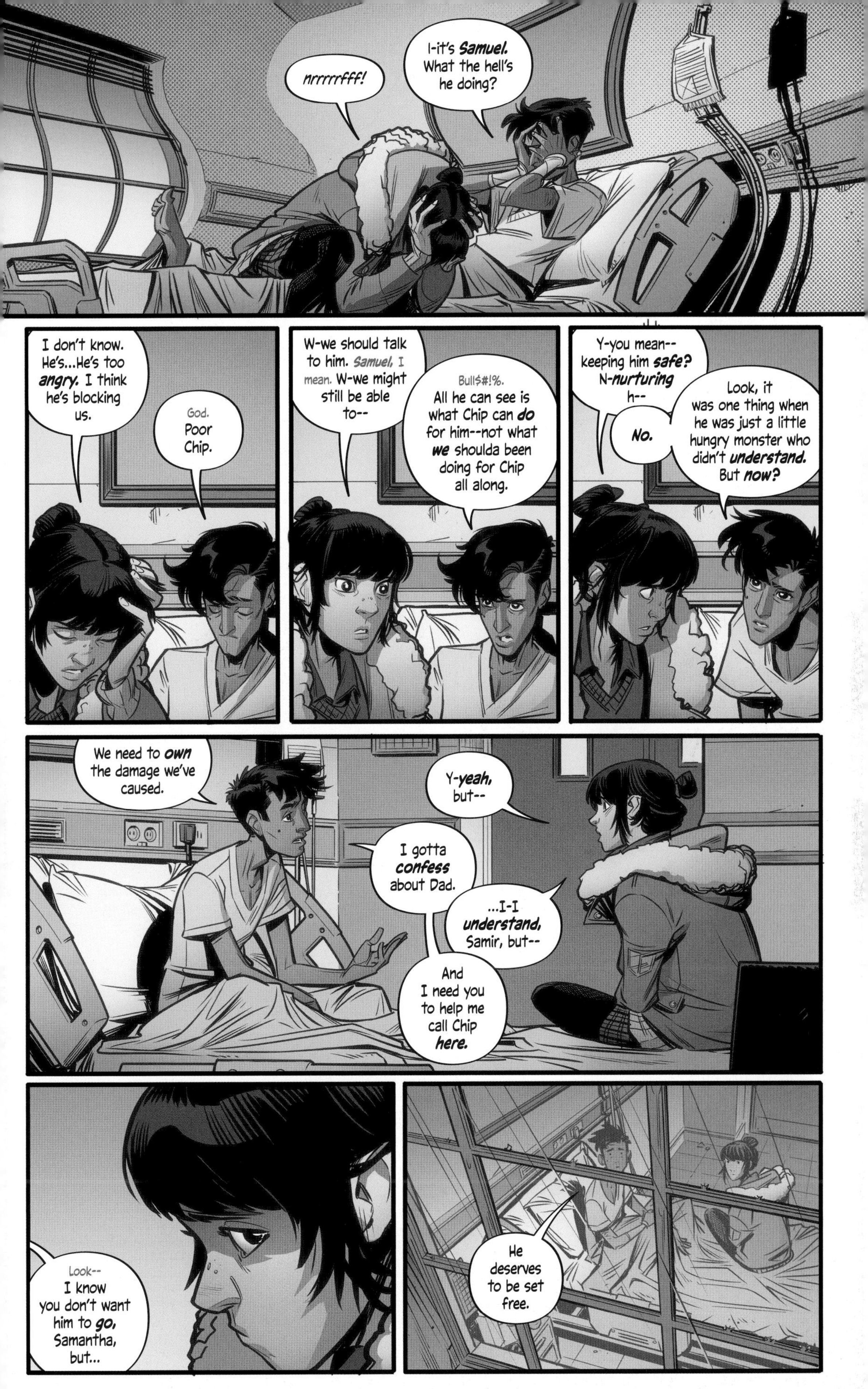
nrrrrrfff!
I-it's Samuel. What the hell's he doing?
I don't know. He's...He's too angry. I think he's blocking us.
God. Poor Chip.
W-we should talk to him. Samuel, I mean. W-we might still be able to--
Bull$#!%. All he can see is what Chip can do for him--not what we shoulda been doing for Chip all along.
Y-you mean--keeping him safe? N-nurturing h--
No.
Look, it was one thing when he was just a little hungry monster who didn't understand. But now?
We need to own the damage we've caused.
Y-yeah, but--
I gotta confess about Dad.
...I-I understand, Samir, but--
And I need you to help me call Chip here.
Look-- I know you don't want him to go, Samantha, but...
He deserves to be set free.

And that's why I believe... I *truly* believe... the future's **bright.**

Well how about *that, huh?* Round of applause, kids!

Round of applause for *Vern!*

Round of applause for his steaming pile of dull, indulgent, lazy-ass **crap.**

Wait-- what?

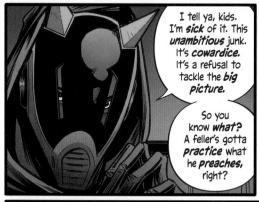

I tell ya, kids. I'm *sick* of it. This *unambitious* junk. It's **cowardice.** It's a refusal to tackle the **big picture.**

So you know *what?* A feller's gotta **practice** what he **preaches,** right?

Pranks. Poetry. It's been fun, folks. But. It's time to *put away childish things.*

It's time to be **seen.**

My name is Samuel Robinson and I'm Waxy.

Thank you. Thank you. Today I need you to listen *real* hard.

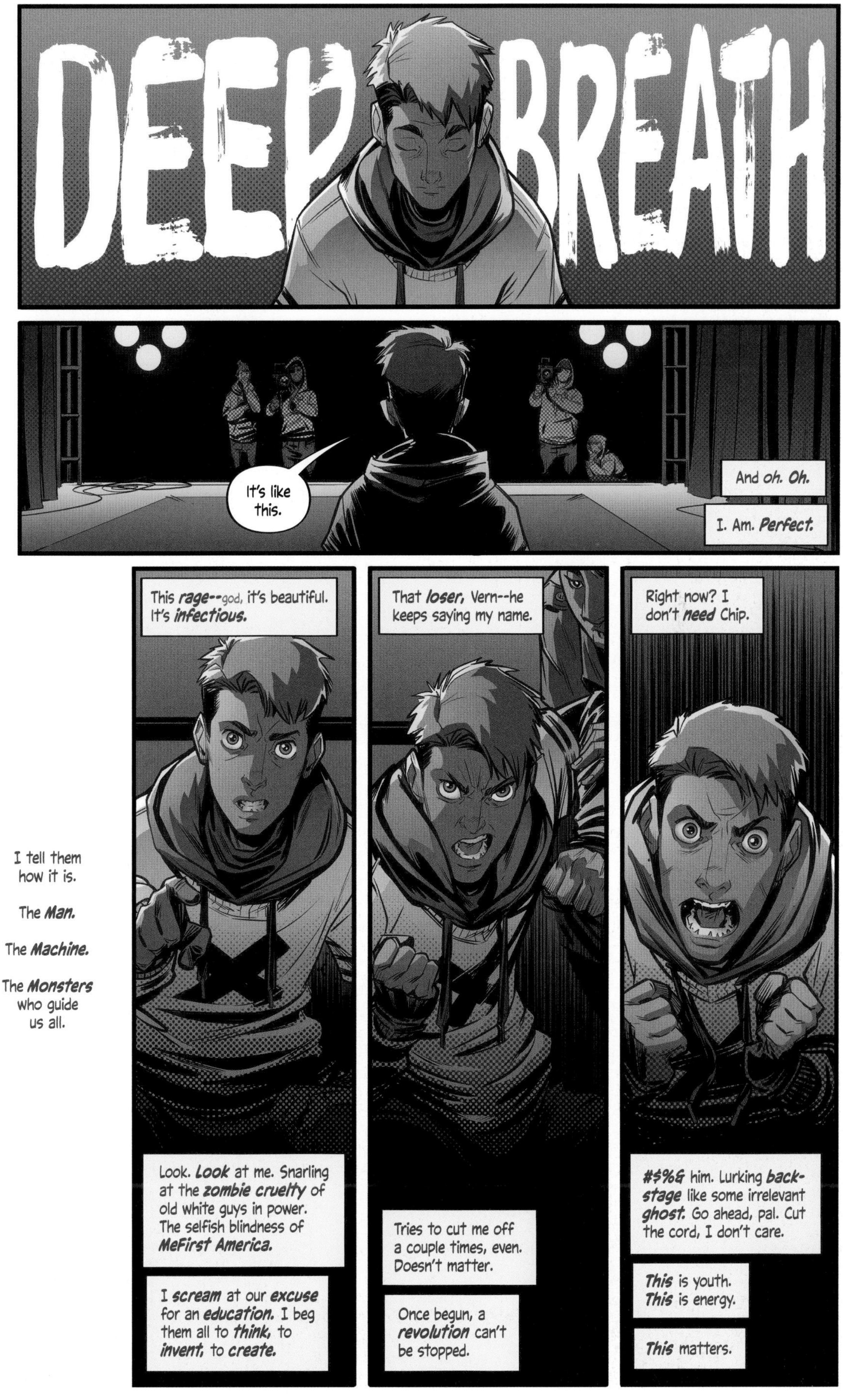
DEEP BREATH
It's like this.
And oh. Oh.
I. Am. Perfect.
I tell them how it is.
The Man.
The Machine.
The Monsters who guide us all.
This rage--god, it's beautiful. It's infectious.
Look. Look at me. Snarling at the zombie cruelty of old white guys in power. The selfish blindness of MeFirst America.
I scream at our excuse for an education. I beg them all to think, to invent, to create.
That loser, Vern--he keeps saying my name.
Tries to cut me off a couple times, even. Doesn't matter.
Once begun, a revolution can't be stopped.
Right now? I don't need Chip.
#$%& him. Lurking backstage like some irrelevant ghost. Go ahead, pal. Cut the cord, I don't care.
This is youth. This is energy.
This matters.

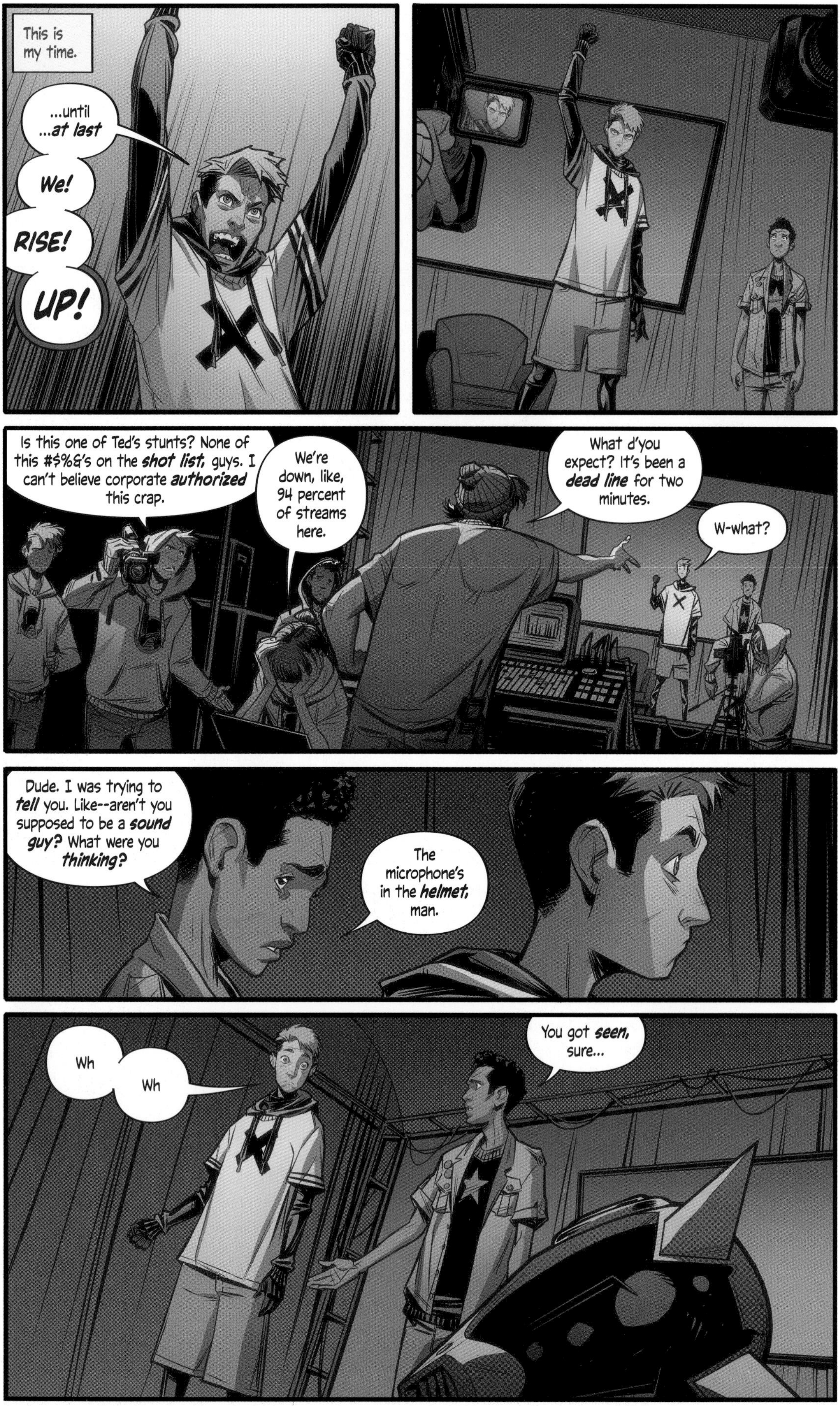
This is my time.
...until ...at last
We!
RISE!
UP!
Is this one of Ted's stunts? None of this #$%&'s on the shot list, guys. I can't believe corporate authorized this crap.
We're down, like, 94 percent of streams here.
What d'you expect? It's been a dead line for two minutes.
W-what?
Dude. I was trying to tell you. Like--aren't you supposed to be a sound guy? What were you thinking?
The microphone's in the helmet, man.
Wh
Wh
You got seen, sure...

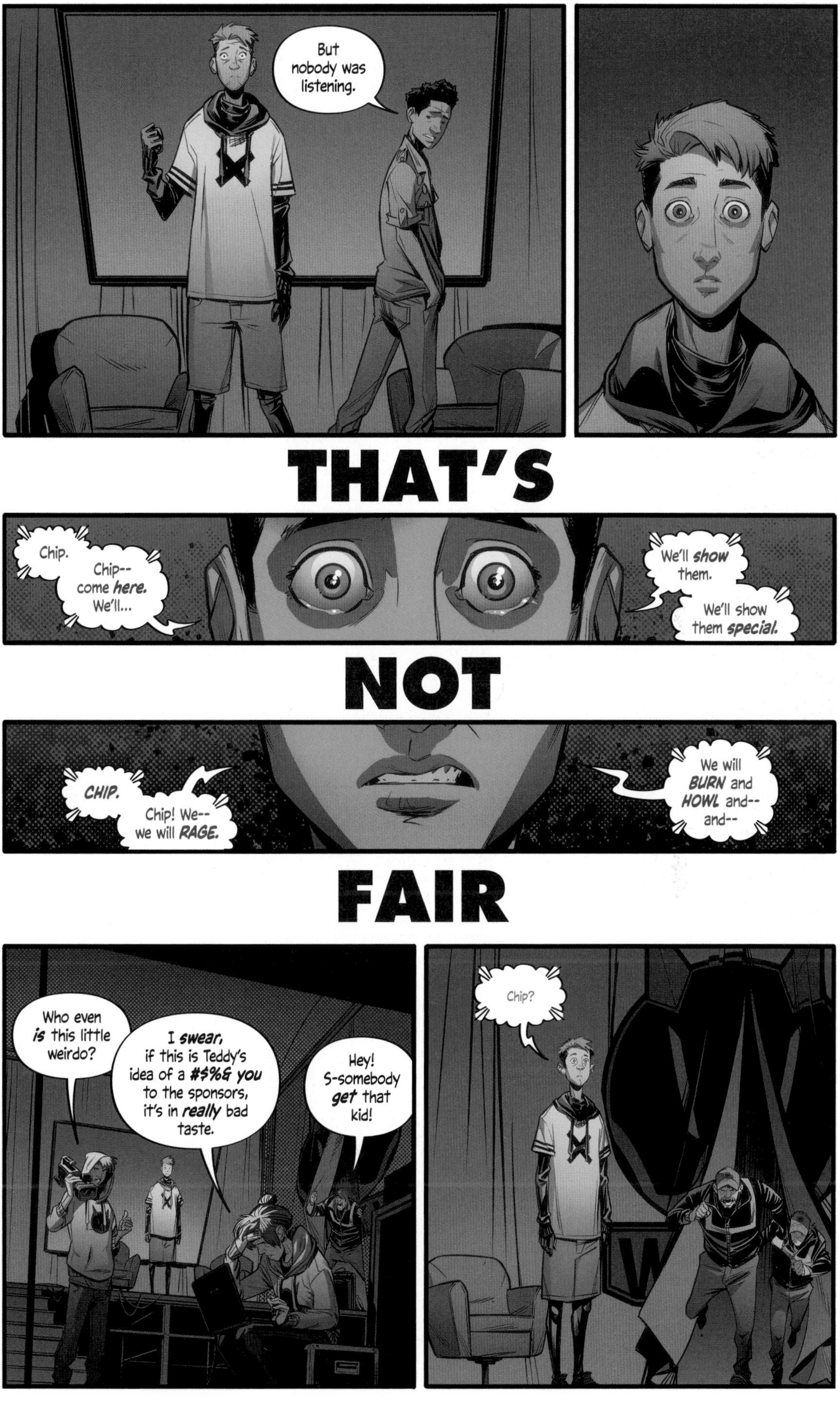
But nobody was listening.
THAT'S
Chip.
Chip-- come here. We'll...
We'll show them.
We'll show them special.
NOT
CHIP.
Chip! We-- we will RAGE.
We will BURN and HOWL and-- and--
FAIR
Who even is this little weirdo?
I swear, if this is Teddy's idea of a #$%& you to the sponsors, it's in really bad taste.
Hey! S-somebody get that kid!
Chip?

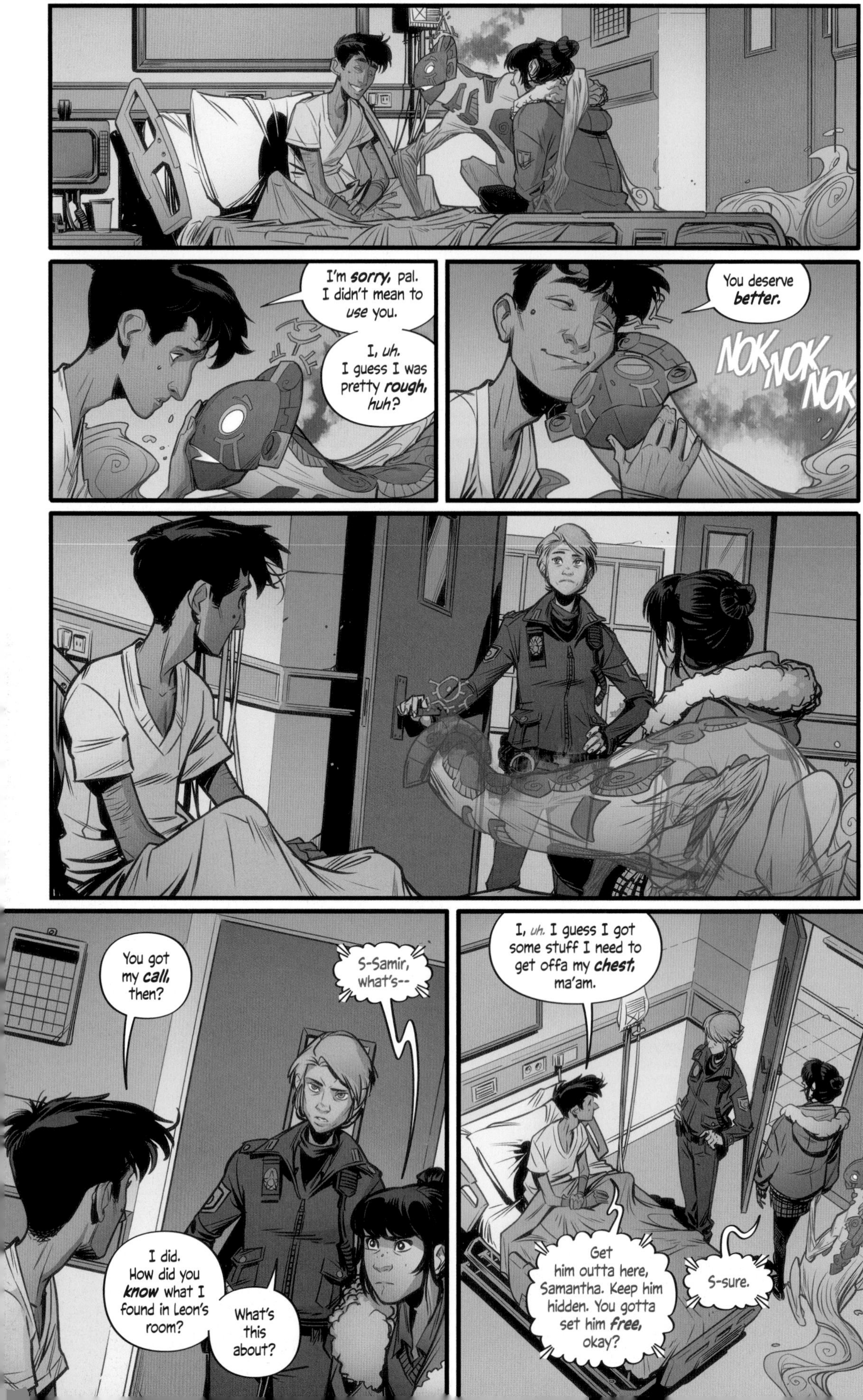
I'm sorry, pal. I didn't mean to use you.
I, uh. I guess I was pretty rough, huh?
You deserve better.
NOK NOK NOK
You got my call, then?
S-Samir, what's--
I did. How did you know what I found in Leon's room?
What's this about?
I, uh. I guess I got some stuff I need to get offa my chest, ma'am.
Get him outta here, Samantha. Keep him hidden. You gotta set him free, okay?
S-sure.

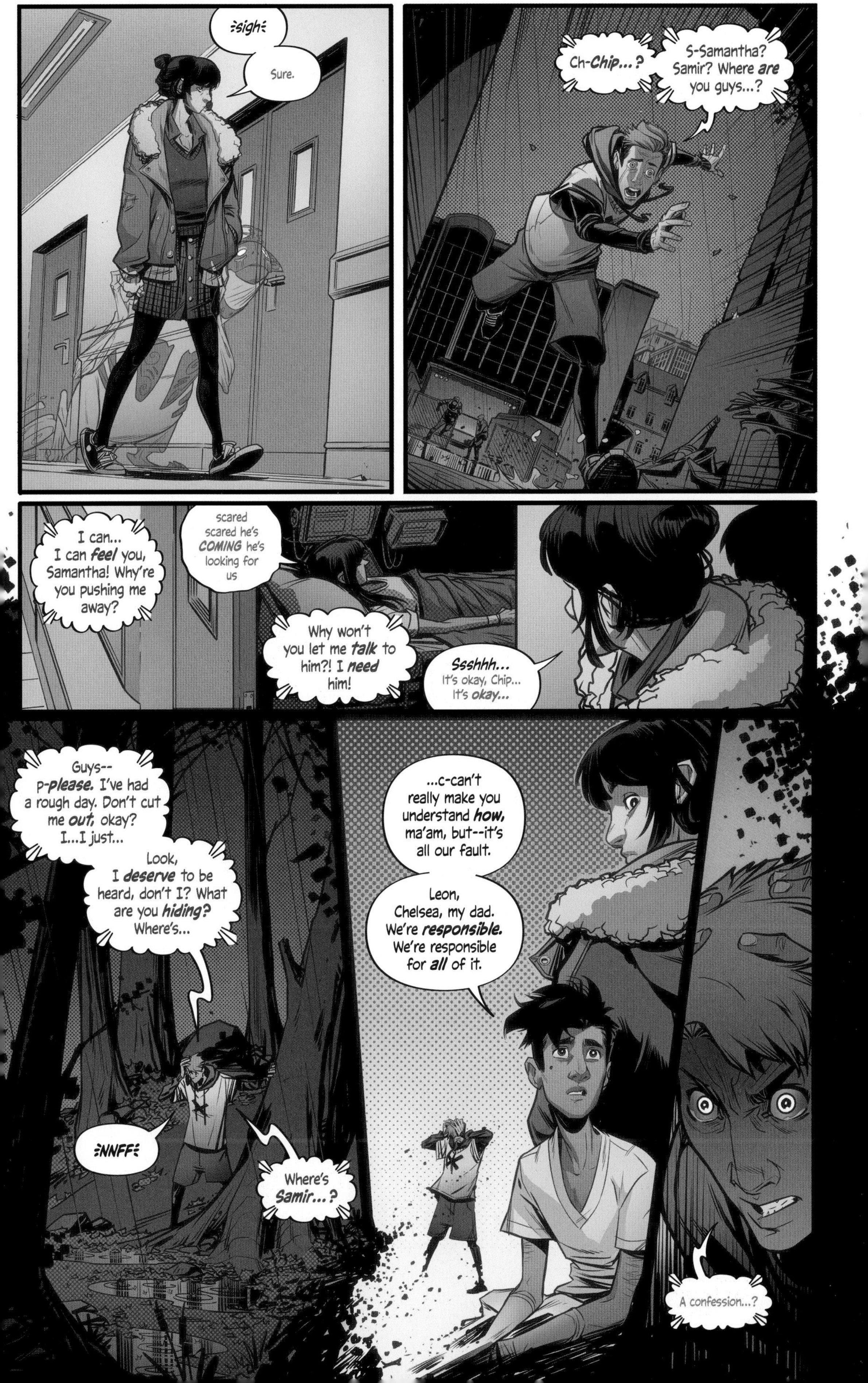
:sigh:
Sure.
Ch-Chip...?
S-Samantha? Samir? Where are you guys...?
I can... I can feel you, Samantha! Why're you pushing me away?
scared scared he's COMING he's looking for us
Why won't you let me talk to him?! I need him!
Ssshhh... It's okay, Chip... It's okay...
Guys-- p-please. I've had a rough day. Don't cut me out, okay? I...I just...
Look, I deserve to be heard, don't I? What are you hiding? Where's...
:NNFF:
Where's Samir...?
...c-can't really make you understand how, ma'am, but--it's all our fault.
Leon, Chelsea, my dad. We're responsible. We're responsible for all of it.
A confession...?

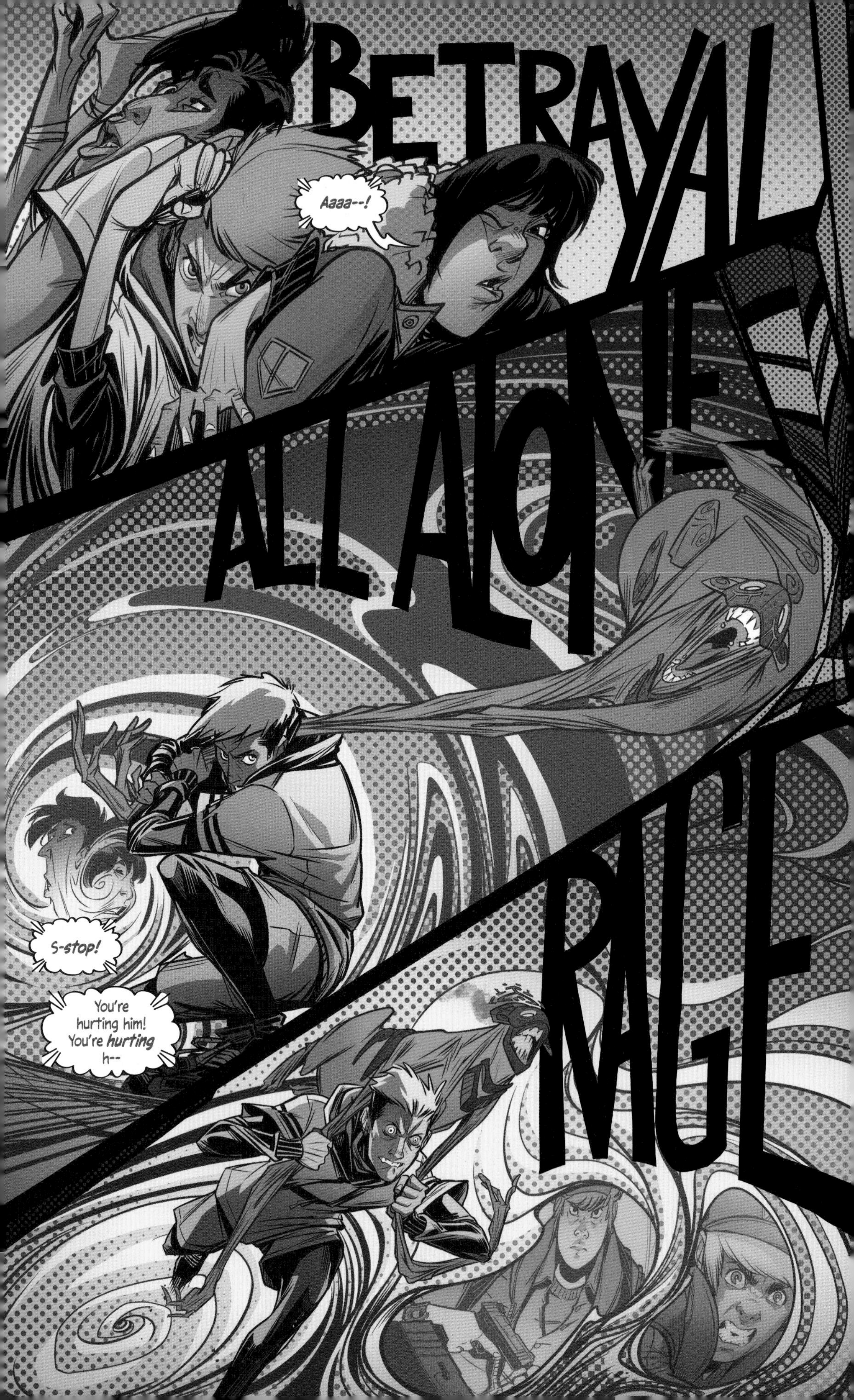
BETRAYAL
Aaaa--!
ALL ALONE
S-stop!
You're hurting him! You're *hurting* h--
RAGE

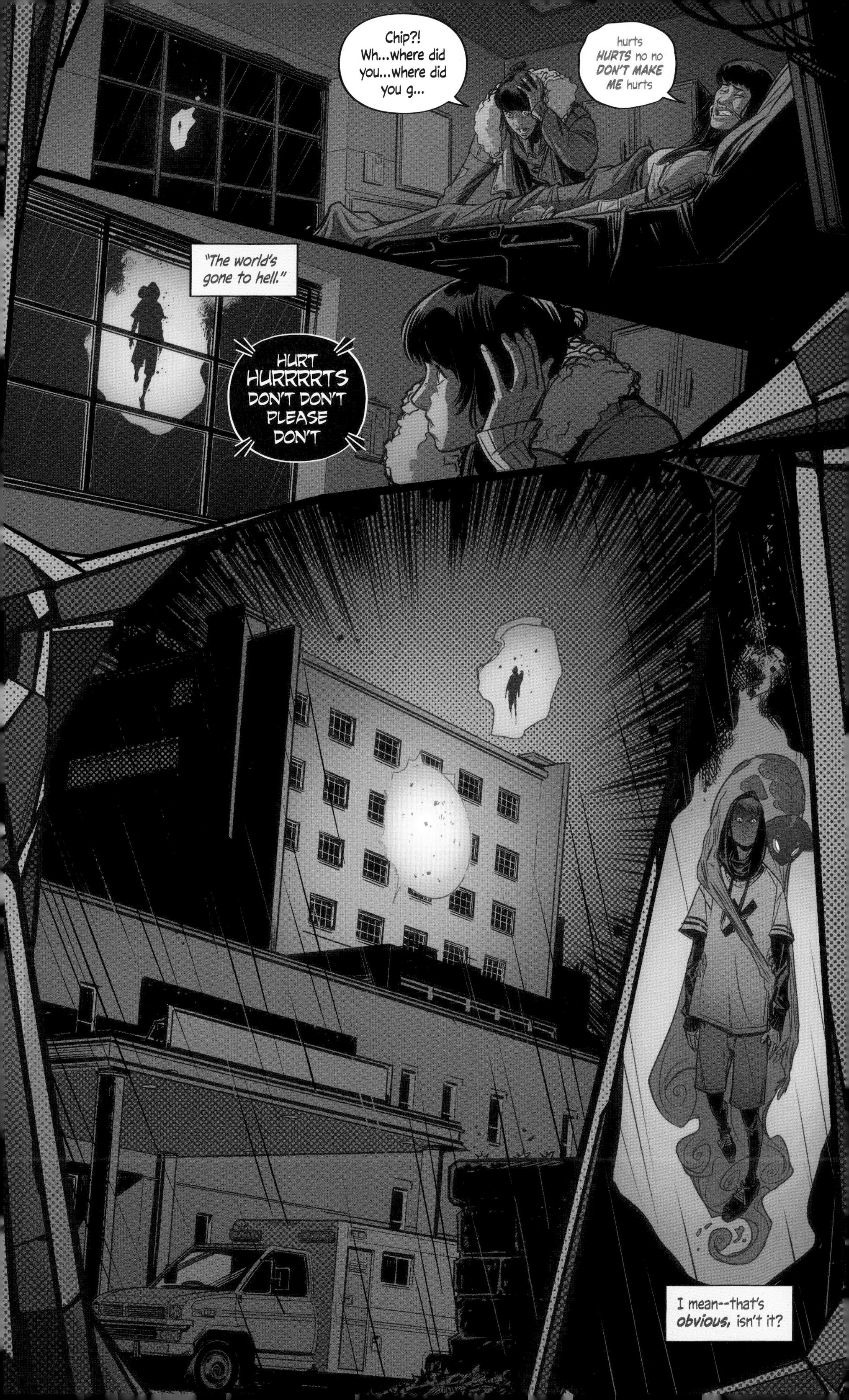
Chip?! Wh...where did you...where did you g...
hurts HURTS no no DON'T MAKE ME hurts
"The world's gone to hell."
HURT HURRRRTS DON'T DON'T PLEASE DON'T
I mean--that's obvious, isn't it?

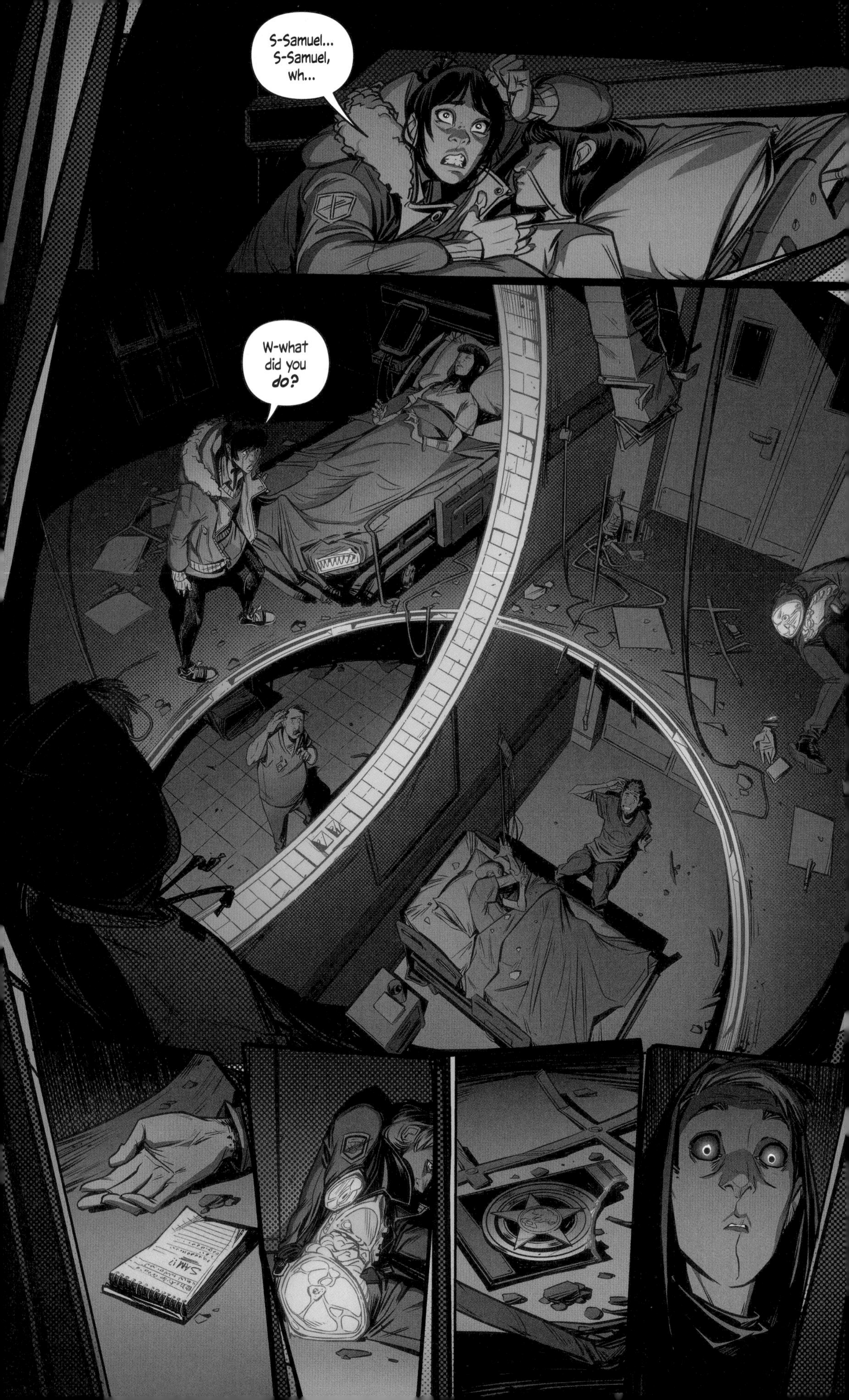
S-Samuel... S-Samuel, wh...
W-what did you *do?*

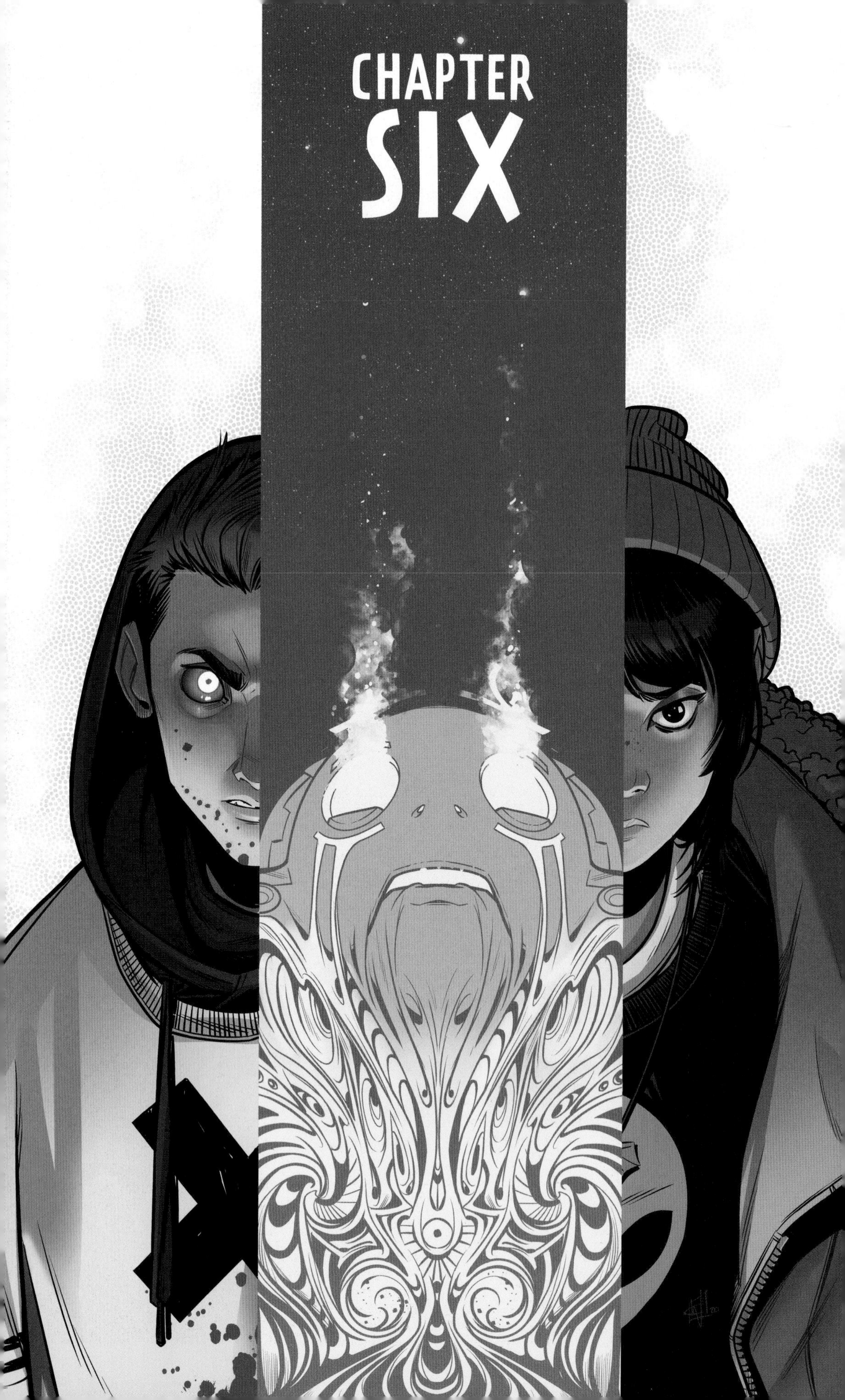
CHAPTER
SIX

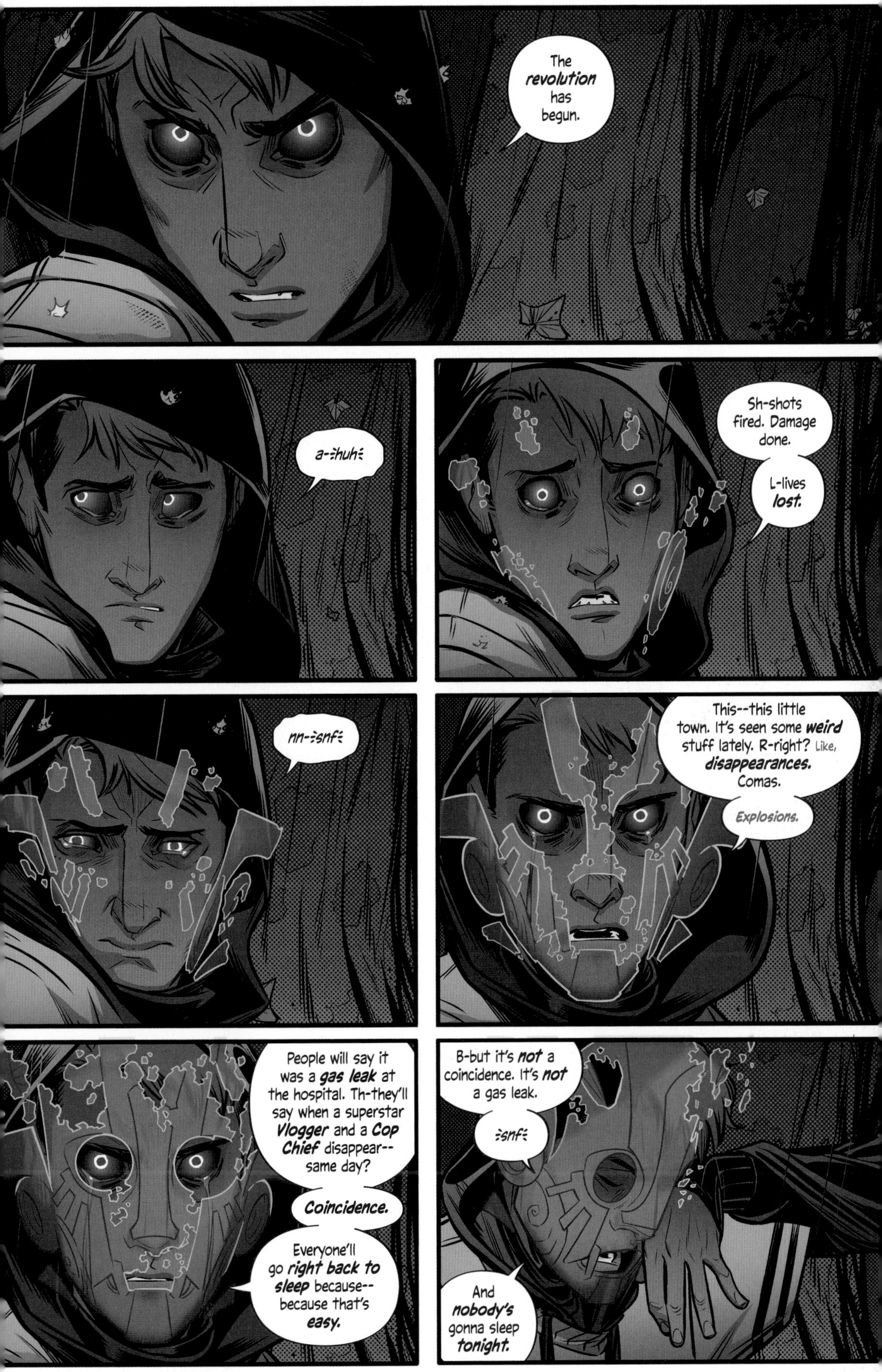
The revolution has begun.
a-=huh=
Sh-shots fired. Damage done.
L-lives lost.
nn-=snf=
This--this little town. It's seen some weird stuff lately. R-right? Like, disappearances. Comas.
Explosions.
People will say it was a gas leak at the hospital. Th-they'll say when a superstar Vlogger and a Cop Chief disappear--same day?
Coincidence.
Everyone'll go right back to sleep because--because that's easy.
B-but it's not a coincidence. It's not a gas leak.
=snf=
And nobody's gonna sleep tonight.

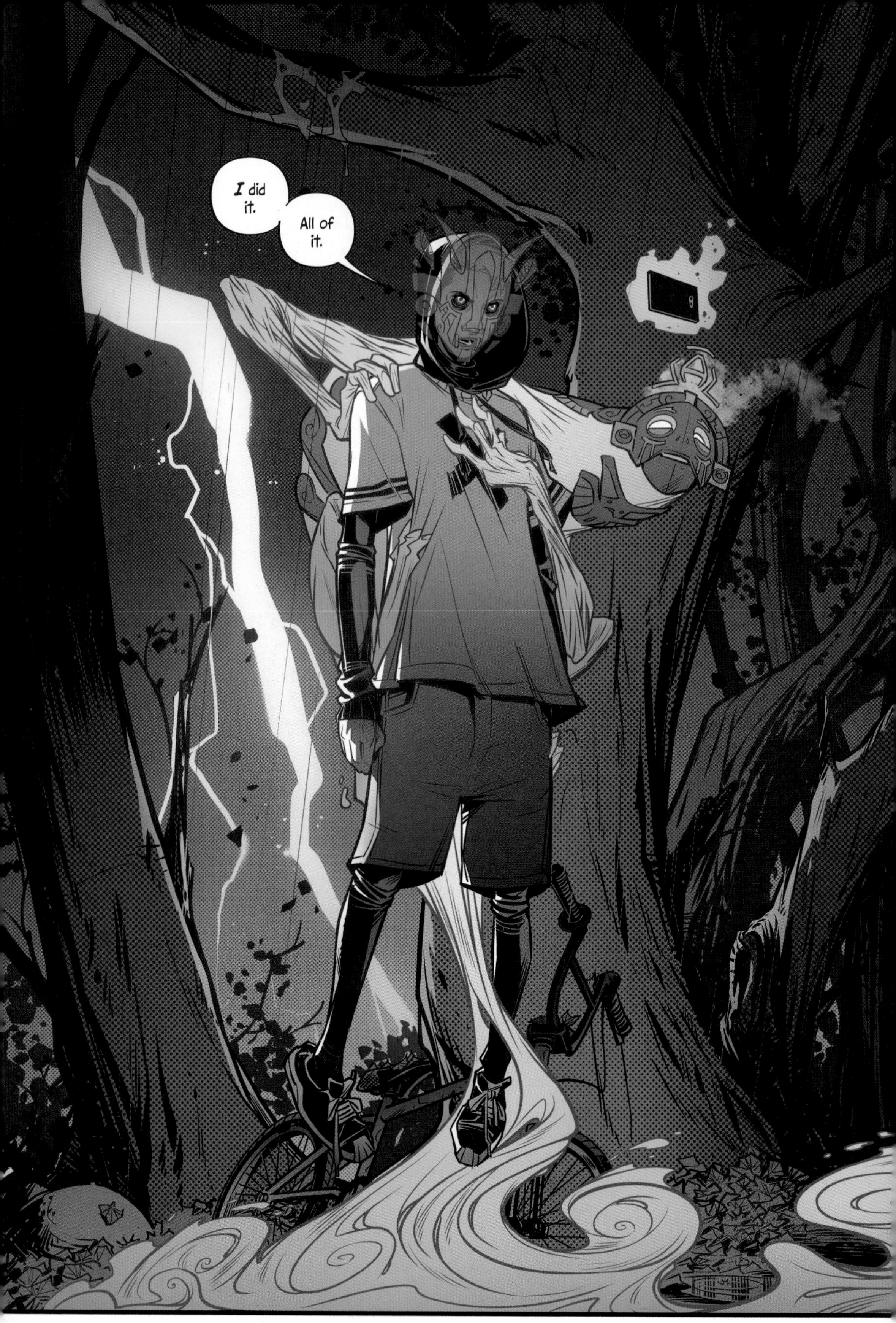
I did it.
All of it.

Chapter 6:
AND ON PURPOSE TOO

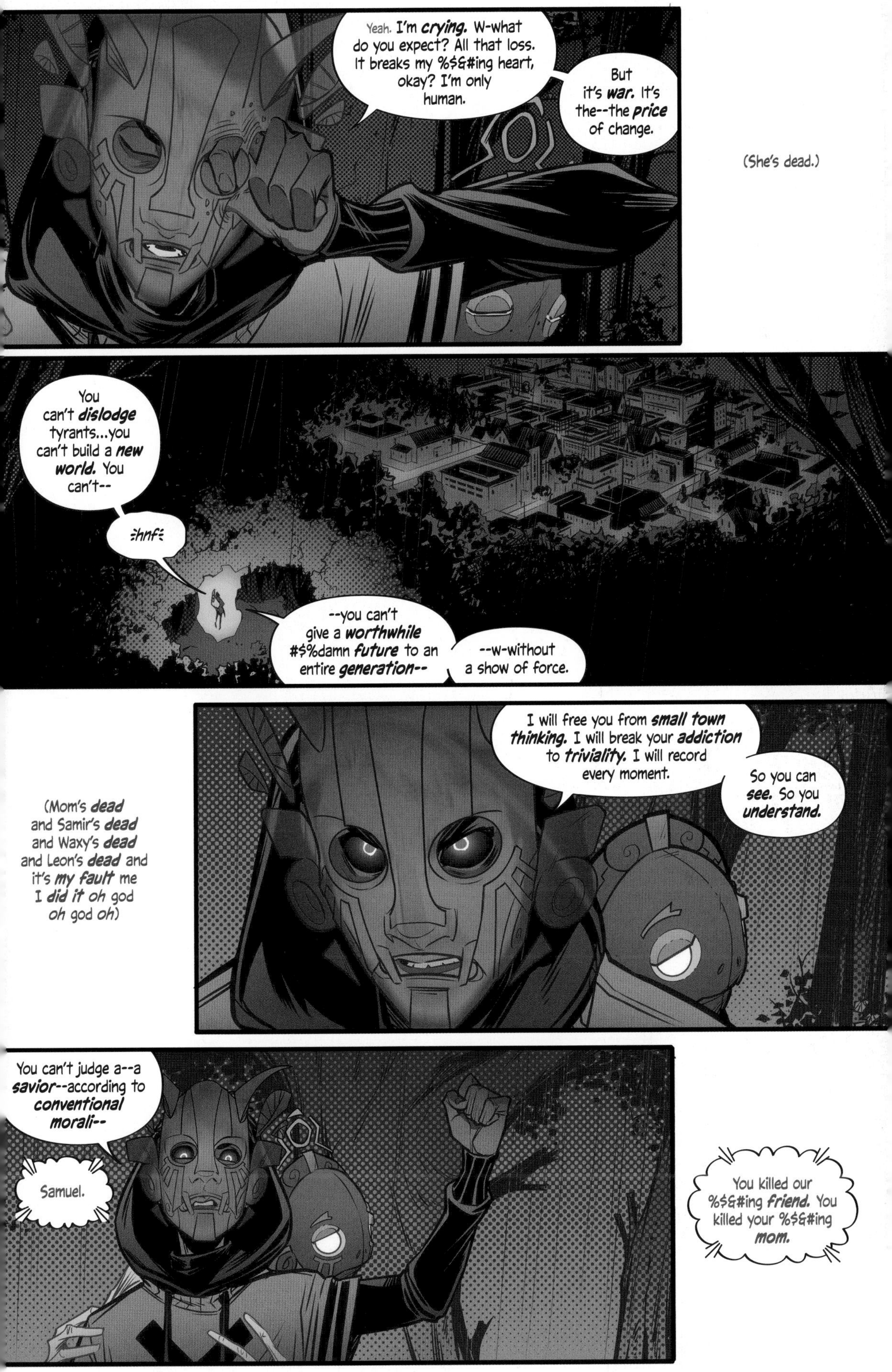
Yeah. I'm crying. W-what do you expect? All that loss. It breaks my %$&#ing heart, okay? I'm only human.
But it's war. It's the--the price of change.
(She's dead.)
You can't dislodge tyrants...you can't build a new world. You can't--
:hnf:
--you can't give a worthwhile #$%damn future to an entire generation--
--w-without a show of force.
I will free you from small town thinking. I will break your addiction to triviality. I will record every moment.
So you can see. So you understand.
(Mom's dead and Samir's dead and Waxy's dead and Leon's dead and it's my fault me I did it oh god oh god oh)
You can't judge a--a savior--according to conventional morali--
Samuel.
You killed our %$&#ing friend. You killed your %$&#ing mom.

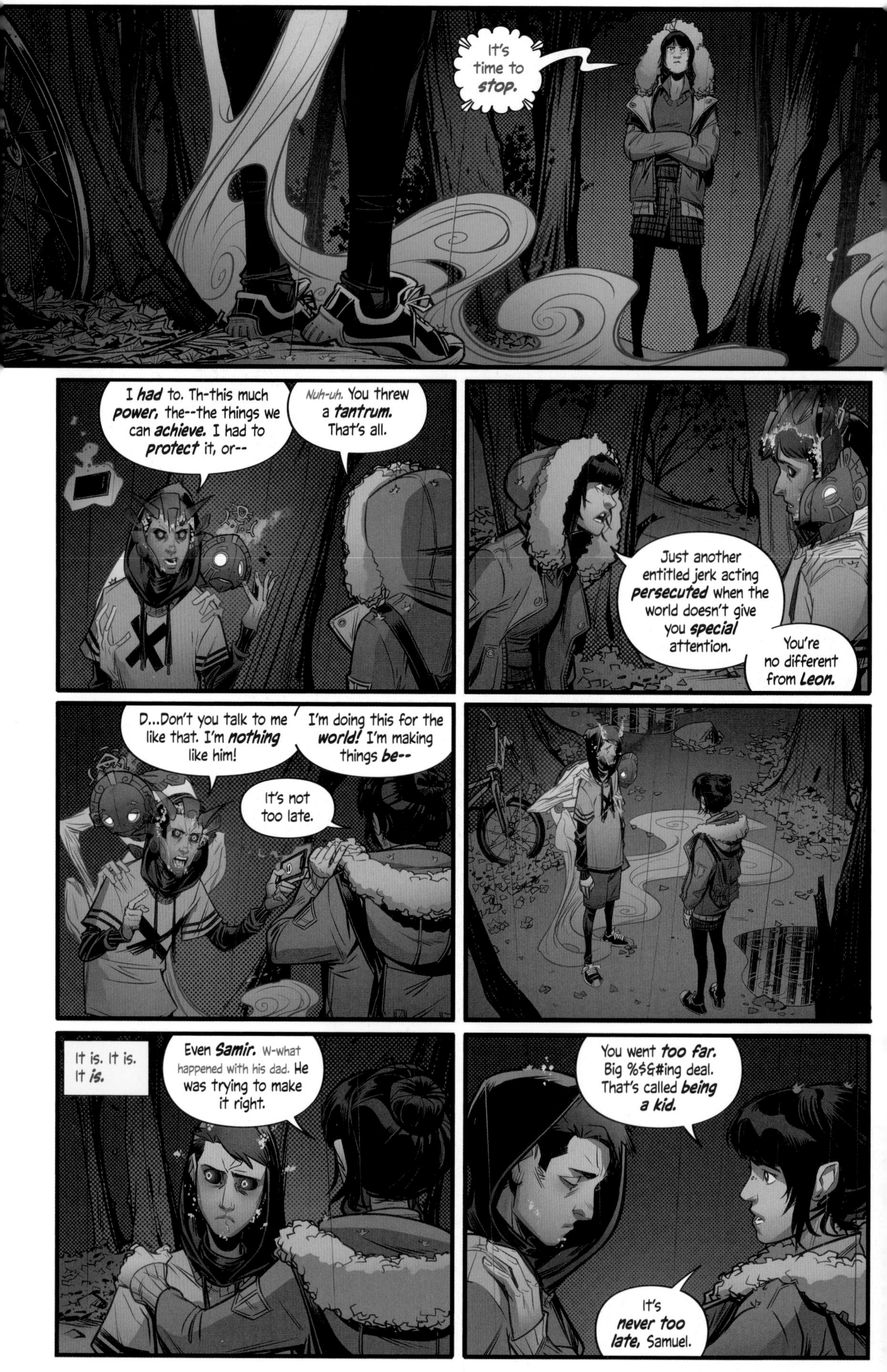
It's time to stop.
I had to. Th-this much power, the--the things we can achieve. I had to protect it, or--
Nuh-uh. You threw a tantrum. That's all.
Just another entitled jerk acting persecuted when the world doesn't give you special attention.
You're no different from Leon.
D...Don't you talk to me like that. I'm nothing like him!
I'm doing this for the world! I'm making things be--
It's not too late.
It is. It is. It is.
Even Samir. W-what happened with his dad. He was trying to make it right.
You went too far. Big %$&#ing deal. That's called being a kid.
It's never too late, Samuel.

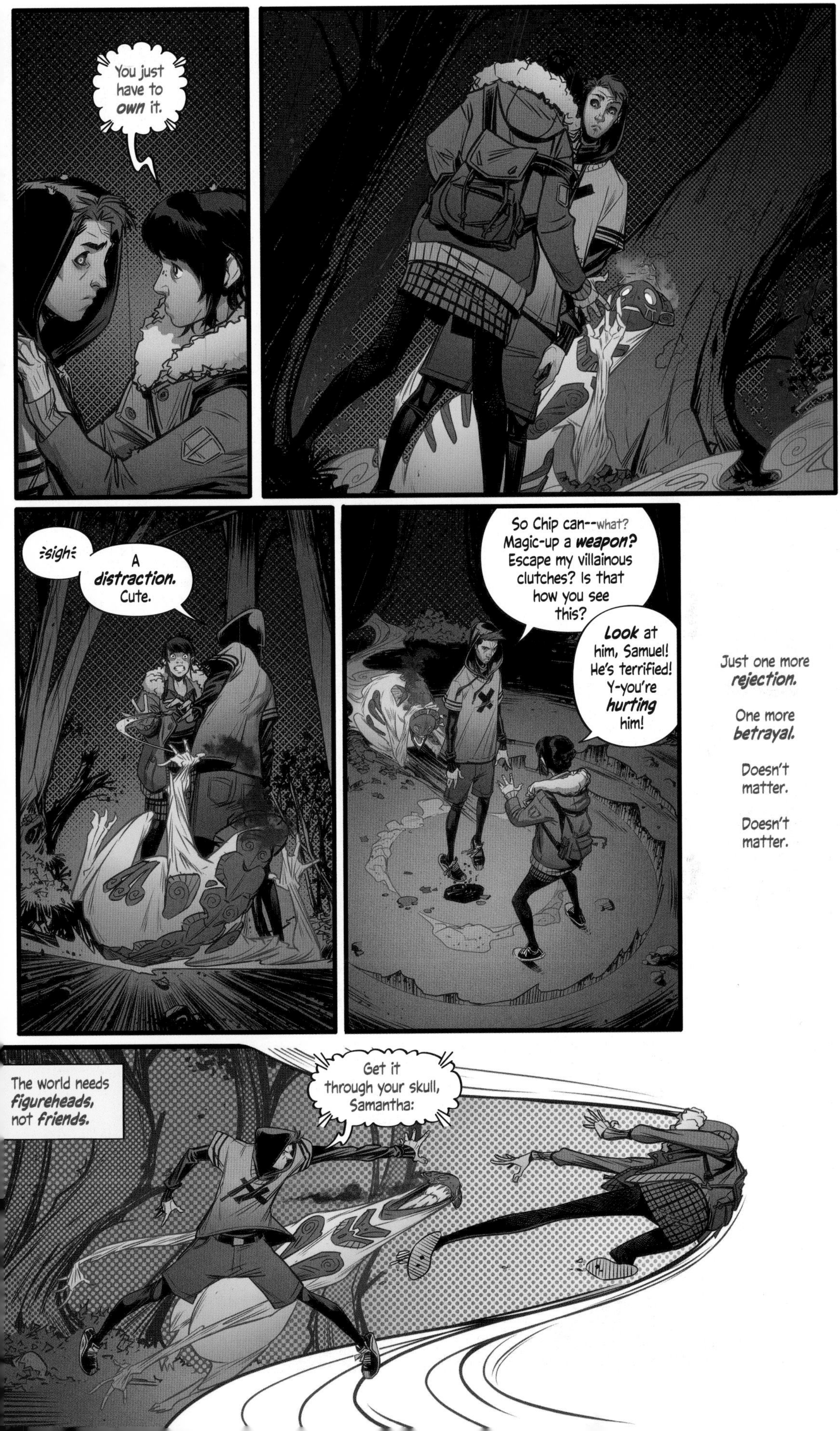
You just have to *own* it.
=sigh=
A *distraction.* Cute.
So Chip can--what? Magic-up a *weapon?* Escape my villainous clutches? Is that how you see this?
Look at him, Samuel! He's terrified! Y-you're *hurting* him!
Just one more *rejection.*
One more *betrayal.*
Doesn't matter.
Doesn't matter.
The world needs *figureheads,* not *friends.*
Get it through your skull, Samantha:

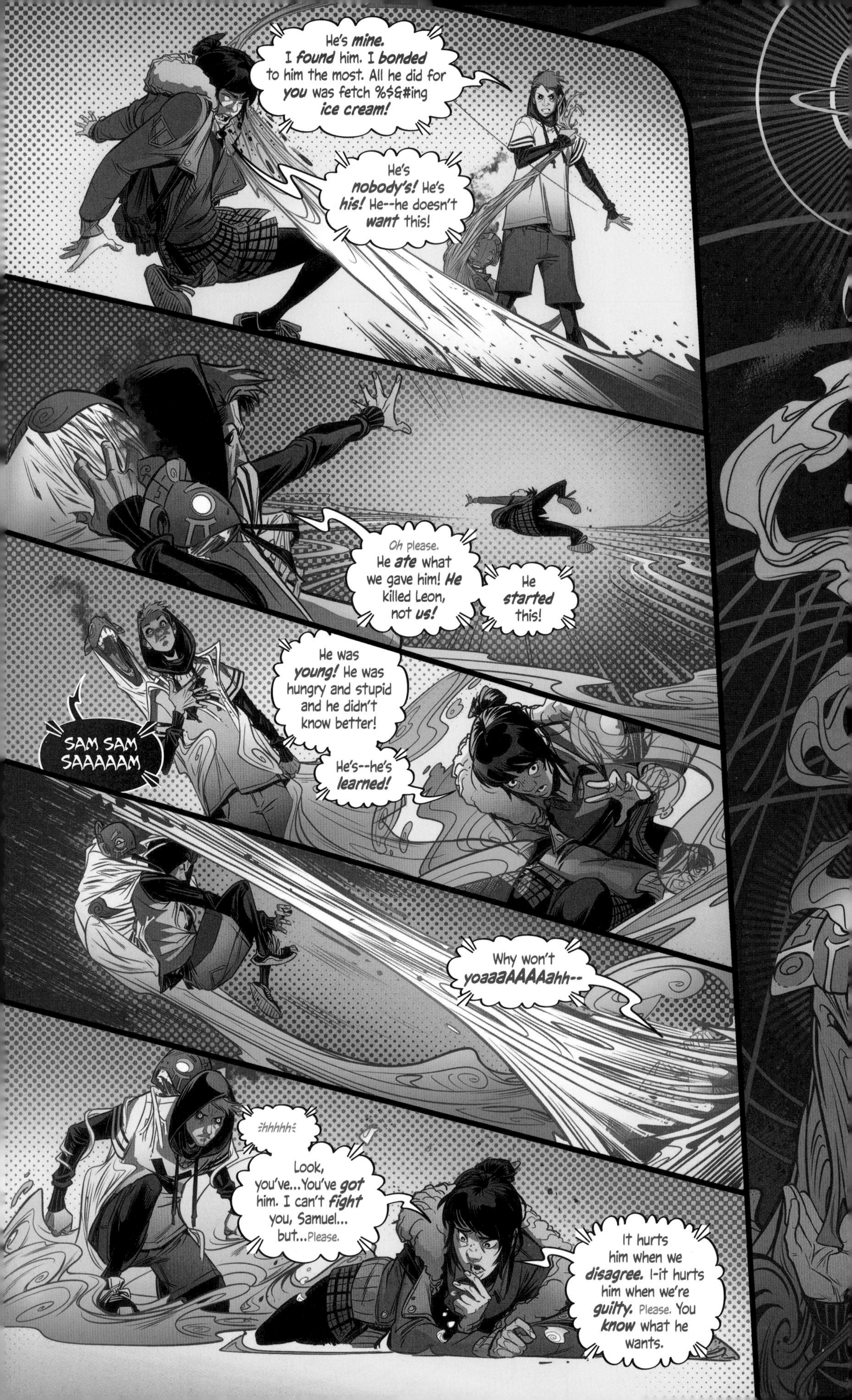
He's mine. I found him. I bonded to him the most. All he did for you was fetch %$&#ing ice cream!
He's nobody's! He's his! He--he doesn't want this!
Oh please. He ate what we gave him! He killed Leon, not us!
He started this!
He was young! He was hungry and stupid and he didn't know better!
SAM SAM SAAAAAM
He's--he's learned!
Why won't yoaaaAAAAahh--
hhhhh
Look, you've...You've got him. I can't fight you, Samuel... but...Please.
It hurts him when we disagree. I-it hurts him when we're guilty. Please. You know what he wants.

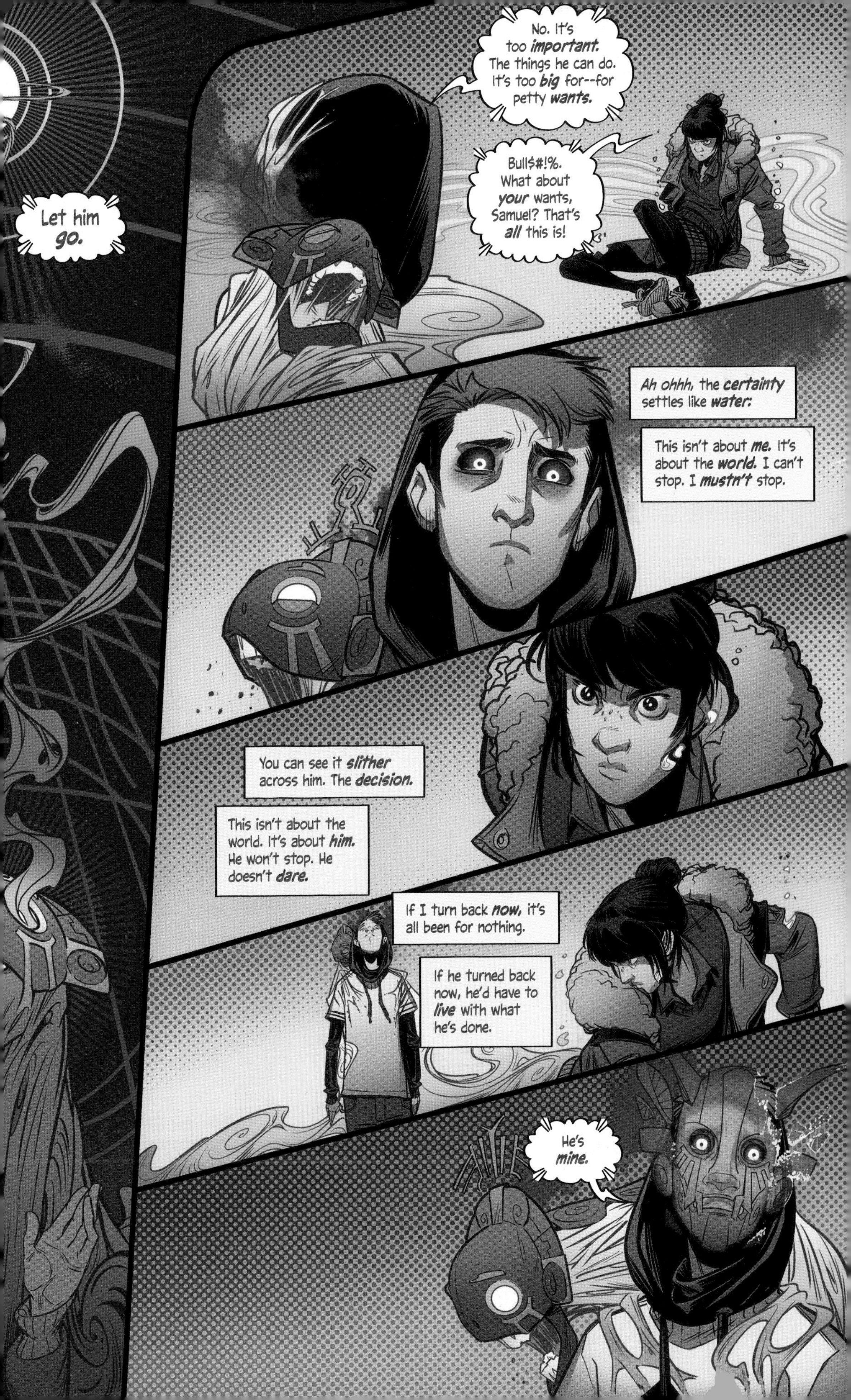
Let him go.
No. It's too important. The things he can do. It's too big for--for petty wants.
Bull$#!%. What about your wants, Samuel? That's all this is!
Ah ohhh, the certainty settles like water:
This isn't about me. It's about the world. I can't stop. I mustn't stop.
You can see it slither across him. The decision.
This isn't about the world. It's about him. He won't stop. He doesn't dare.
If I turn back now, it's all been for nothing.
If he turned back now, he'd have to live with what he's done.
He's mine.

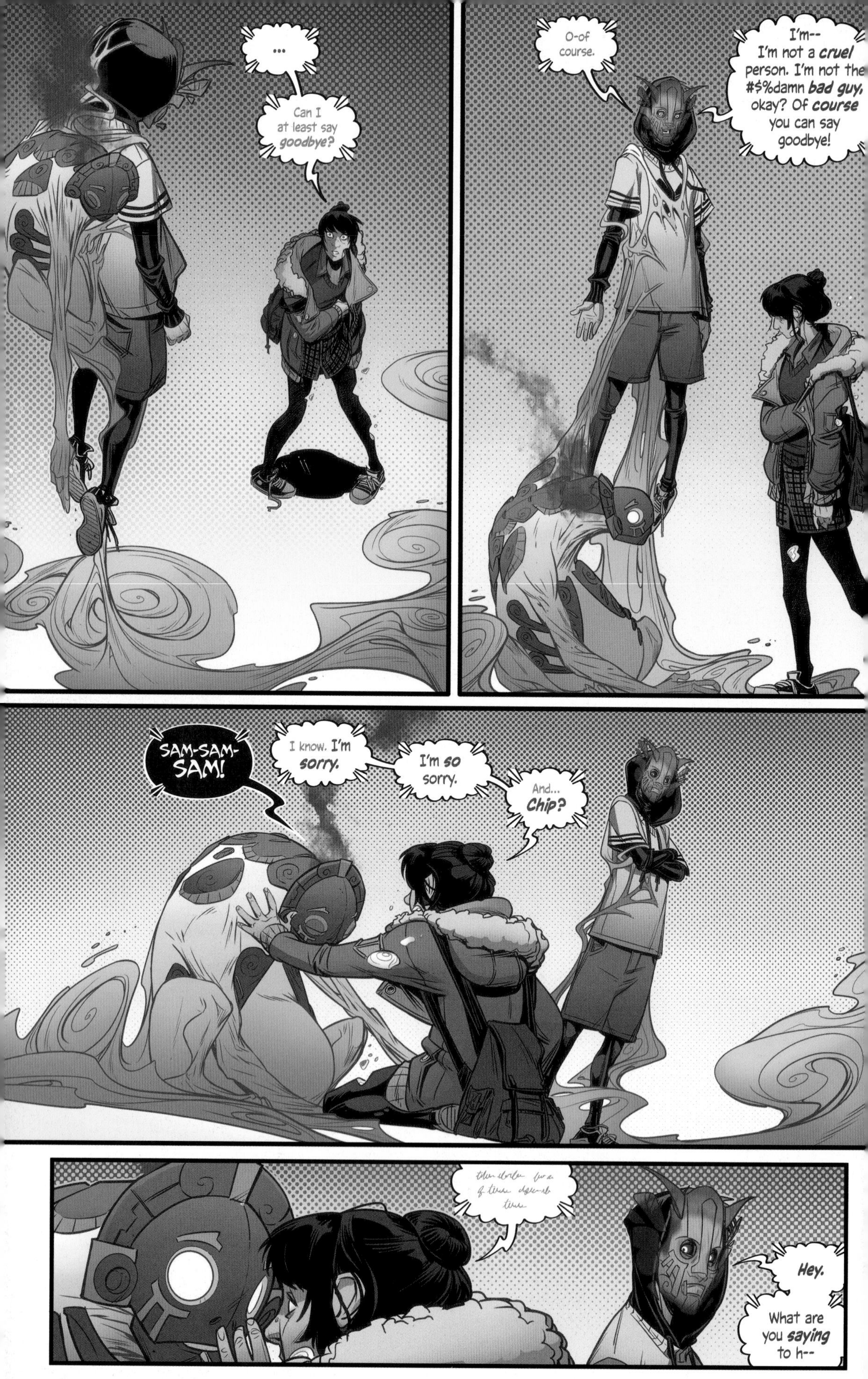
...
Can I at least say goodbye?
O-of course.
I'm-- I'm not a cruel person. I'm not the #$%damn bad guy, okay? Of course you can say goodbye!
SAM-SAM-SAM!
I know. I'm sorry.
I'm so sorry.
And... Chip?
Hey.
What are you saying to h--

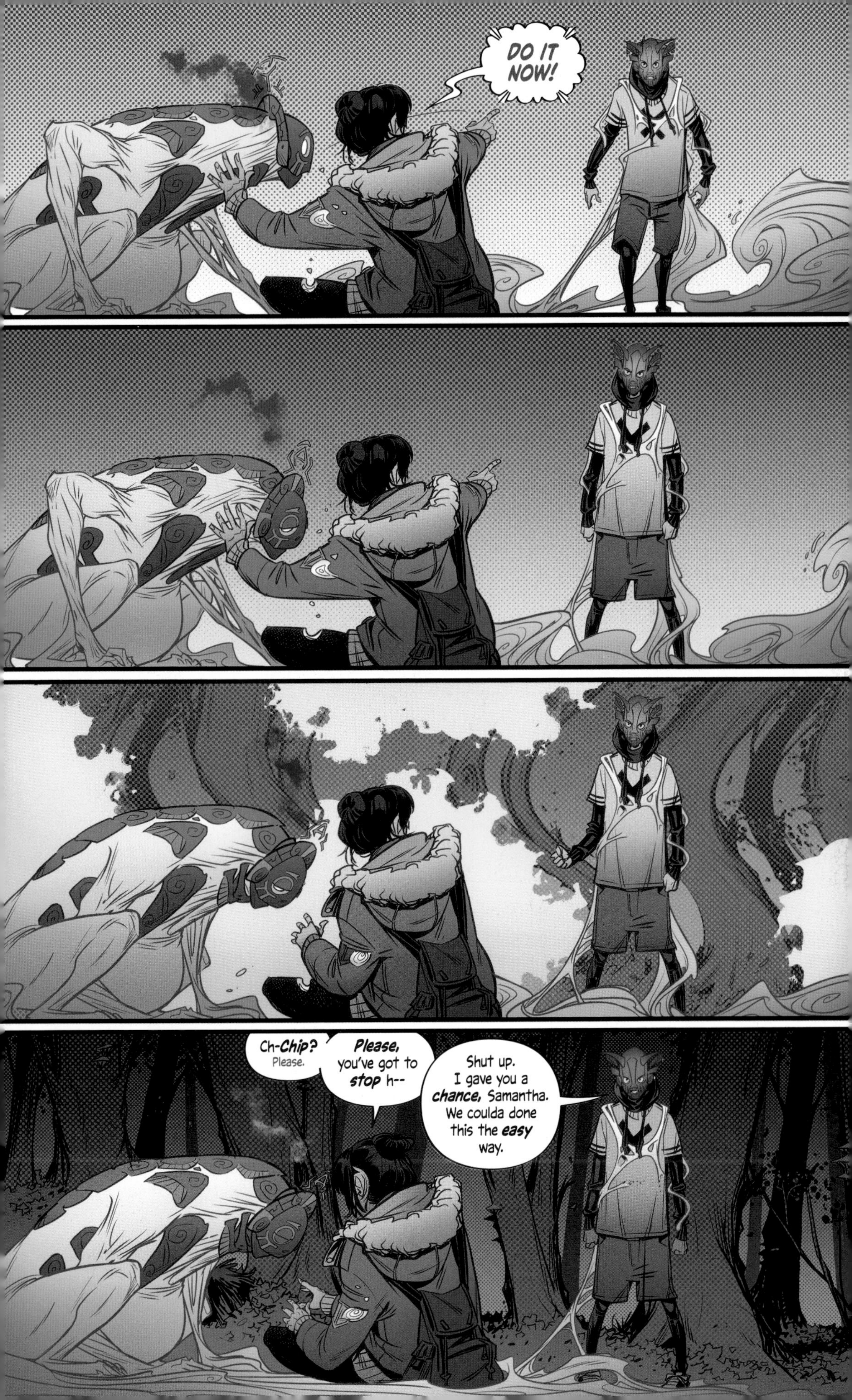
DO IT NOW!
Ch-Chip? Please.
Please, you've got to stop h--
Shut up. I gave you a chance, Samantha. We coulda done this the easy way.

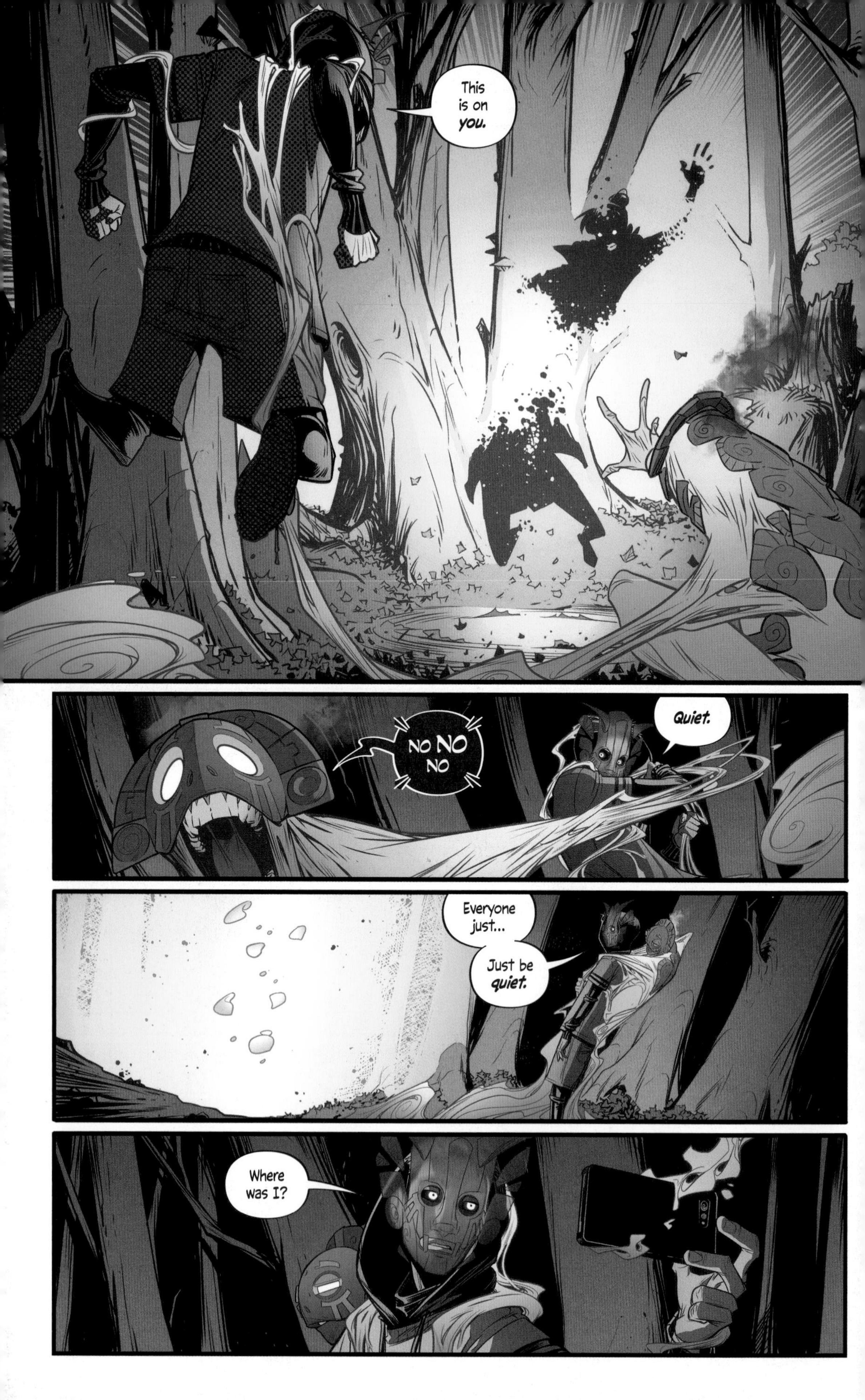
This is on *you.*
NO NO NO
Quiet.
Everyone just...
Just be *quiet.*
Where was I?

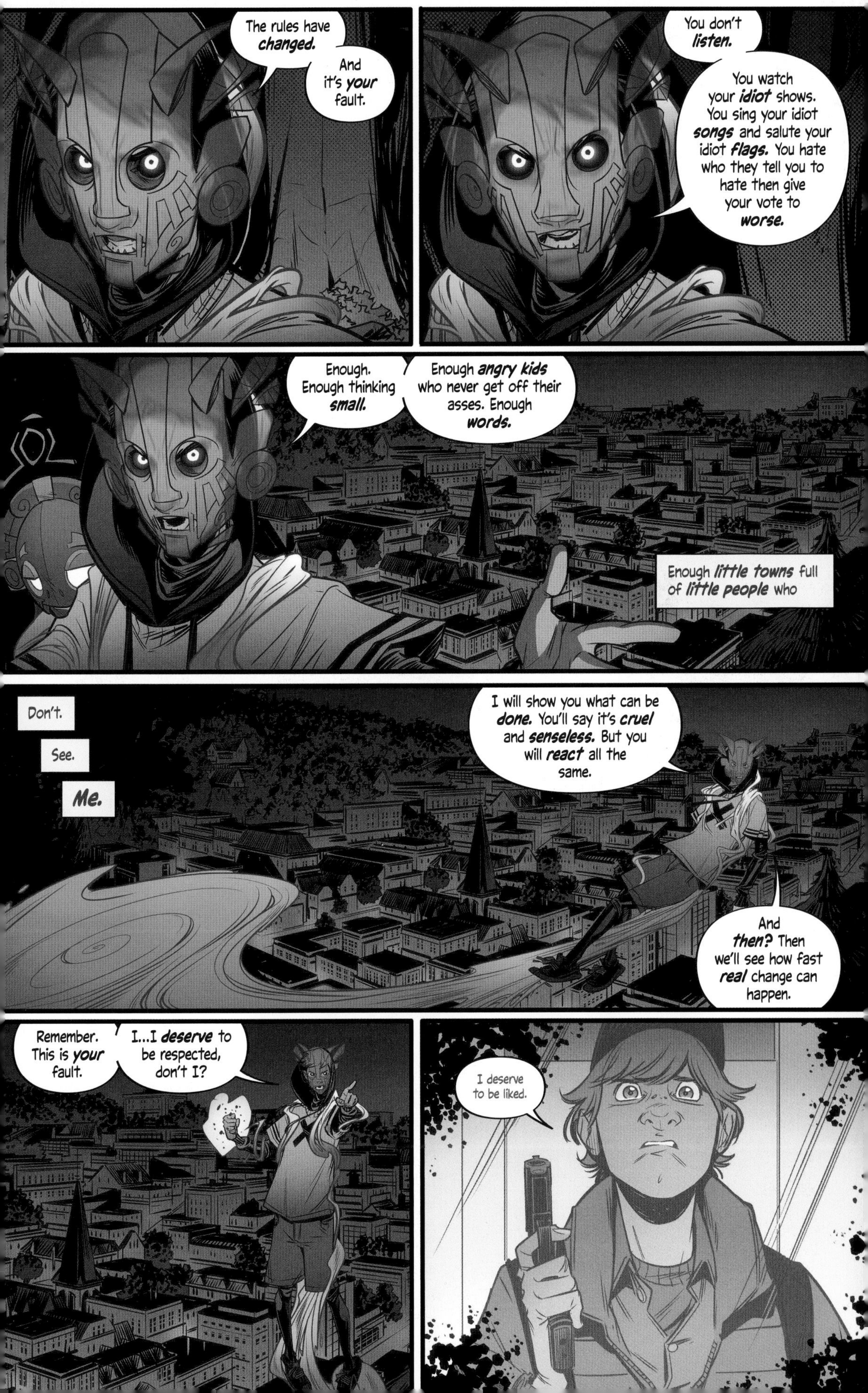
The rules have changed.
And it's your fault.
You don't listen.
You watch your idiot shows. You sing your idiot songs and salute your idiot flags. You hate who they tell you to hate then give your vote to worse.
Enough. Enough thinking small.
Enough angry kids who never get off their asses. Enough words.
Enough little towns full of little people who
Don't.
See.
Me.
I will show you what can be done. You'll say it's cruel and senseless. But you will react all the same.
And then? Then we'll see how fast real change can happen.
Remember. This is your fault.
I...I deserve to be respected, don't I?
I deserve to be liked.

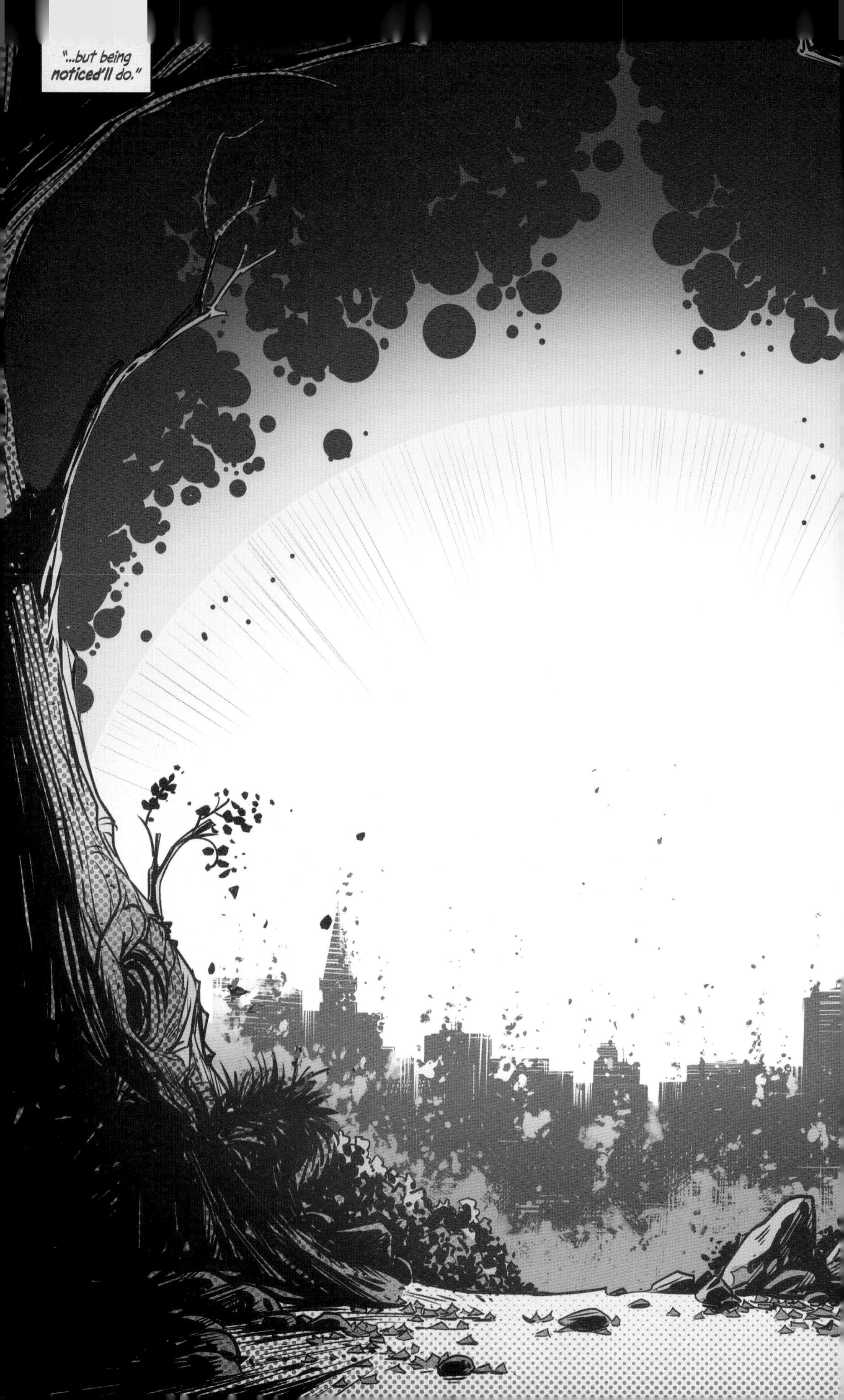
"...but being noticed'll do."

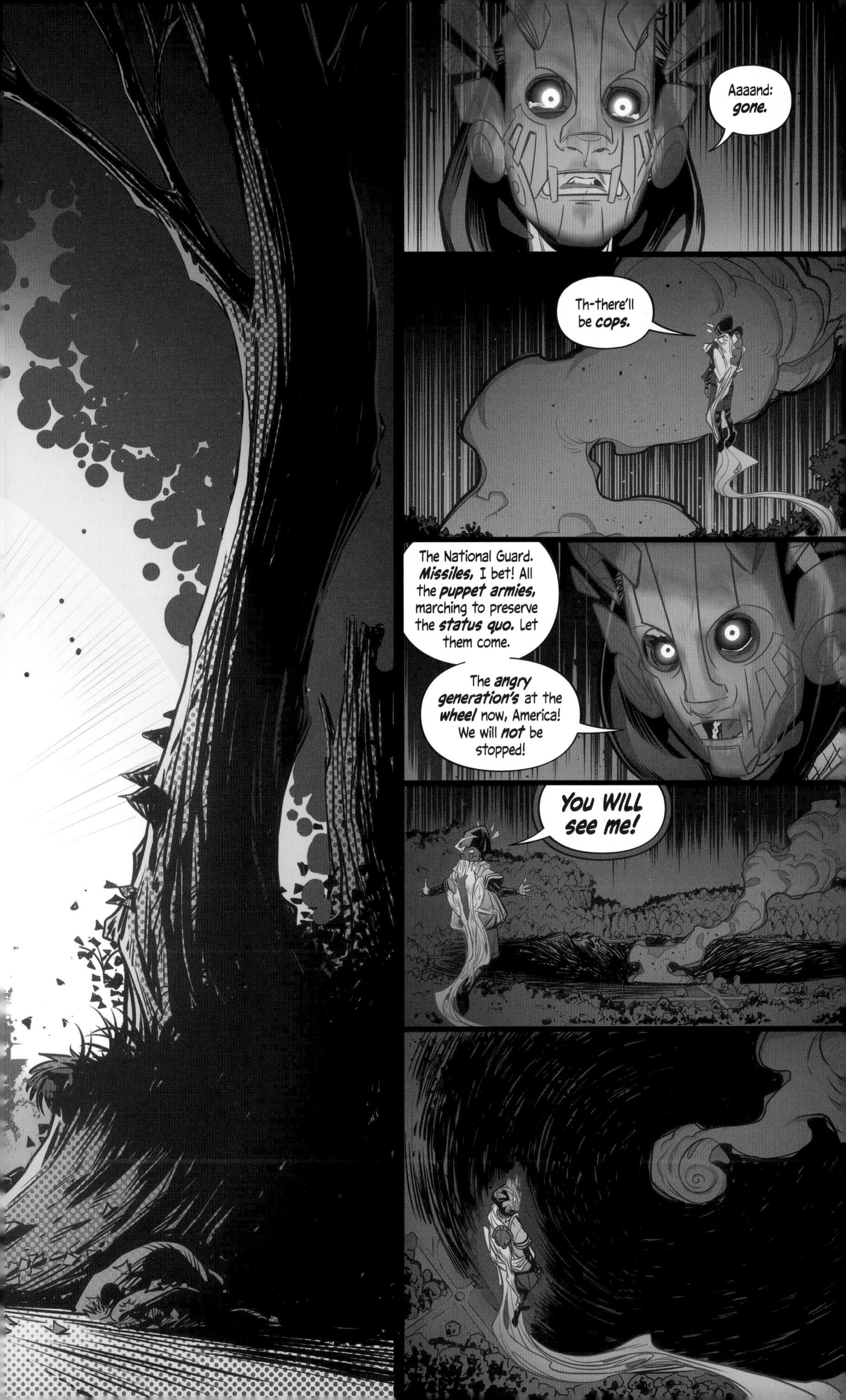
Aaaand: gone.
Th-there'll be cops.
The National Guard. Missiles, I bet! All the puppet armies, marching to preserve the status quo. Let them come.
The angry generation's at the wheel now, America! We will not be stopped!
You WILL see me!

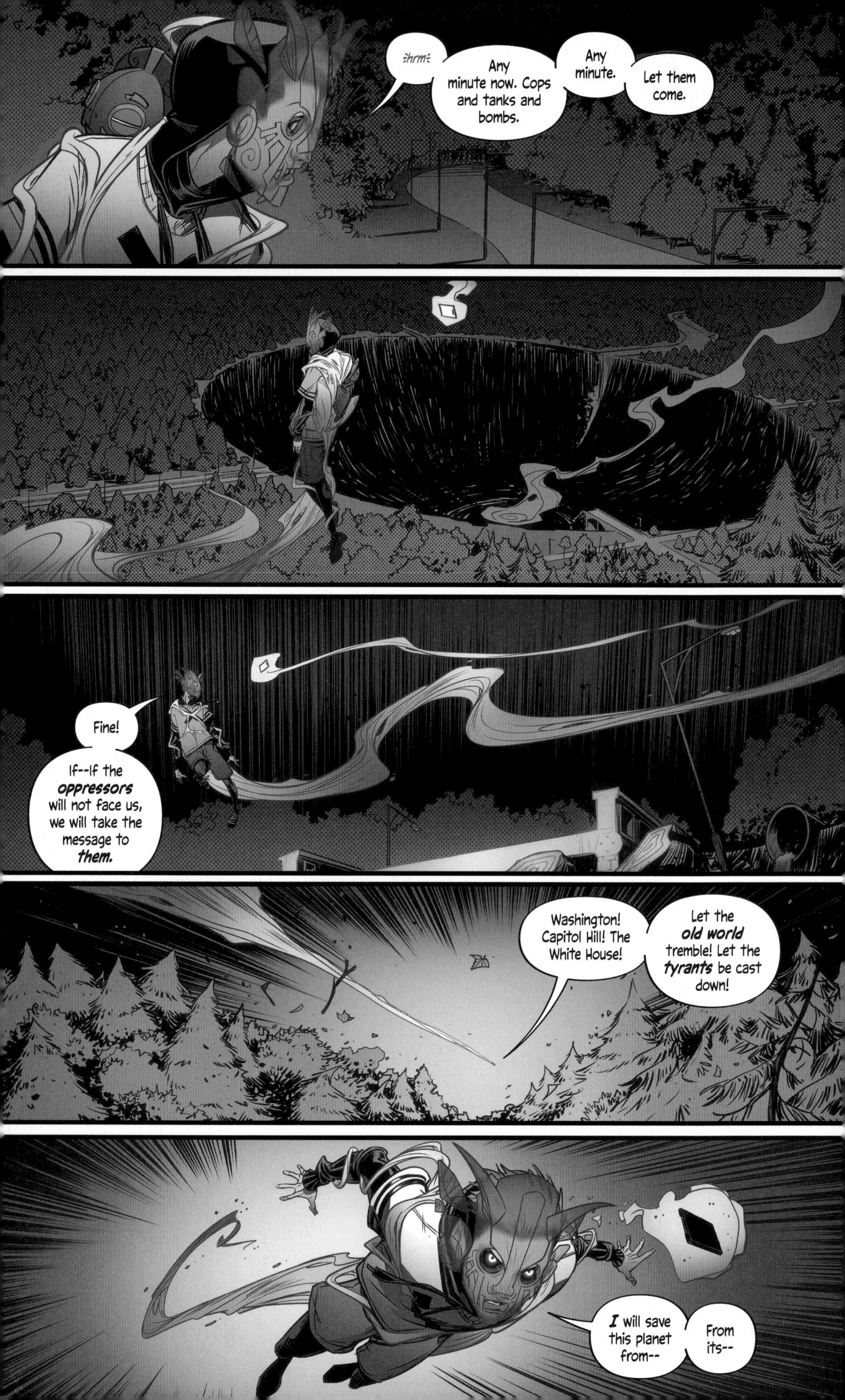

hrm
Any minute now. Cops and tanks and bombs.
Any minute.
Let them come.
Fine!
If--If the oppressors will not face us, we will take the message to them.
Washington! Capitol Hill! The White House!
Let the old world tremble! Let the tyrants be cast down!
I will save this planet from--
From its--

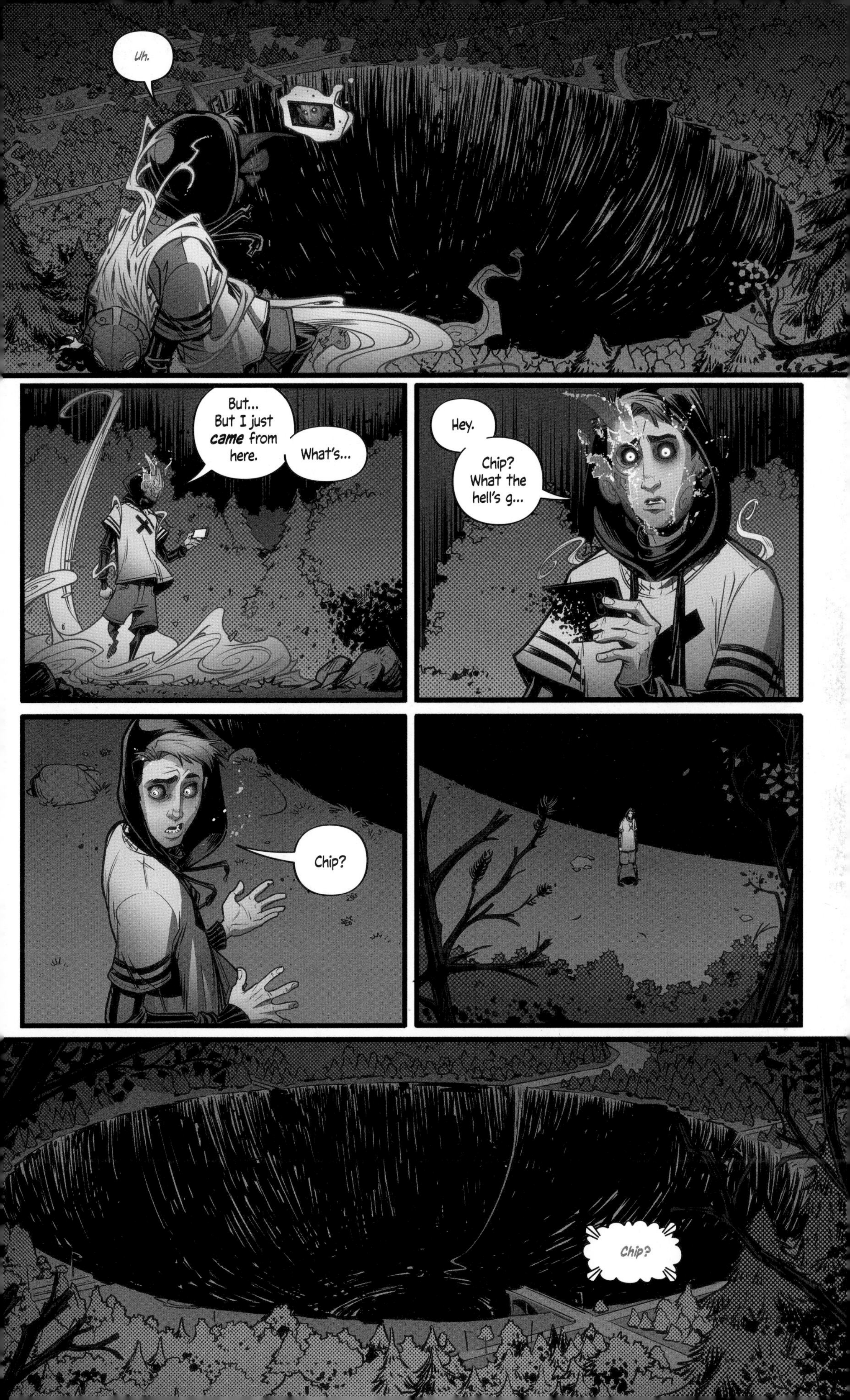
Uh.
But... But I just *came* from here.
What's...
Hey.
Chip? What the hell's g...
Chip?
Chip?

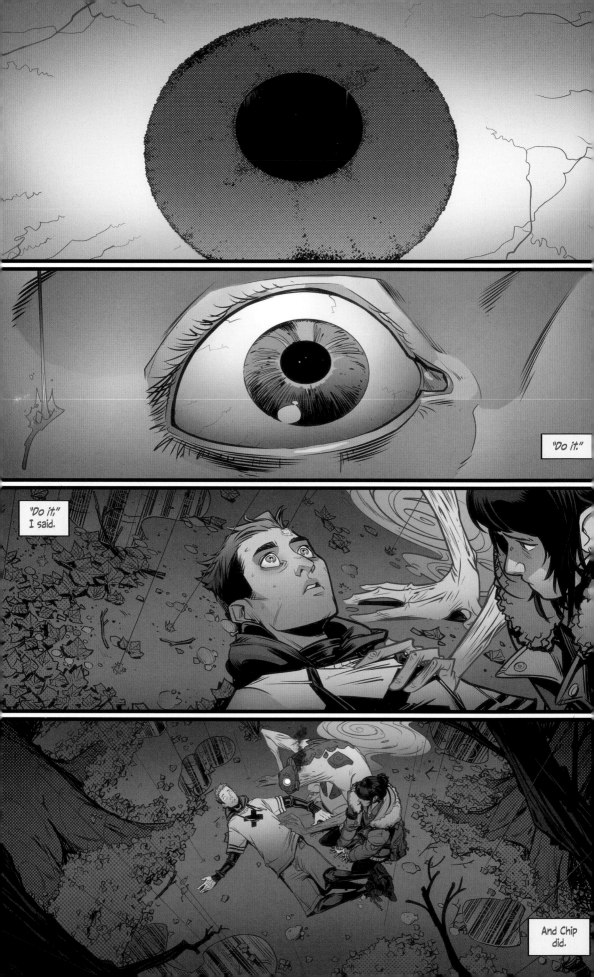

"Do it."

"Do it,"
I said.

And Chip
did.

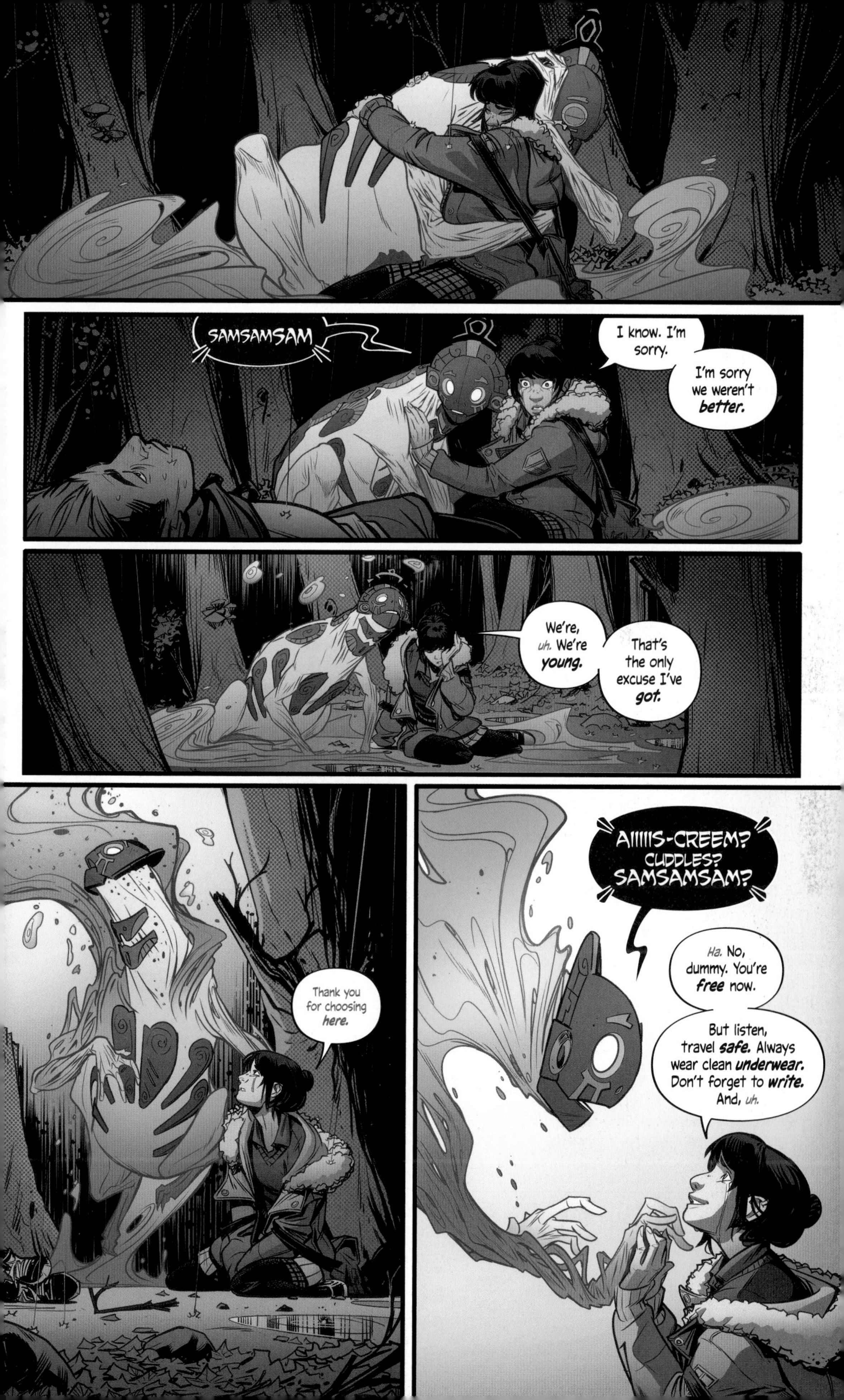
SAMSAMSAM
I know. I'm sorry.
I'm sorry we weren't better.
We're, uh. We're young.
That's the only excuse I've got.
Thank you for choosing here.
AIIIIS-CREEM? CUDDLES? SAMSAMSAM?
Ha. No, dummy. You're free now.
But listen, travel safe. Always wear clean underwear. Don't forget to write. And, uh.

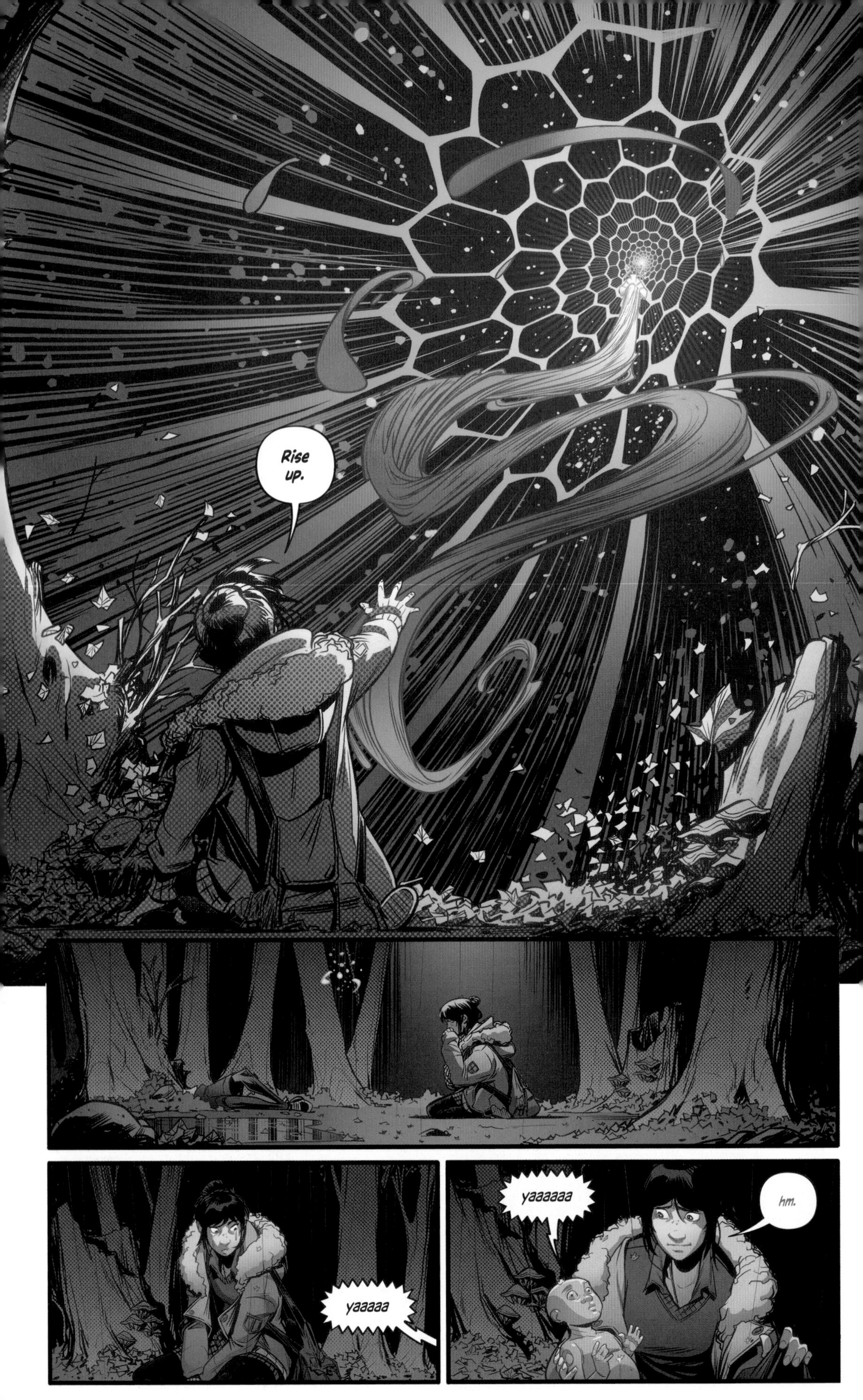
Rise up.
yaaaaa
yaaaaaa
hm.

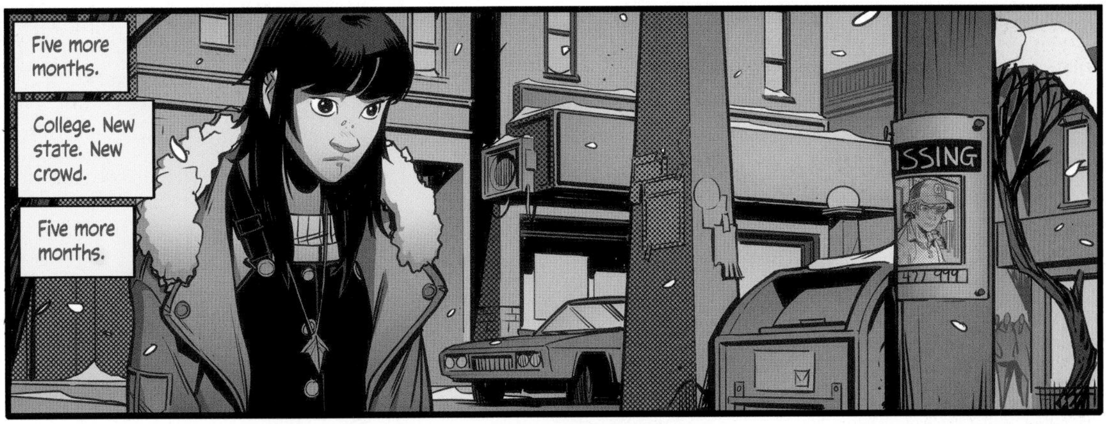
Five more months.
College. New state. New crowd.
Five more months.
ISSING

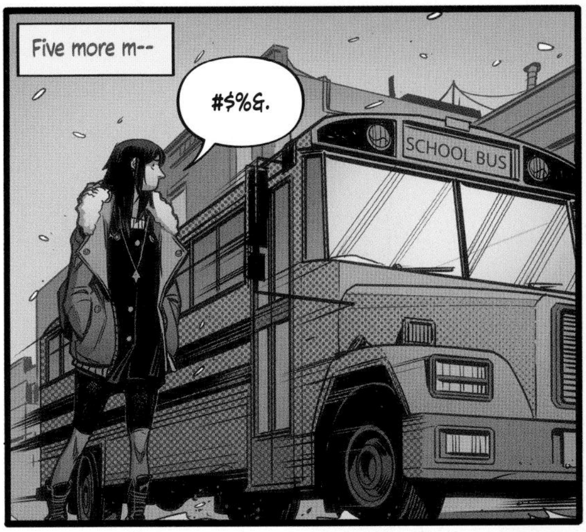
Five more m--
#$%&.
SCHOOL BUS

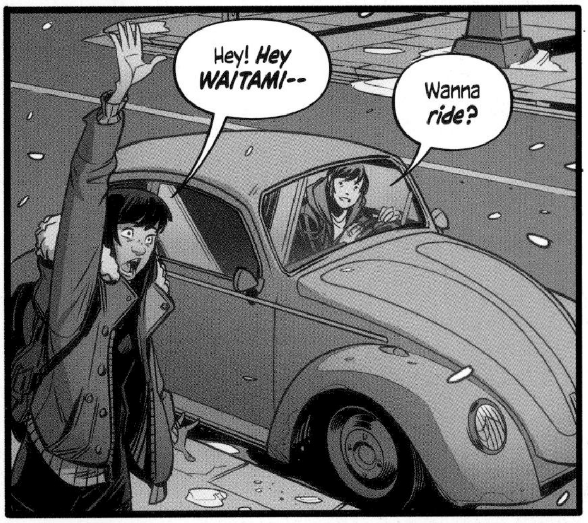
Hey! *Hey* ***WAITAMI--***
Wanna *ride?*

Chelsea. I ***heard*** she woke up.

I heard she broke up with Denny. I heard she cut her hair and redid her look. ***Big changes,*** y'know? Lessons learned, fresh start--***that's*** what she's signaling. ***My*** guess?

Auditioning for the ***Talk Show Circuit.***

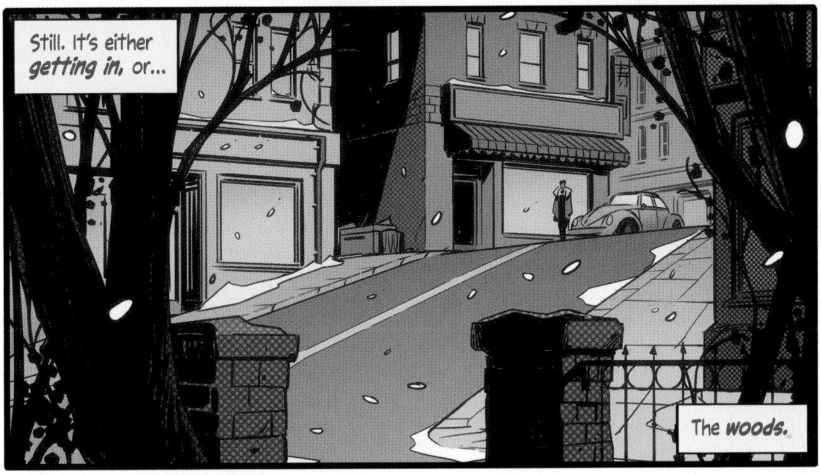
Still. It's either ***getting in,*** or...
The ***woods.***

Epilogue

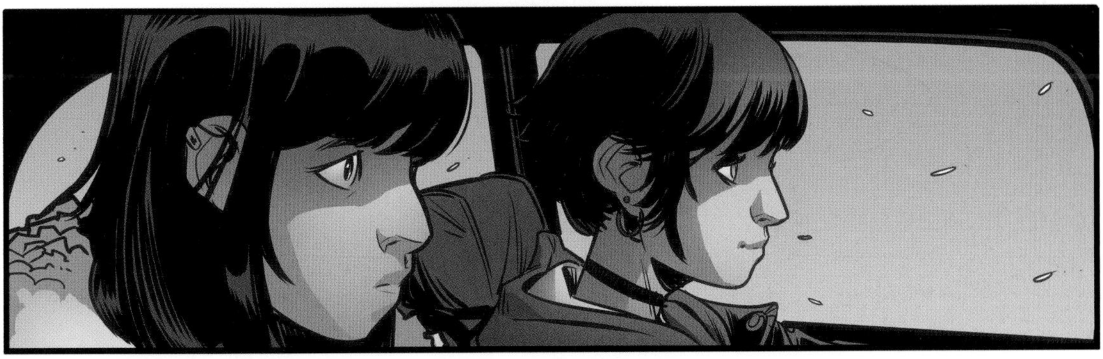

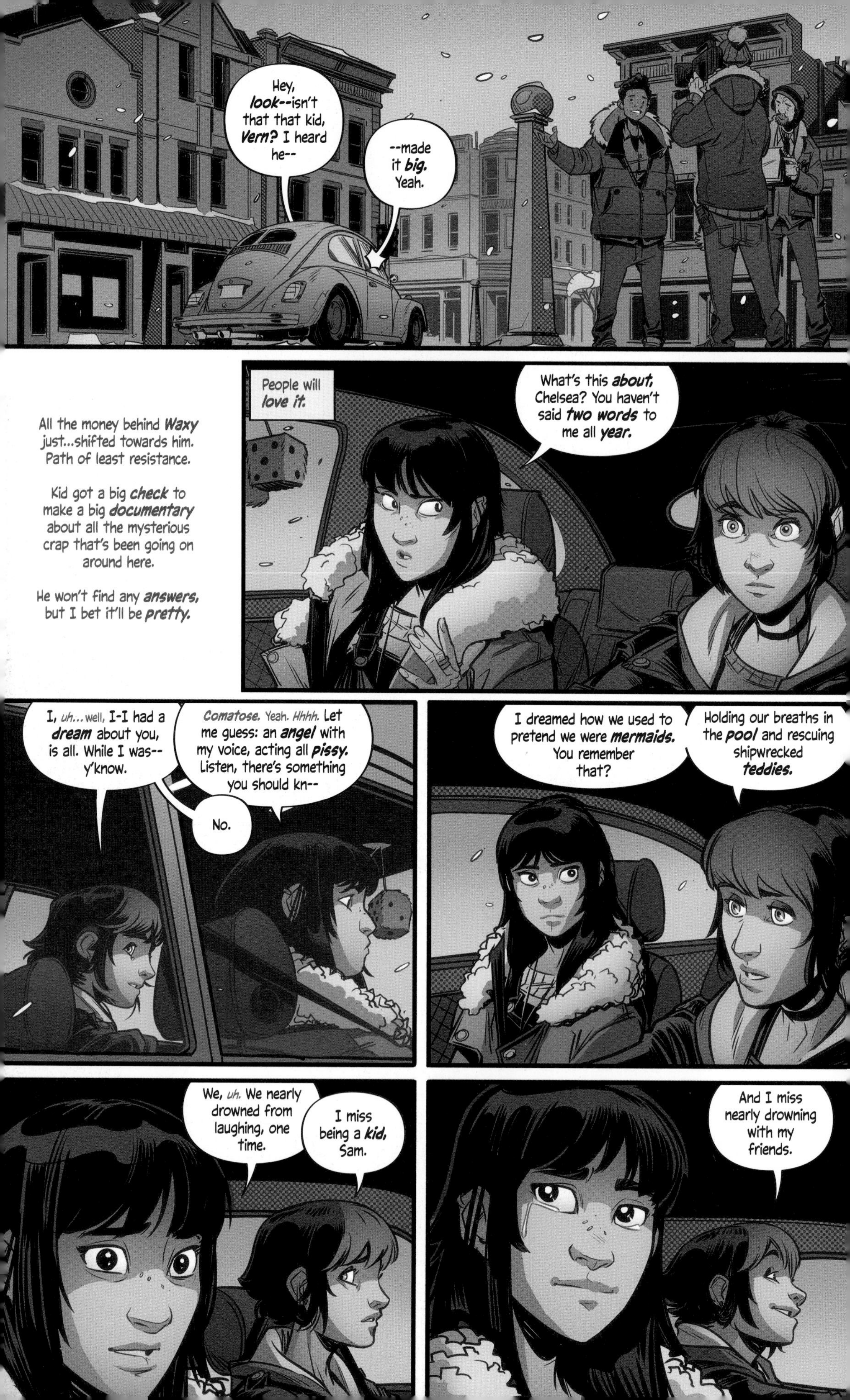
Hey, look--isn't that that kid, Vern? I heard he--
--made it big. Yeah.
All the money behind Waxy just...shifted towards him. Path of least resistance.
Kid got a big check to make a big documentary about all the mysterious crap that's been going on around here.
He won't find any answers, but I bet it'll be pretty.
People will love it.
What's this about, Chelsea? You haven't said two words to me all year.
I, uh... well, I-I had a dream about you, is all. While I was-- y'know.
Comatose. Yeah. Hhhh. Let me guess: an angel with my voice, acting all pissy. Listen, there's something you should kn--
No.
I dreamed how we used to pretend we were mermaids. You remember that?
Holding our breaths in the pool and rescuing shipwrecked teddies.
We, uh. We nearly drowned from laughing, one time.
I miss being a kid, Sam.
And I miss nearly drowning with my friends.

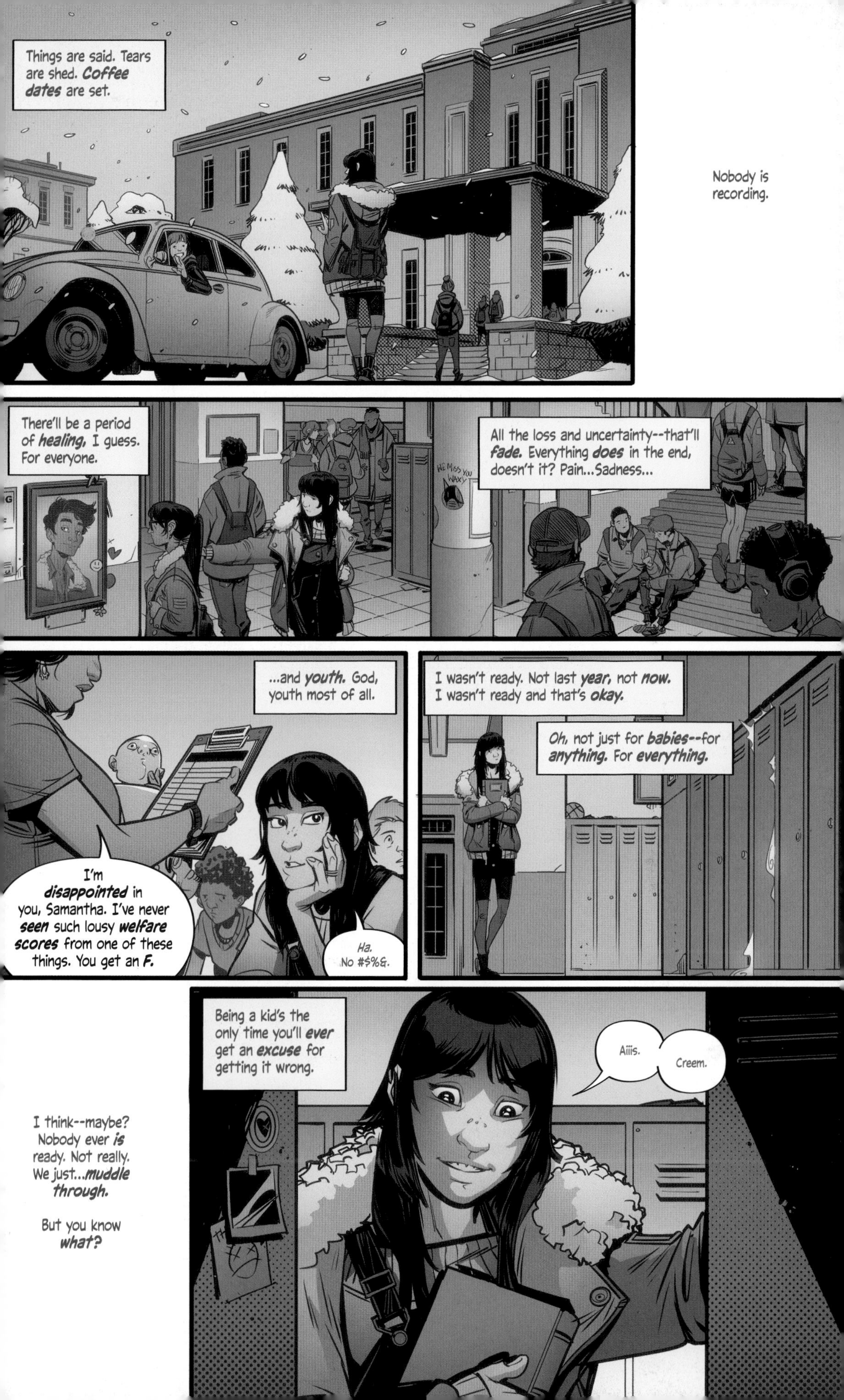

Things are said. Tears are shed. Coffee dates are set.
Nobody is recording.
There'll be a period of healing, I guess. For everyone.
WE MISS YOU WAXY
All the loss and uncertainty--that'll fade. Everything does in the end, doesn't it? Pain...Sadness...
...and youth. God, youth most of all.
I'm disappointed in you, Samantha. I've never seen such lousy welfare scores from one of these things. You get an F.
Ha. No #$%&.
I wasn't ready. Not last year, not now. I wasn't ready and that's okay.
Oh, not just for babies--for anything. For everything.
Being a kid's the only time you'll ever get an excuse for getting it wrong.
Aiiis.
Creem.
I think--maybe? Nobody ever is ready. Not really. We just...muddle through.
But you know what?

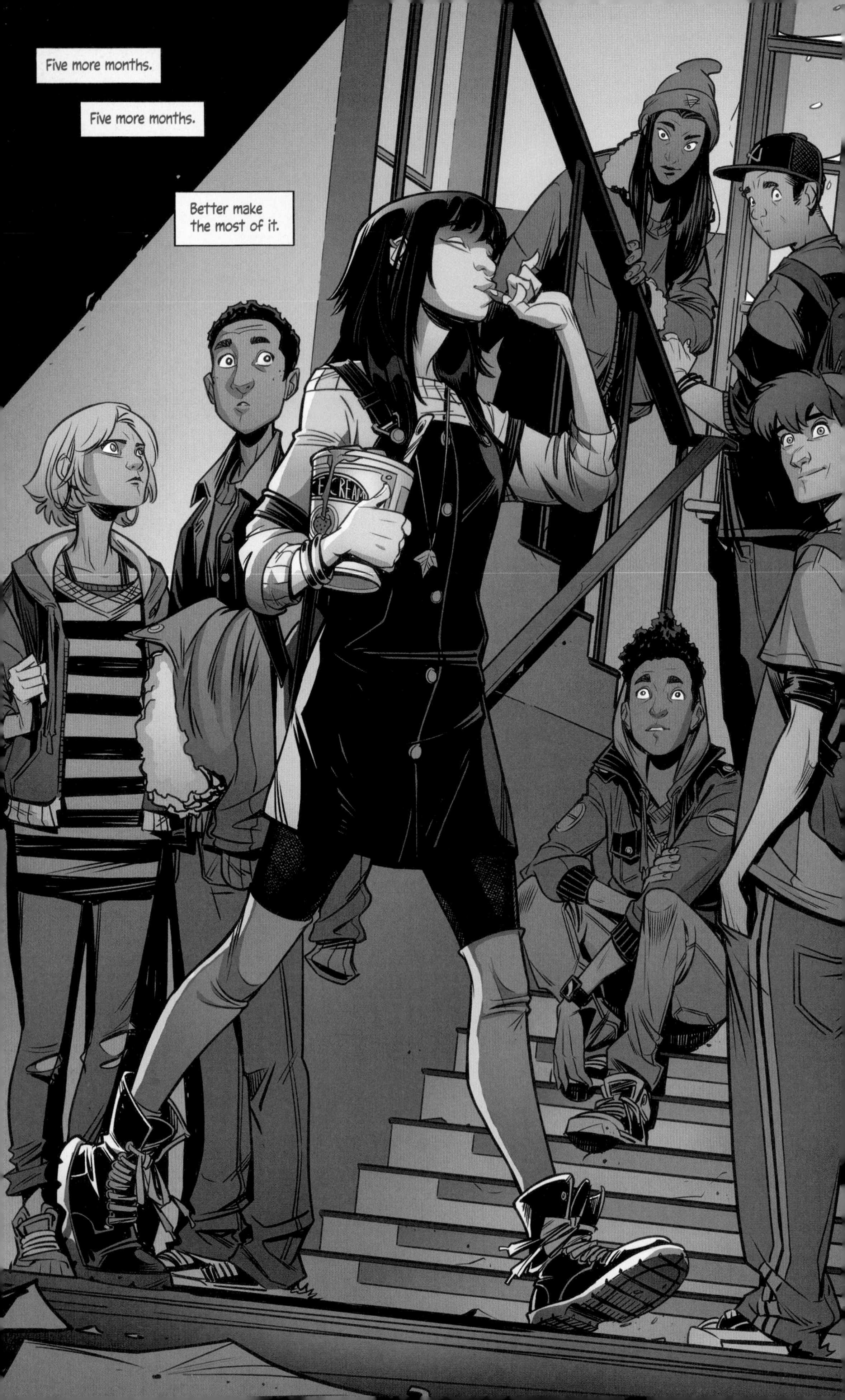
Five more months.
Five more months.
Better make the most of it.

COVER GALLERY

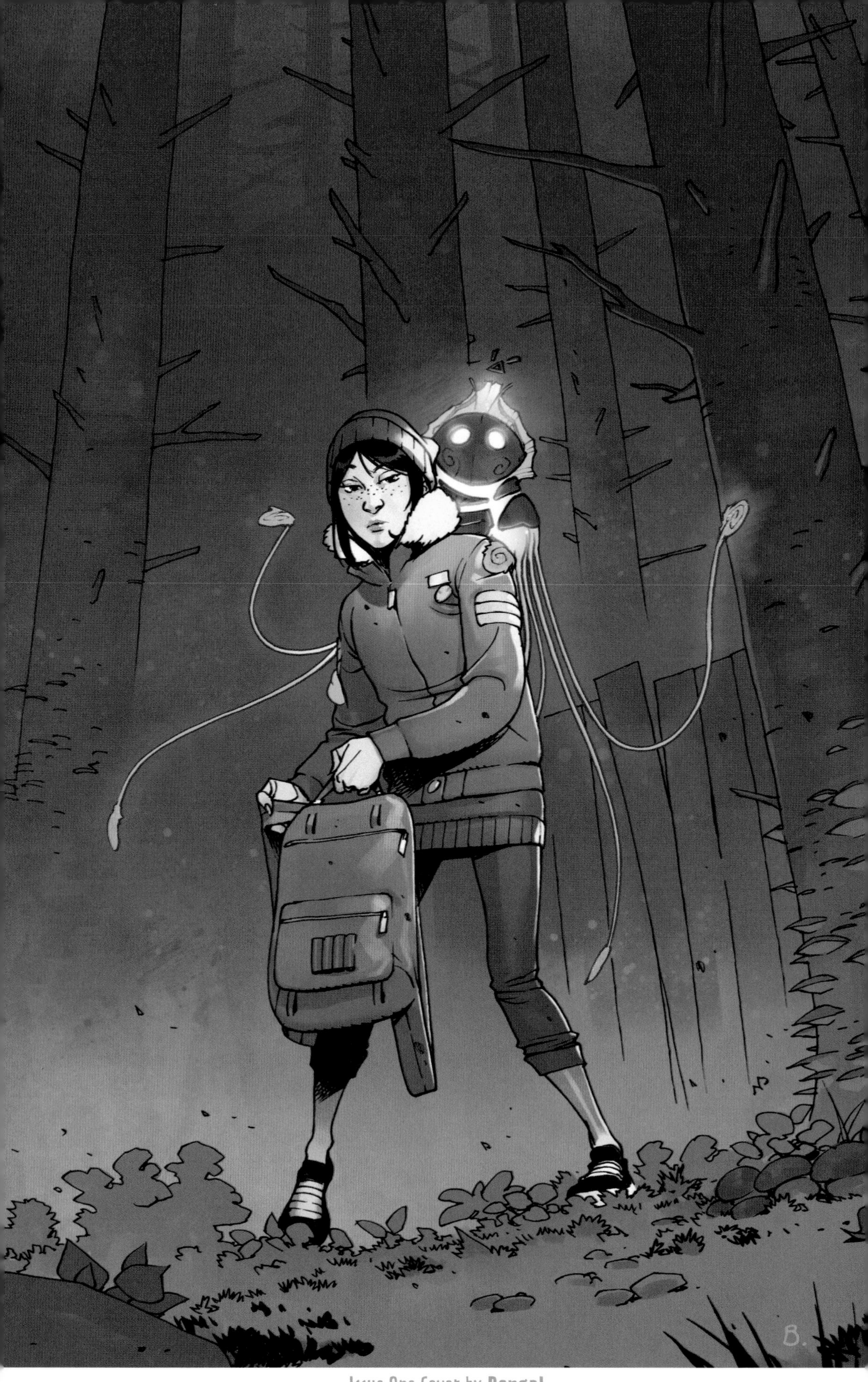
B.

Issue One Cover by **Bengal**

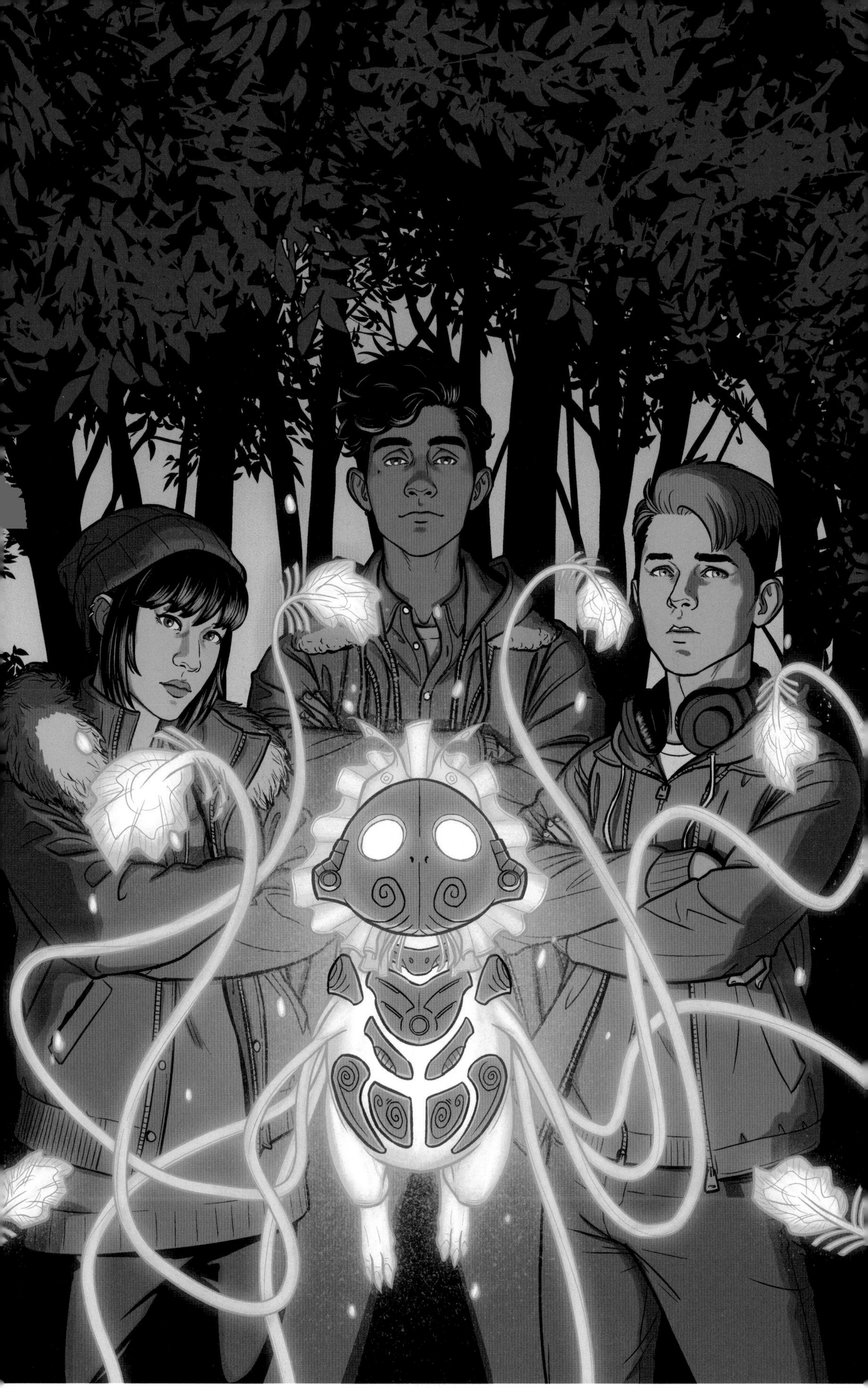

Issue One Cover by **Jamie McKelvie**

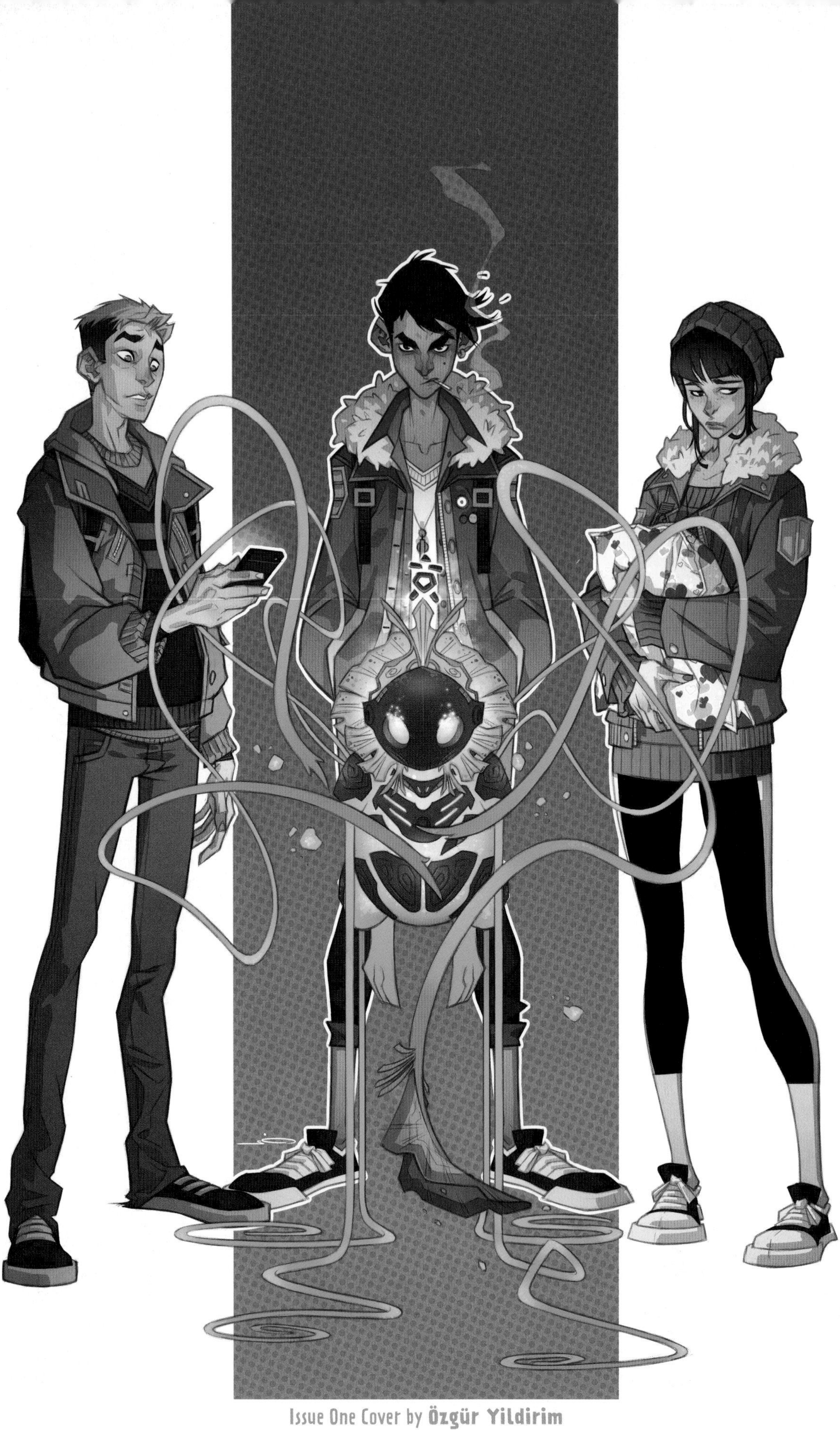

Issue One Cover by **Özgür Yildirim**

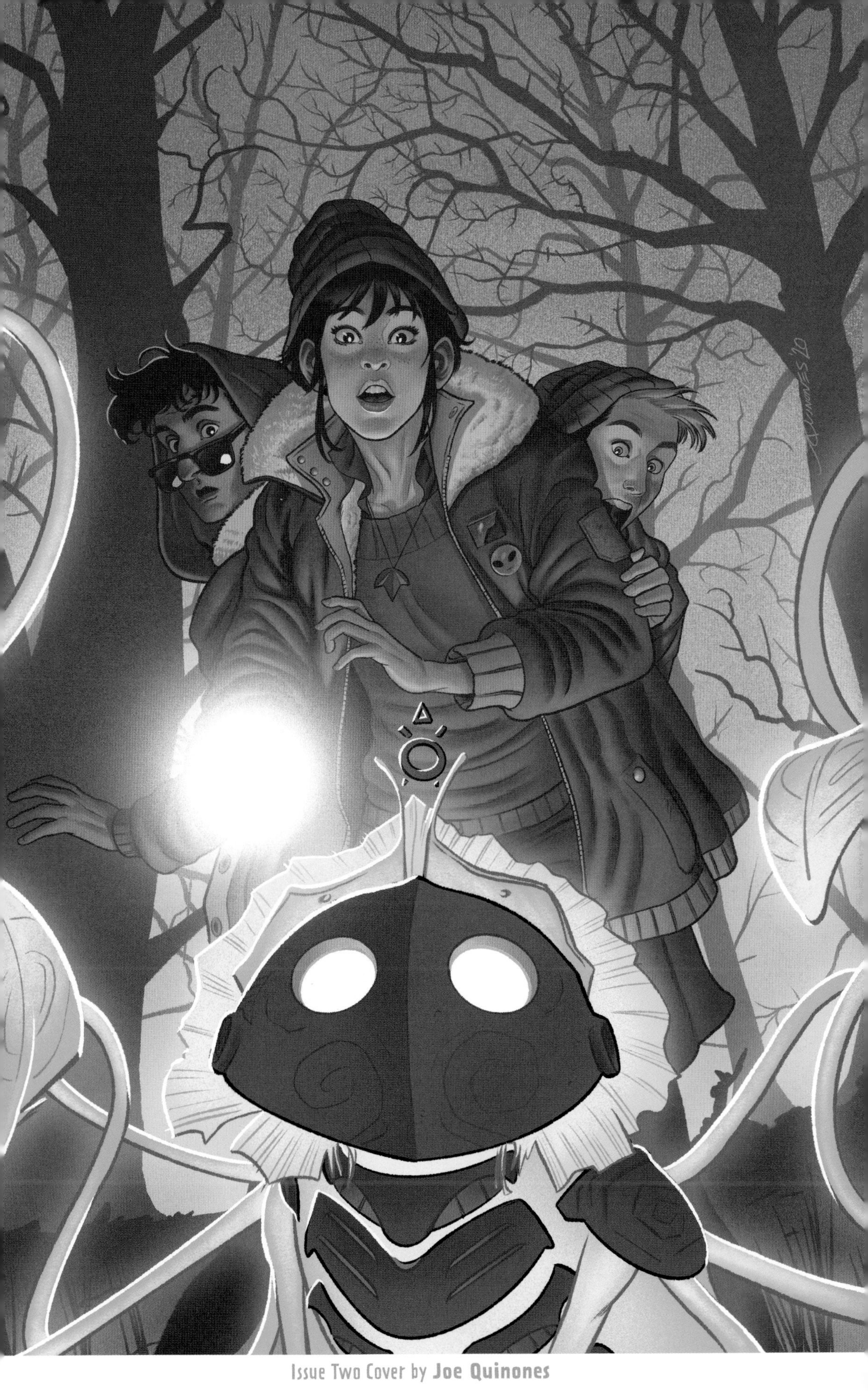

Issue Two Cover by **Joe Quinones**

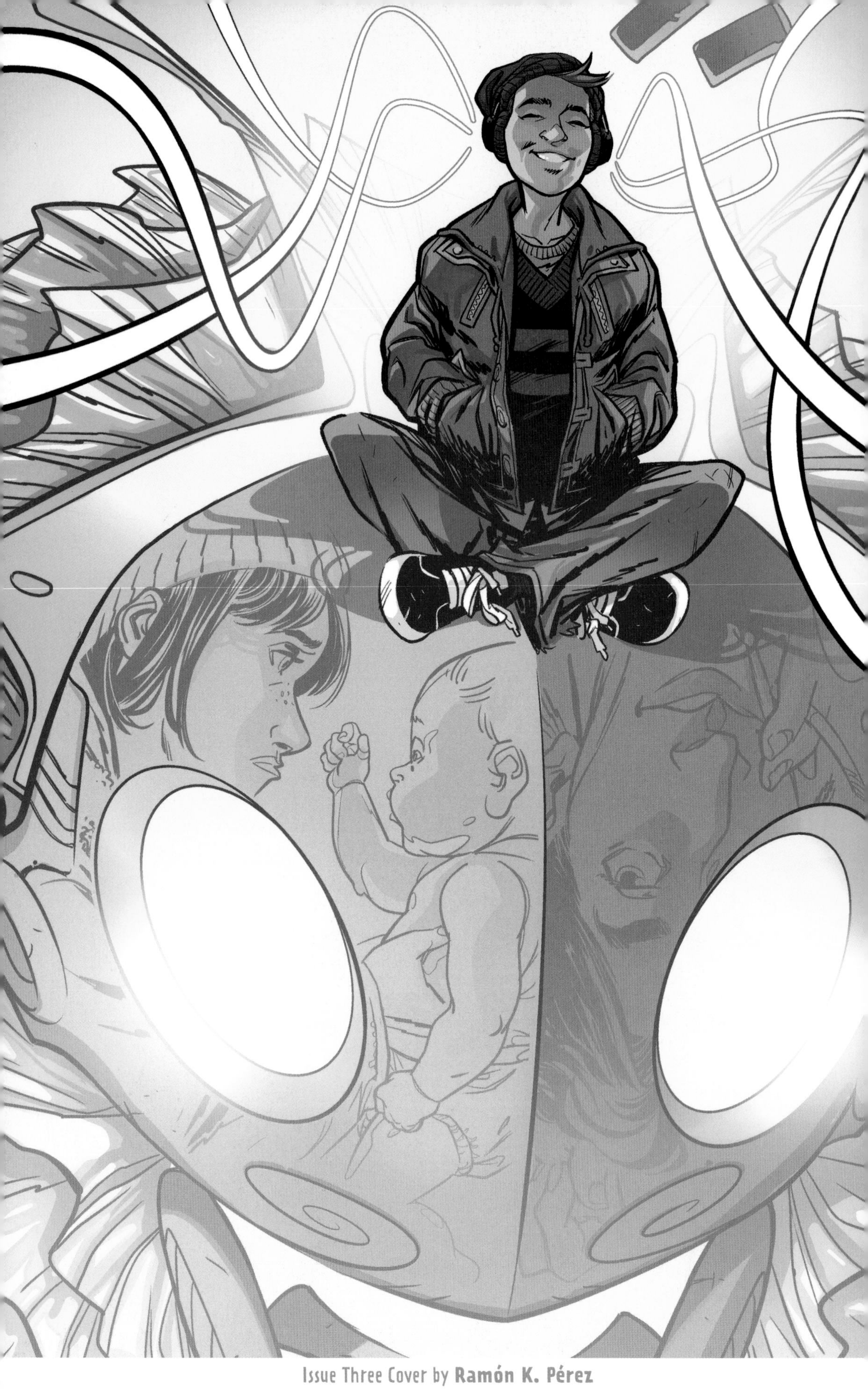

Issue Three Cover by **Ramón K. Pérez**

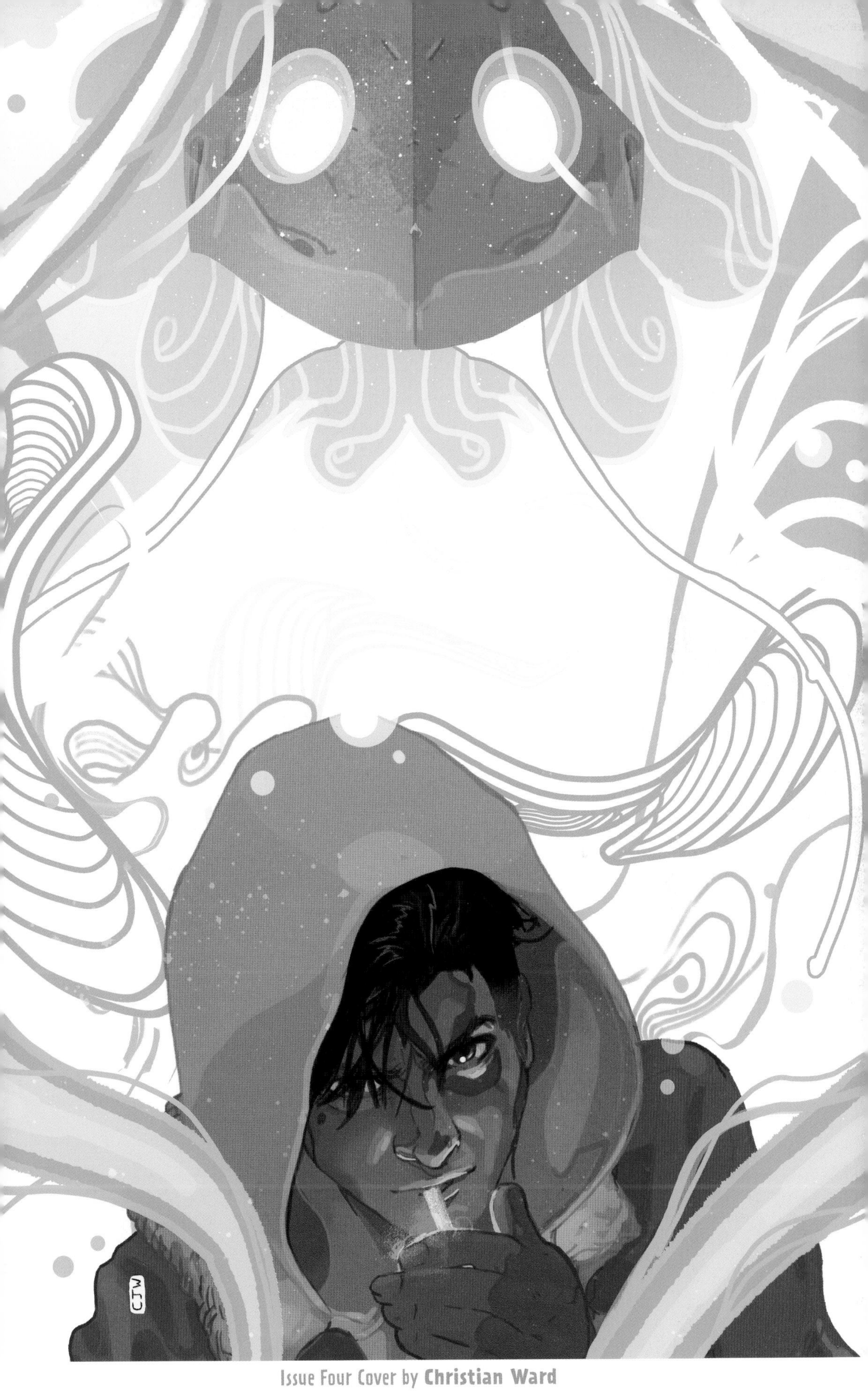
CJW
Issue Four Cover by **Christian Ward**

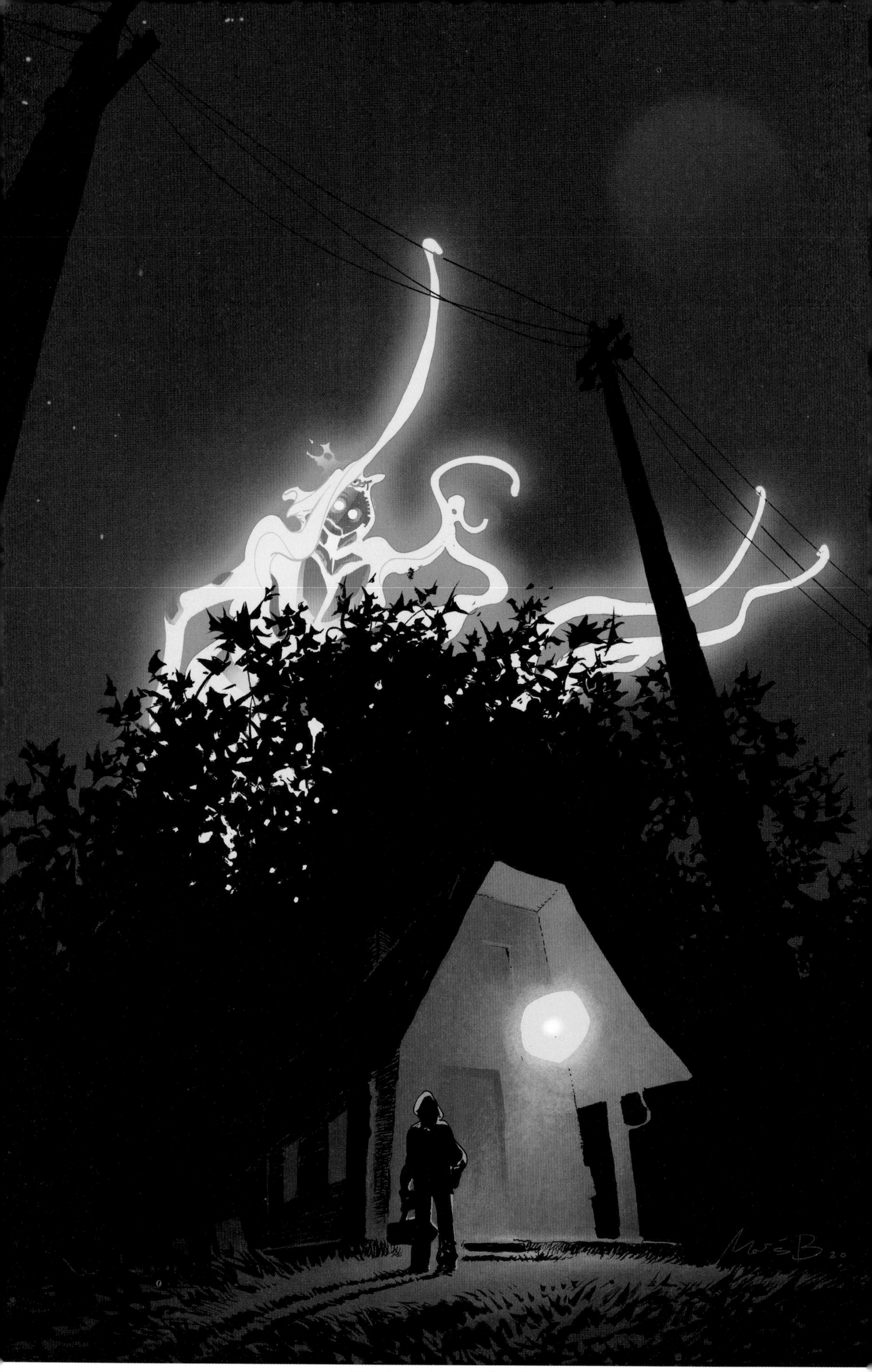

Issue Five Cover by **Matías Bergara**

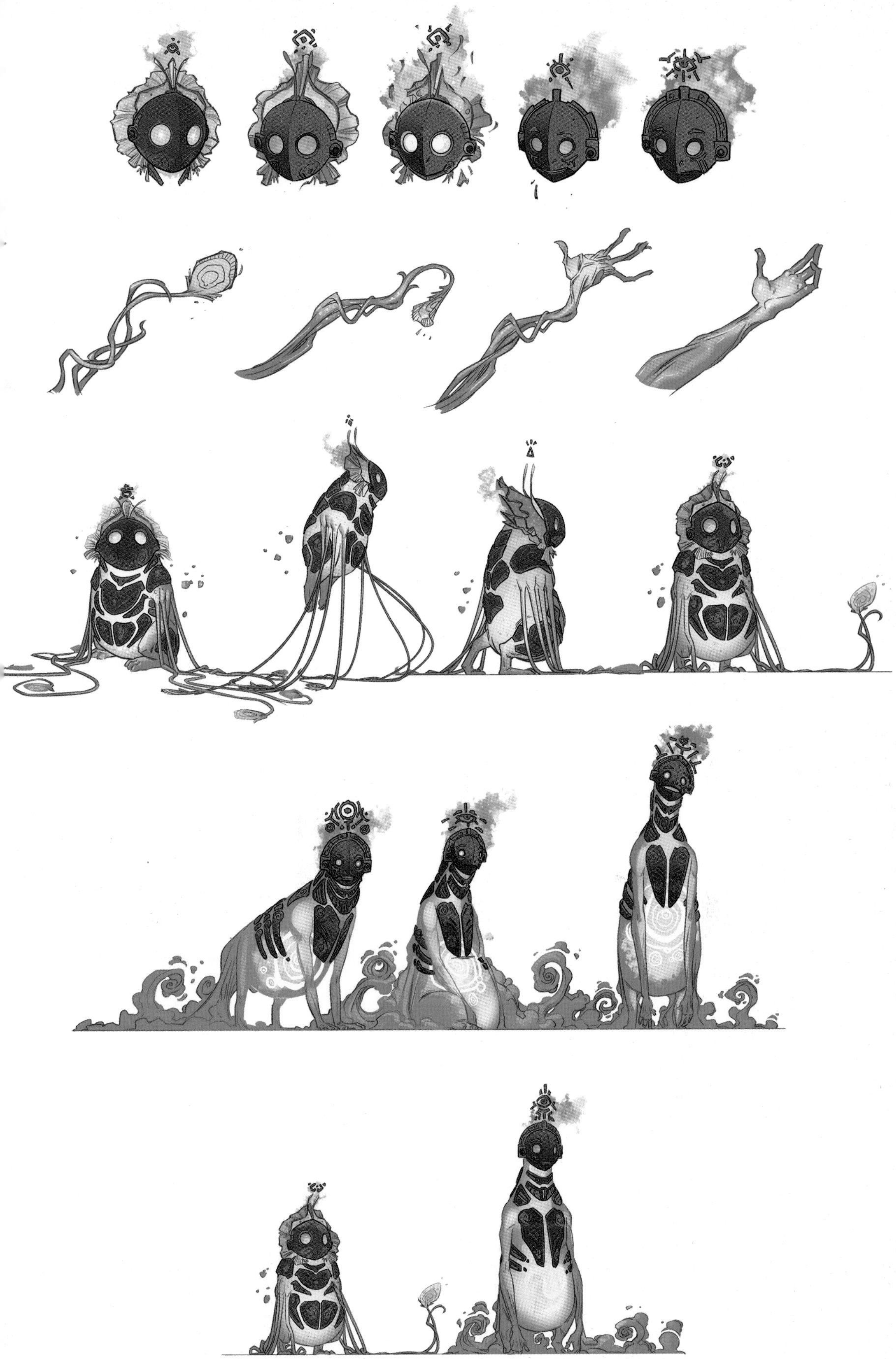

Additional Artwork by **Chris Wildgoose**

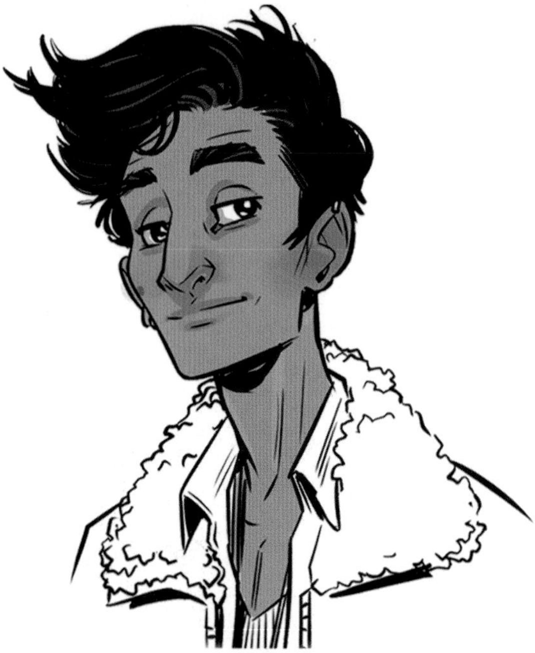

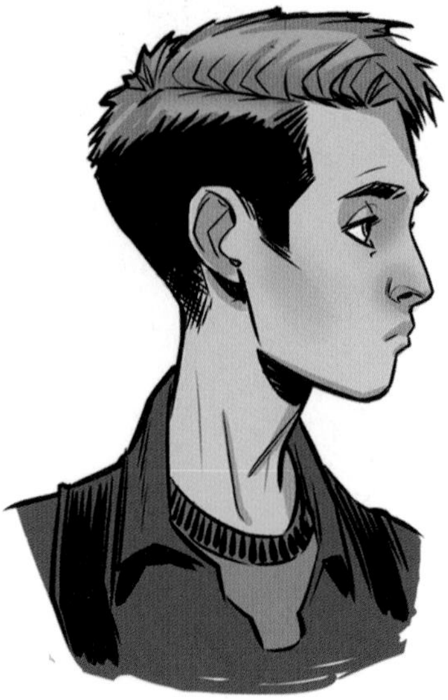

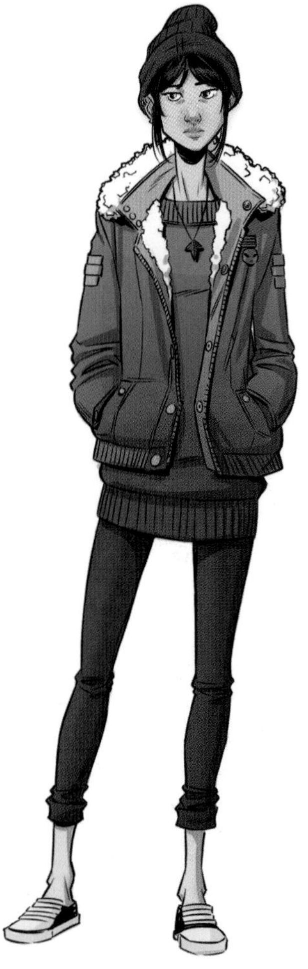

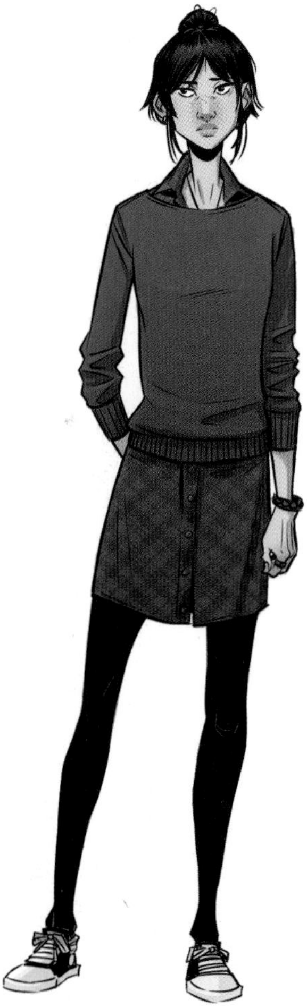

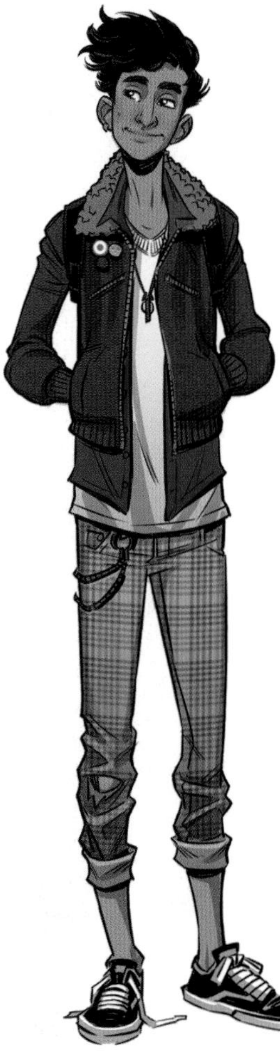

Additional Artwork by **Chris Wildgoose**

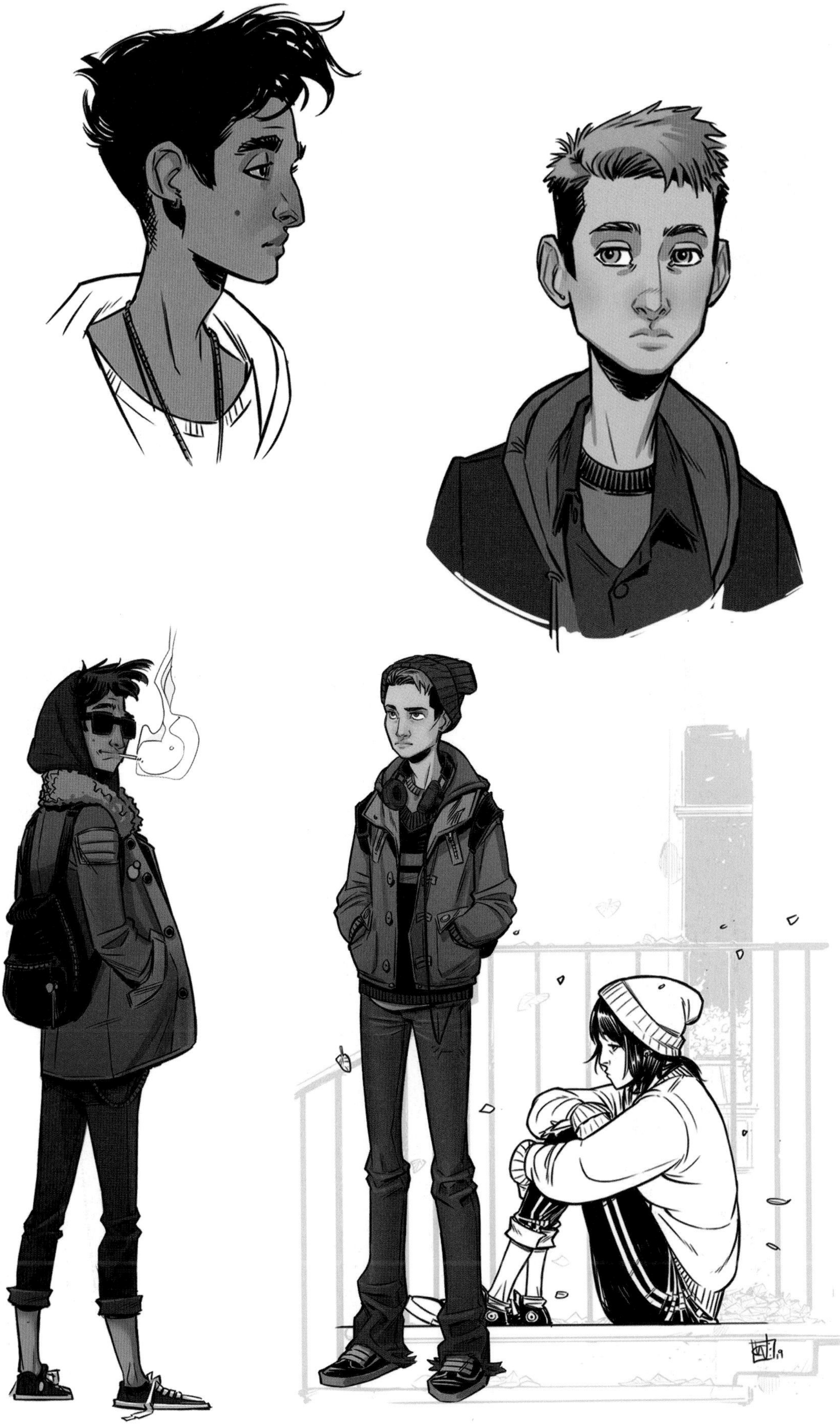

DISCOVER
VISIONARY CREATORS

THE WOODS
JAMES TYNION IV • MICHAEL DIALYNAS
VOL. 1
THE ARROW

"The Spire is fantastic! My kind of genre free-for-all."
—BRIAN K. VAUGHAN (Saga)
THE SPIRE
SIMON SPURRIER
JEFF STOKELY
ANDRÉ MAY
NOMINEE

MARK WAID • PETER KRAUSE
IRREDEEMABLE
AFTERWORD BY GRANT MORRISON

MARK WAID • JEAN DIAZ
INCORRUPTIBLE

MICHAEL ALAN NELSON
DAN MORA
GABRIEL CASSATA
HEXED
THE HARLOT & THE THIEF VOLUME ONE

ABNETT & CULBARD
WILD'S END
FIRST LIGHT
"IT'S REALLY GREAT!"
JEFF LEMIRE

BOOM! STUDIOS

AVAILABLE AT YOUR LOCAL COMICS SHOP AND BOOKSTORE

To find a comics shop in your area, visit www.comicshoplocator.com

WWW.**BOOM-STUDIOS**.COM

James Tynion IV

The Woods

Volume 1
ISBN: 978-1-60886-454-6 | $9.99 US
Volume 2
ISBN: 978-1-60886-495-9 | $14.99 US
Volume 3
ISBN: 978-1-60886-773-8 | $14.99 US

The Backstagers

Volume 1
ISBN: 978-1-60886-993-0 | $14.99 US

Simon Spurrier

Six-Gun Gorilla

ISBN: 978-1-60886-390-7 | $19.99 US

The Spire

ISBN: 978-1-60886-913-8 | $29.99 US

Weavers

ISBN: 978-1-60886-963-3 | $19.99 US

Mark Waid

Irredeemable

Volume 1
ISBN: 978-1-93450-690-5 | $16.99 US
Volume 2
ISBN: 978-1-60886-000-5 | $16.99 US

Incorruptible

Volume 1
ISBN: 978-1-60886-015-9 | $16.99 US
Volume 2
ISBN: 978-1-60886-028-9 | $16.99 US

Michael Alan Nelson

Hexed The Harlot & The Thief

Volume 1
ISBN: 978-1-60886-718-9 | $14.99 US
Volume 2
ISBN: 978-1-60886-816-2 | $14.99 US

Day Men

Volume 1
ISBN: 978-1-60886-393-8 | $9.99 US
Volume 2
ISBN: 978-1-60886-852-0 | $9.99 US

Dan Abnett

Wild's End

Volume 1: First Light
ISBN: 978-1-60886-735-6 | $19.99 US
Volume 2: The Enemy Within
ISBN: 978-1-60886-877-3 | $19.99 US

Hypernaturals

Volume 1
ISBN: 978-1-60886-298-6 | $16.99 US
Volume 2
ISBN: 978-1-60886-319-8 | $19.99 US